THE SHAMAN

William Whitecloud

Animal Dreaming Publishing
www.animaldreamingpublishing.com

THE LAST SHAMAN

ANIMAL DREAMING PUBLISHING
PO Box 5203 East Lismore NSW 2480
AUSTRALIA
Phone +61 2 6622 6147
www.AnimalDreamingPublishing.com
www.facebook.com/AnimalDreamingPublishing
Originally self-published in 2011 by William Whitecloud.

Published in 2018
First published in 2012
Copyright text © William Whitecloud
www.WilliamWhitecloud.com

Cover art by Beau Ravn
www.beauravn.com

ISBN 978-0-6481820-6-1

This book is a work of fiction. All names, places, dialogue and
incidents portrayed are a product of the author's imagination.

Designed by Animal Dreaming Publishing
Printed in Australia

This book is dedicated to my brother, George,
who showed me the crack in the wall.

Contents

Prologue

Back in the days when I lived in Africa, if you asked the colonial old-timers what their worst nightmare was, the first thing they'd likely say was running out of gin on safari. Next would probably be being disemboweled by a leopard as it raked its back claws across their belly while scalping them with its front paws. High on the list, too, would be waking up with one of the house servants holding the sharpest kitchen knife to their throat.

Nightmares were a commodity freely exchanged in the old country clubs. It was the glue that bound the white community together. Once I was having a drink with a bunch of codgers and I asked them their thoughts on dangerous women. The old fellows shifted uncomfortably in their creaky leather armchairs and avoided each other's eyes. Big swigs were taken from iced tumblers, pipes were banged out furiously into ashtrays, and fits of loud coughing were feigned.

A retired major with a big handlebar moustache gave me a sour look. "I say, young chap, there are some things too frightening to mention."

Dangerous women were a cursed species in the eyes of all colonials. A more virulent strain than the sirens in Greek mythology, they came in all shapes and sizes, though they had one characteristic in common, and that was their prowess at seducing men into acts of devastating recklessness. I knew such a woman. This is our story…

CHAPTER ONE

The *Mona Lisa* of Africa

I had not expected to find a vision of beauty in the Manzimwe Mission Hospital but there it was in the form of Dr. Maxine Carlyle treading carefully through a sea of grotesque faces. Dressed in a crisp pair of khaki shorts and a League of Human Rights T-shirt, she made her way toward me, repeating a practiced refrain in Lapedi, "We're working very hard. Yes, there are many sick people. Your turn will come; please be patient."

Suddenly her eyes came to rest on me and her interest in the unfortunate masses died. I was all she could see. "Mark Vale, I can't believe it," she squealed, as if I were a Christmas present she had always hoped for but never dreamed she would ever really get. "My goodness me, how wonderful to see you."

I was sitting inside a cavernous hall that served as a waiting room, though it bore a closer resemblance to a mini refugee camp. The once whitewashed walls were the color of tobacco-stained teeth and the air smelled like rotting corpses doused with paraffin. Many of the patients had been there for days. Knowing the drill, most of them had brought what resources they could to set up camp, along with family folk they had brought to look after them, or those they still had to look after in spite of their own grievous condition.

If only I could say that the stench of the festering bodies around me – and the agonized groaning and wailing that accompanied it – helped take my mind off my own problems. Rather, it amplified them. As I sat on a pew with my back to the grimy wall, wedged between two despairing mothers, both of whom desperately rocked their babies in a futile attempt to hush them, I fully expected the abscess throbbing against my lower right wisdom tooth to blow my head off.

Perhaps it was my lackluster slur and the swelling in my jaw that gave it away, but Maxine was quick to guess my condition. "Oh, no, a sore tooth," she grimaced. "You poor thing, come with me." She led me out of the waiting hall and down a sparse corridor that reeked of disinfectant. Rather than being incensed at my special treatment, the Lapedi natives grinned up at me as cheerfully as they could manage and saluted me by putting their right hand to their temple and their left hand to their right elbow. They seemed momentarily honored to be in the presence of some kind of dignitary.

As relieved as I was to have my own case expedited, I had mixed feelings about being in Maxine Carlyle's care. There is nothing that can magnify the woes of life like a bad tooth, and considering our star-crossed history, I reckoned I already had more than enough grief to deal with.

"We haven't had a dentist here for years," said Maxine, ushering me into a room filled with archaic dental implements. I lay back on a sickly green leather reclining chair covered in thick plastic and eyed a tray full of heavy-duty glass syringes. "You don't use those?" I asked nervously. The needles were as long and thick as six-inch nails.

"No," Maxine laughed, "there's enough HIV around here without our using non-disposables." She looked in my mouth and probed my aching gum with a gloved finger. "Nasty," she concluded. "That back tooth is probably going to need root canal treatment. We can't do that here. I'll organize you a shot of Demerol and some antibiotics. That should kill the pain for a while and settle the infection enough until you get back to civilization."

Maxine took me back to a room adjoining the crowded waiting hall, where African nurses in starched white uniforms were busy stitching and bandaging injured patients. "Sister Sarafina," she called. A nurse turned from the invalid she was ministering to and stared at us impassively. "Can you give Mr. Vale a Demerol injection, please?"

"One amp?"

"That should do it." To me Maxine said, "I'll go and get you the antibiotics."

Sister Sarafina turned sullenly back to her patient and carried on with her operation as if she had not heard her doctor's order. Knowing that the end of my suffering was imminent allowed me to surrender to the excruciating pain I was in. I hopped from foot to foot in agitation as I waited for the nurse to attend to me.

When finally she was done and her patient was helped from the room, the sister directed me to enter a curtained cubicle. I stepped into the tiny plywood compartment and, as per the nurse's instructions, drew the curtain closed. After standing there in bewilderment for a few minutes, I heard Sister Sarafina's thick African accent outside my cubicle: "Take down you pants."

I did as I was told, assuming she would join me in the cubicle to give me my jab. "Now, you see this hole here?" she tapped on one side of the cubicle. I looked down to see a perfectly round hole about three inches in diameter. "Put your bottom against the hole. Whichever cheek, it doesn't matter." There was a mirthful ring to her voice, and I could hear a chorus of giggles around the room.

I did my best to position myself for the injection, but instead of a little stinging sensation, I felt a bruising stab of pain as the needle drove into the muscle above my right butt cheek. I let out a startled cry, much to the amusement of Sister Sarafina and her colleagues. They all laughed loudly.

When I stepped back out of the cubicle, the sister smiled at me warmly. What I had earlier mistaken for resentment I could now see was actually fatigue.

"Thank you," I smiled back at her appreciatively.

"Thank you, sir," she replied humbly. "Dr. Carlyle said you can go outside. She will find you there."

"Outside where?"

"Outside the hospital, by the front." Without making eye contact, Sister Sarafina pointed with a limp wrist over her shoulder.

I walked out of the decrepit building into the feeble warmth of the winter sun. An African dressed in a khaki ranger's uniform stood up from the dirty-white rocks ringing a withered flower garden in the middle of the gravel turning-circle and marched purposefully toward me. He was holding a Remington pump-action shotgun at the ready. Two belts stuffed with buckshot cartridges were slung in an X across his torso. It was my escort, Chollo. He looked at me expectantly.

"We wait...the doctor come," I told him in unpracticed Lapedi. I sat on the stone garden border he had been perched on. Chollo followed me, but he did not sit down. He stood beside me, looking about warily, his nostrils flaring as he sniffed the wind suspiciously.

The pain in my jaw had already significantly subsided. I looked up at the sky. It appeared to me as a giant geodesic dome complete with framed triangular segments. I looked back down at the grounds surrounding the hospital. They seemed frozen – not only by the cold, but also in time. A pair of Lapedi tribal women walked past us dressed in Java-print sarongs. They struck me as the most graceful beings I had ever seen. Their beautiful smiles gleamed like the sun dancing on water, while their feet appeared to be floating off the ground. It was a relief to know the Demerol was kicking in.

My condition quickly changed from fevered agony to a numb and detached melancholy. In my youth this same hospital had been surrounded by the most splendid botanical gardens. Now the gardens were overgrown with weeds and scrub, and the grassless lawns were littered with plastic bags and scraps of glossy newspaper inserts.

In the old days Manzimwe had been a proud district capital. The main street had been lined with every kind of shop imaginable. Throngs of people had bustled about, provisioning themselves with essential supplies and capricious indulgences. Every house and rock border had been glazed with multiple coats of iridescent whitewash, every road and pathway zealously hosed and swept. Back then, even the prisoners took pride in their appearance, being very careful not to get their black-and-white-striped uniforms dirty, and held their heads high, knowing their task of maintaining the civic gardens and parks was an important contribution to the town's image as a hub of national advancement.

These days Manzimwe resembled an archaeological site – the place was in ruins. Hardly a business was left intact. Only enterprises providing the most essential services were open, and then only to offer a pitifully meager range of goods. Most of the buildings had lost their roofs and windows, and their walls were collapsed and crumbling. Those that were still standing were stained a ruddy brown by the local dust and mud. Everywhere people shuffled about forlornly without purpose and stared morosely at the occasional passing vehicle.

From where I sat I could see over to what used to be the actual Catholic Mission. I could still remember it vividly with its gleaming white walls and shimmering tin roofs festooned with orange and magenta bougainvilleas. Now all I could see was a run-down collection of buildings with no windows, and stones holding down the rusted bits of tin that were left. The bell tower appeared to have been decapitated by a mortar bomb in some past uprising.

In the distance I could hear the sound of heavy cannon fire and artillery shells exploding. It was not the first time I had heard the sound of battles raging out of sight. They were something that always seemed to be confined to a distant no-man's-land that never spilled over to affect my family or me directly. Nevertheless, as heavily sedated as I was, I still felt relieved that I was booked on a plane out of the strife-torn Republic.

Maxine appeared from the hospital entrance looking like a blithe spirit. In my Demerol haze, she was not just beautiful, she radiated an aura of divinity. Her face was adorably moonlike – round and luminescent, with a long brow and high cheekbones, between which a pair of lively blue eyes danced with charismatic warmth and intelligence. All of her features were fine: a dainty chin, a small mouth with full lips, and a little button nose that deceptively crinkled with mirth no matter what her mood. The severe, unstyled bob of short hair pulled behind her ears did nothing to take away from the constant cheerfulness she exuded.

It was always easy to imagine that you were very special to Maxine – that was the effect her demeanor had. And that is the effect I felt when she handed me the little canister full of antibiotics and gave me a mug of water to wash down the first dose. "How's the pain now?" she asked gently.

"I'm fine," I murmured dreamily. I felt no need to disguise my admiration of her beguiling qualities. I lazily took in the pleasing sight of her endless legs and small hips and pert breasts.

"Do you have someone to drive you?" she asked. "You're not going to be able to drive yourself, you know that?"

"Too bad," I said, not at all put out. "Chollo here, he can shoot and he can track, but he can't drive."

Maxine stood deep in thought. Her one arm was folded across her stomach and the other pushed a hand into her chin. I sensed her come to a decision, which she tested by looking at Chollo and then back at me. "Why don't you come for a drive with me?" she said. "There's something you should see while you have the time."

"What's that?" I asked.

"An incredible discovery," she beamed. "They're calling it the *Mona Lisa of Africa*."

***

I sat in the backseat of Maxine's Range Rover with my head lolling against the head rest, dreamily watching the world go by outside. Maxine's driver, a well-spoken Lapedi man named David, was behind the wheel. Chollo sat beside him, an intense presence scanning the terrain ahead for the slightest hint of anything untoward. Though I did not look at her, I could feel Maxine's eyes regarding me from her seat on my right.

My wish that we could just keep on driving and never arrive anywhere reminded me of that same feeling I used to have in childhood. Some of my first memories were of sitting in the backseat of the family Wolseley as it bumped its way along some corrugated country road. I would look wistfully out the window, hoping that the scenery we were passing would somehow freeze and that we would never have to move on from it. Whether it was a herd of wildebeest on a savannah plain or some half-naked tribal folk waving from their thatched huts, I never wanted the sense of anything I beheld to be lost.

"I'm sorry to hear about Stan," Maxine said, breaking the blissful silence we had been driving in. I didn't feel inclined to respond. There were many issues and sentiments from the past that I was happy to let lie. "I was hoping to be at his memorial, but the casualties from the fighting along the border have made it impossible to leave the hospital. It's only because a Médecins Sans Frontières doctor arrived yesterday that I'm getting a break today – and only for as long as the fighting doesn't escalate."

"I understand, Max," I said, still keeping my gaze on the scenery beyond. "It was just the family, anyway."

"I know," Maxine said warmly. "If times were different, your father would have had a state funeral."

Maxine's words unleashed a torrent of subterranean emotions. I regarded my own feelings with an objective curiosity, as if I were studying novel pieces of art at an exhibition. She had breached the wall that divided me from everything I didn't feel up to facing and, seen through the Demerol veil, it all didn't seem so unbearable. Finally I turned to look at her.

"It's funny," I said, "I remember an exact moment when I was seven or so, when I imagined what it would be like to be grown up. I pictured myself with a beard – a symbol of my conclusive maturity, I guess. In that moment I assumed without a doubt that, just as my physical body would fill out and reach its ultimate dimensions, so too would I automatically fill out emotionally and psychologically. I used to look at my father and think, 'One day I'll be that self-assured, infallible man of the world.' I figured that by the time a person left high school or university, they'd naturally be in sync with life."

"Stan's a hard act to follow," said Maxine.

"Oh, look, I wouldn't want to try," I replied. "I just never figured I'd be hitting my forties and still looking for answers, or faced with issues that I didn't feel man enough to face. Now that Dad's gone, there's a gulf between me and what I'm looking for. I feel like the foundation I was standing on has been washed away."

"What are you talking about, Mark?" exclaimed Maxine. "You're the man who teaches people how they can rise above their limited mindset to create whatever they want. You wrote the book on how to deal with all this stuff, didn't you?"

"It's okay, Max," I said, feeling like she was the one who needed reassurance, "it's just the truth." I let out a pleasant sigh. I felt good and righteous admitting my inner quandary. "I don't know how much you know but, yes, I did write a book on living life by magic – *The Magician's Way* – and it was a big success." I paused for effect, and then went on. "The chairman of the Continental Banking Group and one of our country's most famous artists, Melissa Matheson, spoke glowingly about me and the book at the launch. People were lining up to attend my seminars; I was in hot demand for speaking engagements. I was the man."

I thought wistfully back to those times for a moment.

"So what happened?" said Maxine.

"Well," I mused, "my whole premise was predicated on

the idea that we have a natural ability that can create what-ever we want with absolute ease."

"I know," Maxine laughed encouragingly, "I've read your book. That stuff works without fail. As long as you're able to hold a picture of what you want in your mind, it will manifest every time."

"Yes, but here's the thing," I countered hastily, without even stopping to question how she had gotten ahold of my book. "*The Magician's Way* did a great job in waking people to the fact that they're the predominant creative force in their life and that they can create brilliant outcomes totally outside of what they ever believed was possible. I know many people who have manifested all sorts of amazing things using the very magic I've taught them. Hell, I've done it myself – I've written a best-selling book without knowing the first thing about writing and publishing; I've turned dire business circumstances into massive moneymaking oppor-tunities. But there's an insidious side effect to magic that people don't expect."

An expression of alarm flitted across Maxine's face. "What side effect?"

"I call it the Hitler Effect," I said languidly, not letting on that the term had just then come to me.

"The Hitler Effect?"

"Yeah. If you think about a megalomaniac like Adolf Hitler, and observe his creative arc, you will see what I'm talking about." I could feel myself warming to my subject, as if I were syphoning words from some glowing reservoir of eloquence deep within myself. "To begin with, you see him taking massive action in favor of his vision. His initial success is phenomenal. His fierce will is supported by an uncanny psychic foresight; destiny is totally on his side: plots against him fail, his actions lead to overwhelming victories. To begin with he seems so invincible. The image he projects is one of superiority and power. Yet it is well documented that his ambition was driven by a deep inferi-ority and powerlessness complex. That's the hidden picture in his mind that all of his power-mongering was trying to bury, and in the end that is the picture that prevailed – he was crushed so utterly and decisively."

I paused to catch my breath. "And on a much less dramatic and sinister level, we are all the same when it comes to pursuing our desires and ambitions. I had a massive life coaching business following the success of *The Magician's Way*, and I've seen this happen to so many people, including myself. Almost always when people start to use their will and direct their natural ability to create outcomes of their own determination, they do see startling results. Like with Hitler, the initial success bodes very well; it's very encouraging. But sooner or later the flow of serendipity dies, as if someone upstream has cut off the supply. Whatever was gained is lost, maybe; or it becomes a struggle to maintain or build momentum; or it comes at a cost in other areas of the person's life. Someone might become spiritually awakened, for instance, but then find the material side of life difficult; the delightful soul mate that fell down from heaven turns into a heartbreaking, fire-breathing dragon; piles of money build up, but health and human connections wither.

"Now psychological tension builds in the fledgling magician's mind as a result of this oscillation, and he begins to make up beliefs about what the problem is: using my will is bad; there's a negative belief blocking my desire – I'm not positive enough; I don't have enough resources yet – I have to know more, try harder, get motivated; stuff like that. To resolve the tension, the would-be magician does what he assumes has to be done to fix whatever is supposedly responsible for cutting off the flow. He might surrender his will to fate, or start navel-gazing or searching for more knowledge. Whatever he does, though, just disconnects him from magic more than ever."

"How is that?" Maxine frowned.

Her question took me by surprise, jolting me out of the stream of consciousness I was giving voice to. I had to dig back down into my fogged-up mind to find my train of thought again. "Well, because there is never anything wrong with our natural ability to begin with. It can create whatever it's directed to with perfect ease. The idea that there is some condition that has to be fulfilled before we can create is a total red herring. It's a distraction that unharnesses our creative faculty.

"Here's the thing that people don't seem to get. Our natural ability is always creating an exact replica in our external world of whatever picture is being held up in our internal world. So, when we experience unwanted realities in our life – circumstances or things at odds with what we deliberately intended – there isn't anything faulty with anyone or anything, it's just that the picture being held up to our natural ability isn't the same one as we're seeing in our self-conscious mind. We're just blind to the actual message our creative faculty is getting. If it got a different message, if it saw a different picture, it would create that just as easily.

"This is a fundamental secret of magic. Whoever knows this secret and can operate at a level beyond self-conscious awareness is the true magician. They have the power to see the true picture and decide whether that is a good representation of what they want to create or not, and if not, to change it. That is why, to be able to work masterfully with magic, you have to know yourself. Every mystical tradition, from Christ to the Oracle at Delphi, they all say the same thing. It's by far the most important principle of self-mastery."

"Know thyself," Maxine nodded her head thoughtfully. "How does that fit in with your point?"

"Well, my point is," I said with a loud sigh, "that to be able to consistently manifest what you love, you have to know what that is. We assume we know, but mostly we don't. Love, as I use the word now, is a vision of something we have a pure connection to, something we desire for its own true sake. What we want can sometimes be the same as what we love, but mostly it's what we believe we need to have before we can have what we love. More often than not, we're mistaking what we want for what we love. It's the Hitler Effect. In his heart, the guy most probably longed to paint and enjoy being part of some bohemian crowd, but in his mind he didn't feel safe to be that unless he ruled the world. Let's say he loved expression and belonging, not power; but he lusted after power – that's what he wanted. Don't ask me why, it's just a human tendency that rather than going directly for something that's an end result in and of itself, we try to resolve or fix something we imagine is wrong with ourselves or others or the world. Then we think our visions are positive because of the rosy picture we see in our minds as we imagine life with all of our wants, little realizing that what our natural ability is looking at is the negativity or limitation motivating the wants.

"You know the saying, 'Be careful what you wish for'?" I snorted humorlessly. "I don't think it's a caution that what you want might not be cracked up to what you expect it to be; it's a warning that your desire might be promoting some-thing other than what you might self-consciously expect. Let's face it, we humans don't naturally have the awareness to distinguish between our loves and wants. That kind of clarity rests on a plane of consciousness outside of our ratio-nal, self-conscious awareness, which is fanatically biased in favor of our wants. And that's the wall people eventually hit when they take up magic. They're left half-wise, where they've been let into the secret of their superhuman potential and maybe know a lot about the mechanics that drive magic, but not much about the wisdom that sustains and enriches its outcomes.

"Being half-wise is dangerous, believe me. It's like handling a double-edged sword. Sometimes you're moving mountains using only the force of your will, then at other times your life is turned upside down by all kinds of strife that you have absolutely no answer to. It's like the old Hermetic alchemists' admonishment: 'And they shall be dashed against the rocks by reason of their own folly.' The folly being, of course, applying the formulas without know-ing thyself, which means without distinguishing the forces at play in your consciousness, without knowing what's motivating your choices, what your true target is."

"So what specific side effects have you suffered, if you

don't mind my asking?" I wasn't facing Maxine right then, but I knew she would be wearing an expression of gentle concern to match her tone of voice.

The shame I had been keeping hidden from everyone in my life danced unselfconsciously to the foreground of my mind. "Well," I readily confessed, "the truth is, I never met anyone who could tell me the secret to 'know thyself.' I have very good magician friends who know me well, and they can often tell me whether I'm on track or not, and when they guide me I can create anything; I'm on fire. But without them, I'm hopeless; I can't see the forest for the trees. I don't know by myself.

"In the beginning, the problem wasn't apparent. After *The Magician's Way,* I also had my spectacular initial success. I was the flavor of the month with the human potential crowd. I was thriving, doing what I love. Business was booming; referrals were flooding in as all of my clients made great strides forward in their lives. Then one by one they began getting slammed by the Hitler Effect and I didn't have a meaningful solution for them. They began drifting away, trying out other empowerment modalities and going to all of the usual inspirational talks looking for the answers. But there's no one out there, as far as I know, who is teaching the vital insight that will be of real, permanent value to them. And believe me, it's no consolation to me that my clients aren't going to find the secret to 'know thyself' from someone else. I'm as hungry for it as they are.

"Where I got caught is making big leveraged lifestyle investments based on the money I was making when things were booming – big houses, expensive cars, the usual traps. Now that business has dried up, I'm finding it a real struggle to make the repayments on my loans. So my dilemma is, do I try to soldier on in the self-empowerment business, trusting I will make the breakthrough I need to make, even though I can't imagine where that will come from, or do I go back into the corporate world? If the answer is back to the corporate world, then what can I do? The information business I used to be in got taken out by the Internet ages ago; it's dead and buried. That's the thing, relying on your natural ability is all well and good when it comes to straightforward physical outcomes like finding a parking spot in the city or playing golf. But it's a lot trickier when you're dealing with the strategic issues of your life. My confidence to make choices was shot well before my father's death – now I'm more stuck than ever. I feel so powerless, I'm virtually paralyzed. I never expected that his passing would rattle me so badly.

"You know, Max, there is a very real possibility that I'll end up a complete nothing, just like my family here in the Republic always half-expected me to. They never valued *The Magician's Way*; they thought I was selling snake oil. Now the hole I'm in just confirms their suspicions. You can't imagine what a fool I feel, having set myself up as a guru with all the answers and now being on the verge of losing everything – and above all, my credibility."

"I'm sure things will work out, Mark," Maxine said soothingly. My sense was that she was beginning to regret engaging me in conversation. "Tell me about your family – your wife and kids, I mean."

"Uhhh," I moaned feebly, "another disaster. Isn't that the case, though? When one thing's out in your life, everything else is too. My wife, Kirsten, and I, we've separated again. It's awful because of the kids, and knowing that she and I still love each other terribly, but we're just back in the same financial stress and creative doldrums we were in before *The Magician's Way*. We just don't know if being together is the right thing, or whether we'd be better off making new lives for ourselves."

"Oh, I'm sorry to hear that," said Maxine. Her eternally uplifting countenance had morphed into a look of profound solicitude. She touched my arm gently. "You know what? I think you're going to be very impressed with what I'm going to show you. It may very well be connected to what you're looking for."

I reflected with no bitterness, thanks to the synthetic morphine high, that Maxine had always had the effect of buoying me and then leaving me deflated. The truth was that I had loved her for…well, forever. She was one of the first white children outside my family that I had ever met. We had been inseparable in our first years at school. We used to tell people that we were going to get married.

The effects of that innocent love had never left me. Later, in my teenage years and early adulthood, it seemed I always managed to bump into Maxine at some low point in my life, and she, in turn, always rushed in like a fresh summer breeze to fill me with hope. She had a knack of doting on me and encouraging in my heart the vision of a wonderful life that could be forged from the chemistry between us. And then she would inevitably reveal her unavailability. Maxine was a mirage that had confounded my empty heart for as long as I could remember.

Even though I now felt the full force of her energetic charm, this time I was under no illusion that there was any hope of finding comfort in Maxine. My family had already told me that she was currently engaged to a League of Human Rights activist by the name of Roger Stratton. Apparently it was an open secret that she and her fiancé were bent on rescuing some high-profile prisoner of conscience and spiriting him or her out of the country. "In the middle of a civil war!" everyone sighed, rolling their eyes in exasperation.

If the rumor was true, I did not envy Roger Stratton. Going by Maxine's form, the poor guy was doomed to meet a sticky end. His intended was what the old colonials feared more than anything else – a dangerous woman.

By appealing to their innate chivalry or machismo, and, in some cases, stupidity, Maxine had managed to get more than her fair share of men into trouble. To cite a more extreme example, there was the boyfriend from medical school who was murdered by river pirates while escorting her on an excursion up the Orinoco. Maxine herself had been badly wounded in the fracas, but other than a thin scar across her throat, had survived the experience without any noticeable permanent damage.

Back home she had been arrested and thrown into prison twice that I knew of for inciting civil unrest. Though the jails of the Republic were among the most notoriously brutal in the world, Maxine always seemed unfazed by her time inside. In each case her detention coincided with some young male expatriate idealist being violently ejected from the country for allegedly collaborating with "reactionary elements threatening state security." Never mind that this ominous rhetoric might refer to someone whose greatest sin was to attend a union meeting where better wages for teachers might have been discussed – in the Republic that could get you killed.

***

I was jolted out of my reverie as the Range Rover hit a huge pothole in the mountain track we were following. First I was thrown into the air as the vehicle went nose down like a bucking horse, and then I slammed into my door as the car rolled almost completely on its side. Maxine squealed with fright as she practically slid into my lap. Once the vehicle steadied, she disentangled herself from me and shifted back into her seat.

"Jesus! That was close," she said breathlessly, fastening her seat belt. "Are you trying to kill us, David?"

"Yes, madam," her chauffeur laughed agreeably.

Usually this would have been no laughing matter for me. We were now driving perilously close to the edge of a massive precipice. Given the shaky condition of both our vehicle and the road we were on – not to mention my fear of heights – I should have been filled with horror. Instead, I stared with fascination into the chasm on my side of the track.

The miserable excuse for a road edged away from the top of the escarpment we had been traversing and led onto a small plateau perched a few hundred feet below the main tableland of the Lesoti mountain range. On Maxine's side of the car, nestled into a cliff face, was a small cluster of weather-beaten huts. Their grass roofs were frayed through to the stick rafters and were in bad need of rethatching. The geometrical Lapedi motifs that adorned the rounded mud walls of each hut were chipped and faded to a mere hint of the bold primary colors they had originally been painted in.

David stopped the car in front of a crude boom gate fashioned from forked tree branches stuck in the ground with a pole – weighted by a rock at one end – resting between the forks. Why he had come to a halt when there was nothing to stop him from driving around either side of the gate, I could not fathom.

A youth of indeterminate age appeared in the shadow of one of the doorways. He wore the short, red, ochre-caked dreadlocks of an *ndotsi* – an apprentice sorcerer. Cradled in his arms was an AK-47 assault rifle, with a spare ammunition clip taped to its curved magazine. Chollo stiffened at the sight of the ndotsi and then, after studying the boy's attitude for a moment, relaxed again.

Before long a gray-haired man emerged from one of the other doorways and approached us. He was dressed in an unbuttoned great coat and a threadbare Java-print sarong. For shoes he wore a pair of homemade sandals with car-tire soles and straps made from strips of inner tubing.

Maxine and David got out of the car to greet the old man. "Hello, father," they both said in the native tongue.

"Yes, children of our people," came the formal response. The old man held his left hand to his right elbow and raised his right hand to his temple in the traditional salute of respect. "I see you," he said in a level voice, looking into the car to include Chollo and me in the greeting.

David returned the salute and then led the old man to the back of the car. There was a brief exchange of words, after which the back hatch of the Range Rover clicked open and they began unloading sundry supplies of food and clothing that Maxine had packed back at the hospital. While the ndotsi and a couple of malnourished but nevertheless smiling children carried the supplies to the huts, the old veteran produced a tattered receipt book and laboriously wrote out a receipt for Maxine. Once the exchange was complete, David and Maxine jumped back in the car, the boom gate was opened for us, and we drove through and parked on the other side of the gate.

"What was that for?" I asked in amazement.

"For their dignity," replied Maxine.

"A toll gate at the end of the road," I marveled. "Now I've seen everything."

"You haven't seen anything yet," said Maxine. "That's an entry fee to one of the most spectacular art galleries in the world."

"Art gallery?" I looked around the bleak plateau.

"Up there," she smiled, pointing to the boulder-strewn mountain face at the far end of the field. "Wait till you see the *Mona Lisa of Africa*."

David and Chollo waited with the car while Maxine and I wandered off toward the sheer mountain face armed with two flashlights. We passed a pair of topless maidens harvesting wild spinach in a withered corn patch. They stood up to wave and giggle with the mock coyness tribal girls use to flatter strange men. "How much do you know about shamanism?" Maxine asked me, dismissing the girls with a friendly wave.

"Are you talking about witch doctors?"

"No, shamanism."

"Aren't they the same?"

"That's like saying Pan and the Devil are the same."

I stopped walking. "What are you talking about, Max?"

"Well, you know how Pan was the pagan god of nature. Pagans were nature worshippers, and when the Roman Church wanted to eradicate paganism in Europe and supplant it with their own doctrine, they discredited Pan by personifying the Devil in the image of Pan – hence the horns and tail and cloven hoofs. Clever, huh? They were masters of propaganda, those early Christian proselytizers.

"Come on, let's keep walking." Maxine tugged at my shirtsleeve. "So, of course, when the Catholic missionaries arrived in Africa, a similar whitewash was called for. They took all the superstition and hocus-pocus, all the voodoo beliefs and practices, and presented this as evidence of a primitive, Devil-crazed culture. Shamanism was associated with the dark side of tribal magic. So a very refined and sophisticated spiritual connection and healing art was perniciously snuffed out."

"Well," I said, "I've never seen anything high and mighty about witchcraft. All I've ever been aware of is ritual murder, psychosomatic illnesses, and people being stood over by the voodoo caste."

"Yeah, but that's because the balance has been lost," said Maxine. "Don't you get it? We've taken away their connection to soul and healing. We give them Bibles and antibiotics, but we take away their power, so of course they become prey to superstition. They've lost ownership of magic, so now they're victims to it."

Maxine's proposition was unexpected and startling to my drug-muddled mind.

"You say 'we,'" I protested, "but what's this got to do with us? You and I didn't corrupt an entire people's culture, and besides, how could we undo the harm you suggest has been intentionally done?"

Maxine stopped and fixed me with a look that let me know my words were on record. There was a hint of sneakiness in her ever-uplifted expression. "We'll see," she said. "First you have to see this."

We attacked the slope diagonally. It was not as steep as it had looked from where the car was parked, though we did have to use all of our limbs to haul ourselves up. Halfway up I turned and looked back. I was surprised to see how far away the Range Rover looked. I noticed for the first time that the car had a red cross stenciled on its roof as well as its front doors. "How much difference will they make when the bullets start flying?" I wondered.

From where I stood I had a great view of the surrounding country. Looking south beyond the miniature plateau below us, I could see almost all the way back to Manzimwe. To the north, the great Lesoti mountain range stretched out like a lion lying on its belly. In line with the lion's shoulder, at the foot of the mountains, I could vaguely make out the green expanse of the vast irrigation scheme I had grown up on. Two thousand feet directly below me, the great cattle ranches and tribal reserves of the Republic spread out like a dull gray blanket to the west. Beyond the plains, I imagined another mountain range climbing up into the clouds where once, as legend had it, the Lapedi kings sat in council with the gods.

"This is it," Maxine called from a little way above me before disappearing into the face of the mountain. When I reached the spot where she had vanished, I found the entrance to a small tunnel not much wider than my shoulders and only as high as my waist. Warily, I got down on my hands and knees and began crawling into the tunnel. To my relief, the passage was not very deep. I was soon able to stand upright in a cave about the height, width and breadth of a decent sized bedroom. The walls of the cave all curved up to the ceiling – except for the northern face, which was a big, flat slab of rock.

Maxine had her flashlight on, though she kept it facing down in an obvious attempt to obscure from me the surprise she had waiting. In spite of her attempt at theatrical suspense, I could make out some distinctly man-made images on the wall in front of us.

"Shamanism," said Maxine once she was satisfied that she had my full attention, "is about a journey to another realm, where the forces at play in that dimension can be harmonized to create a corresponding harmony in our world."

Maxine paused to make sure I would appreciate the import of her subsequent words. "Or," she said, "to find guidance for misguided souls." I knew that was supposed to make an impression on me, but I couldn't imagine a wall of bushman paintings being too edifying.

As if reading my mind, Maxine aimed her torch beam at the cave wall and shined it around to reveal a large mural crowded with a variety of figures. "For a long time, European settlers thought that paintings like this depicted the hunting stories of a stone-age society, or accounts of clan warfare. But now we know that in every case these are an account of a shaman's journey into the spiritual world for the purpose of guidance, healing, or rainmaking."

Maxine traced her torch beam back to the far left side of the cave wall. "One of the clues," she continued, "is that the San – or Bushmen as we used to call them – hunted hundreds of species of animals, yet they only ever painted three: their favorite, the eland, the largest member of the antelope family; lions, sometimes; and very occasionally, catfish. These were their totems, the sacred animals they associated with their trances, their spiritual dream-state. Over here—"

Before Maxine could go on, she was interrupted by a loud, rolling, thunder-like noise that reverberated around the cave walls as the earth shook violently underfoot. Instinctively we both reached out with our free hands for the support of the wall in front of us. The rumbles and tremors subsided and then erupted again.

Maxine glanced at me solicitously. "Artillery fire," she called out. "Nothing to worry about; it's miles away. More than likely around the Gola-Gola border post. There's been a big buildup of Fighters inside Portuguese Territory lately. The offensive had to start sooner or later."

"Jesus Christ," I muttered, contemplating with awe the force of an explosion that could rock the ground dozens of miles away.

"Most probably hit an ammo dump," said Maxine nonchalantly. "You okay? Shall I go on?"

"Yeah," I murmured, even though my mind was stuck on wondering what it would have been like for the combatants at ground zero.

Maxine searched for her starting point with her torchlight, and once the beam had settled on a cluster of images, she resumed her commentary as if nothing had happened. "This is a classic piece of rock art," she gushed, "painted by a master metaphysician six thousand years ago. To give you some idea of how remarkable that is, consider that Rome was only founded three thousand years later. I get goose bumps every time I look at this painting."

Personally, I was yet to see what was so astonishing about the etchings, as I thought of them. Again, Maxine seemed to read my mind.

"You'll be amazed at how well this was painted," she said, seemingly in defiance of my lack of appreciation. "Some of the images are photographic in their depictions, despite the crude materials and surface the artist had to work with. The most amazing thing is that this artist, like all of his historical colleagues, was never trained in any art form and in all likelihood never had any practice before he created this masterpiece. There is no evidence that he painted anything before or after. There was only this one time, six thousand years ago, when a lifetime of ritual devotion culminated in this…this…person, let's call him, making – or experiencing, more like it – an unimaginable leap in consciousness, fully bridging his mortal coil to the Divine, temporarily equipping himself with an artistic technology five thousand years ahead of his time. This is the work of a genius, a man who attained something philosophers and modern physicists have only talked of in hypothetical, theoretical terms: that most transcendent state of being where one is pure emptiness, nothing but a channel, an instrument of the Divine."

Maxine's goose bumps were contagious – I could feel them tingling up and down my arms.

"How he achieved…I mean, how he opened himself up to this quantum transformation is depicted here in the scene he painted." Maxine circled the cluster of images with her torch beam. "At the beginning we see the image of a human in shamanic regalia dancing. But look at the progression of figures moving on from him. First, a creature that has the head and torso of a man and the legs of an antelope. Next, the creature has the head of an antelope, the arms and torso of a man and the legs of an antelope. This is to signify that the days and days of dancing, clapping, and chanting are taking effect. The shaman is going into trance; he's beginning to shape-shift, to take on the demonic nature that can travel between worlds.

"See these red streaks projecting from the snouts of the therianthropes, the composite creatures? Those are nosebleeds, a very common symptom of the initial trance state. See the eland and the lions that follow in this sequence? See how they have nosebleeds, too? Here we see the shaman connected to his totem animals through trance. They're passing on their spiritual resources to him so he can do battle on the Other Side."

The torchlight lingered on the scene of shamanic preparation and then slowly began climbing the rock face following the trajectory of the mural.

"This thin red line I'm following obviously plots the shaman's journey, and at the same time, it appears to be an astral cord that anchors him to his human domain, the physical dimension."

"What's an astral cord?" I interrupted.

"Oh," Maxine laughed, "it's a luminous thread that spiritualists say links our spirit essence to our physical body. They often appear in San rock paintings. As we see here in this picture, the cord always cuts through a crack in the cave wall. The crack represents a fault-line in the normally immutable structure of our reality. It's a glitch, a portal into the Other World that the shaman can pass through. This theme survives even in contemporary myths and fairytales, like Alice going down the rabbit hole into Wonderland, or the wardrobe in the Narnia chronicles that leads into a strange land of fauns and satyrs and talking lions. Only this isn't a fairytale, this isn't Enid Blyton; this here is a firsthand account of a factual Other Worldly journey.

"This particular journey was a healing assignment. There's no indication of what the shaman was treating. It could have been blackwater fever or a bad snakebite, something like that maybe. Whatever it was, the epic scale of the saga portrayed here suggests that it was a grave condition. As soon as the shaman goes through the crack into the Other Side, he is immediately set upon by evil spirits. Look at these archers letting loose this barrage of arrows; they're far too diabolical to be human. Whereas the shaman, nimbly avoiding his attackers thanks to the powers of eland and lion, he's perfectly human. The creepy guys are definitely evil spirits, metaphysical symptoms of the affliction he is treating."

Maxine spoke with an unabashed delight. Something of the innocence of our childhood association touched me and I felt a twinge of guilt that part of me was so wary of her. All the while she spoke, she did so apparently oblivious to the subdued drumming of mortar fire in the background and a mild trembling of the earth. Momentarily, a shocking clatter drowned the cave. It was the sound of a giant drill boring into the granite roof above our heads. I instinctively shielded my head with my arms.

"What was that?" I asked in astonishment once the noise had subsided.

"Helicopter gunship," replied Maxine with a little laugh that released her own fright. "Lucky there aren't any Fighters in the area; otherwise, the choppers would be napalming the caves."

"Lucky us." My sarcasm made me realize that my Demerol high had most probably already peaked. I had enough objectivity to recognize that I should be registering some degree of concern.

"Are you alright, Mark?" said Maxine.

I was struck by how such a mild question could carry so much empathy. It conveyed the impression that my welfare was the most important thing in that moment – the rest of the world could wait. All good doctors are practiced in giving that impression when attending to their patients, but it came naturally to Maxine.

"Evil spirits," I grunted dismissively, gesturing to the mural for her to go on.

"Yes, evil spirits," she confirmed. "Look how the chase continues all over this side of the wall. These fiendish creatures ambushing our hero wherever he goes are the implicate causes of the malady affecting his patient in the physical world. After flushing them all out, the shaman turns around and counterattacks. Now he lets loose his own salvo of arrows. Eland and lion medicine – the animals' spiritual energy – is too strong for them. His arrows find their mark and not one evil spirit is left standing. Now all he has to do is follow the astral cord back through the crack in the wall and slip back into the physical world."

Maxine considered the mural for a while before going on.

"The amazing thing is, this isn't a fairytale. This really happened. The man who painted this spent days fasting. The effect of that physical depravation was probably amplified by his whole clan dancing and clapping and chanting along with him. Slowly but surely, his consciousness would have become unhinged from its rational seat and carried higher and higher by the incessant hypnotic rhythm. His nose would have begun bleeding. He would have fainted repeatedly until he had lost all consciousness and fallen into the trance state.

"It's true that aboriginal people universally believe the Other World to be more real than our own. Even in Lapedi mythology they talk about the Land of Dreams, a kind of imaginative or extra-conscious plane that we exist on simultaneous to our earthly life, but whose reality is more substantial than waking, self-conscious reality. So, imagine the impact of waking up in an alien and hostile world, where the most frightening demons are standing by for the kill. As the mural attests, this was an epic battle, an odyssey from which the shaman returned victorious – back in our world someone was cured of some dreadful illness as a direct result – but you have to appreciate that this battle might have lasted days, every detail of which the shaman experienced as a vivid reality."

"Sounds like a bad acid trip," I quipped.

"You can snicker, but you're going to eat your words," Maxine laughed lightly. "This is the best part. What happens next can't be denied, nor can it be rationalized away. Listen to this. The shaman found his way back to the physical world. He followed the astral cord home through the crack in the wall and came out of his trance with his experience burning in his imagination so brightly that it was still his spirit self rather than his human self occupying his waking mind, if you know what I mean. A force outside of his biological programming was driving him. Some deep, atavistic urge compelled him to affirm the events and outcomes of his ordeal, to validate his experience here in the physical plane. Who knows, we can only guess his motivation, but it was there, blazing in him like a forest fire.

"In his transfigured state, the shaman began to fossick for artistic materials. Remember, this was a spontaneous act. The man never had any desire to paint until this moment. There was no pallet of ochre conveniently at hand. He had to go off and mine them. Let's hope he had some help, because not only did he have to collect his materials from scratch, he had to carry them up the same steep slope we've climbed to get here. He had to have a fire to light up the cave, ostrich eggs filled with water, ochre, painting sticks, kindling and wood, flints, all that kind of stuff.

"Finally he would have been ready to paint. In the dim light of the brushwood fire, he began transferring the vibrations in his mind onto the granite walls. He could barely see what he was doing. Neither he nor any of his clan ever realized that he was painting what scholars now refer to as the *Mona Lisa of Africa*. Six thousand years had to pass before this cave could be illuminated by a light bright enough to reveal the genius of this work. These images are as real as photographs. This is virtually photographic evidence of a journey to hell and back."

Maxine fell silent, letting the gravity of her words hang in the caustic air of the cave. While I had been more or less unmoved by her literal interpretation of the shaman's bizarre odyssey, the theme upon which my childhood friend finished her commentary sent a chill up my spine. I was gripped by an eerie excitation that I was familiar with from visiting hallowed archaeological sites like pyramids or ancient cathedrals. It was the sense of an imminent transcendent combustion, a higher intelligence on the verge of stepping out of the ether and revealing itself to me.

"Go on, take a look," Maxine urged. "You've got the

bright light."

I pressed my thumb down on the switch of the chunky twelve-volt flashlight in my hand. The wall before me was suddenly bathed in an unnaturally brilliant light. Crouching, I began inspecting the images depicting the shaman going into trance. Neither Maxine's passionate exposition nor what I had seen in the dimmer light could have prepared me for what I now beheld. To anyone watching, I would have come across as a gaping child mesmerized by the kaleidoscopic wonder of an underwater aquarium.

"Oh my god!" I whistled softly.

My vision had been arrested by a three-dimensional image of an eland. Not only did the eland appear perfectly proportioned and lifelike, the artist had managed to capture it in one of Africa's quintessential poses: that of an antelope looking back over its shoulder at something it has stopped running from. While the portrait was only about nine inches high, the eland's attitude was infused with the classic antelope qualities of vulnerability and curiosity. It appeared not to be fixed flat against the wall, but to float in relief.

"How could someone paint something as incredible as this without being able to see what they were doing?" I marveled. "Using a stick and some ochre, for God's sake!"

"What did I tell you?" Maxine laughed gleefully. "They don't call it the *Mona Lisa* for nothing."

I stared at the eland again. The real *Mona Lisa*, as far as I was aware, was famous for her enigmatic smile, but it was not so easy to decide what was most unique about this beauty. There was the bovine innocence in the eyes, the sweet character of a tame horse written all over the face, yet I was equally impressed by the rich folds of dewlap and the coiled tension in the flanks. It seemed as if the painted antelope could dart off in a flash.

"It's phenomenal," I conceded.

Having given me room to absorb the brilliance of the animal portrait, Maxine now stepped forward herself and began examining the rest of the mural. I tore myself away from the eland to share my light with her. We studied the various images in awed silence. Eventually, I could not contain my fascination any longer.

"None of these images are as photographic as the eland," I said, "although many come close. But they're all fantastic. They're all in perfect proportion and express such realistic movement and emotion. Look at this guy here, how he's straining to get away from the demons. He's running so fast, he's beginning to stumble. And look at the terror on his face; he thinks he's had it.

"Even the mythological characters look like something that's real. They express such powerful archetypes that you don't question their authenticity. There's something so noble about the shape-shifting creature, something messianic or saintly. Not like the evil spirits here. Their malevolence and fiendish intention are so clear. They are hideous, no doubt about it, though not by virtue of their monstrous or macabre features, but because of their coldness."

My words surprised me. A second look at some of the images made me question whether my praise was not exaggerated. None of the figures exhibited a detail that might justify such a rich description. Yet there was no doubting that the qualities I attributed to the works were embodied in the impression the images evoked.

"How can it be possible that this is the only painting the artist ever did?" I wondered aloud.

"What you have to understand," Maxine replied, "is that this man's forebears took up rock art twenty-seven thousand years ago in Spain. If this had been a widely practiced art form handed down from generation to generation among the San clans scattered across Africa and southern Europe, can you imagine how many thousands of sites like this there would be? Except, with the number of sites that are known, there isn't any evidence to suggest that there existed even one artist in every generation anywhere in the whole world. They were not prolific. Some artists did paint multiple works, but there's no rock art for hundreds of miles of here, other than this painting."

"So they just popped up here and there independent of

any continuous artistic tradition," I mused. "Kind of like if random pigeons were born with the instinct to weave nests."

"Exactly," said Maxine, "except with rock art there's more to it than instinct, more than innate knowing. There actually is a particular process that is handed down through the generations: the art of healing and rainmaking. None of this art was produced other than as the product of trance – being able to go into the spiritual dream-state. There was a skill being employed – the ability to journey into and harmonize the Other World. I don't believe that painting was their talent – their talent was connecting with the Divine."

I felt the hairs on the back of my neck stand on end. A spooky sensation crawled over me like a cold hand feeling for my soul. My imagination was gripped by a palpable sense that the mural was a sentient personality standing by expectantly, waiting to engage human intelligence.

"And do you think that this talent could be learned by you or me?" I said, my voice trembling.

"Well," Maxine hesitated, "talent implies a natural gift. No doubt we could be instructed in the process. Whether you or I could apply it to the point that we could be the Leonardo Da Vinci of our time is another matter."

"But still," I persisted, "what you're saying is that this supernatural ability is the result of an applied formula, which means that there exists a practical bridge to a super-creative state of being."

"Oh, absolutely!" Maxine agreed. "This is a bridge to actualizing an unlimited super-conscious potential beyond anything you and I can conceive of, to knowing everything we need to know to realize that potential."

I shined my torch back and forth across the ancient fresco. "That's amazing," I laughed, tantalized by the recognition that there existed a mysterious force in the universe so powerful that it could, through human contact, miraculously express its existence in the physical world. Equally enthralling was the unshakable impression I had that on the other side of the crack in the wall before me lay a world in which loves were clearly distinguished from wants. I was too elated to be disturbed by an underlying sense that something of the mural's demonic personality had attached itself to my psyche.

"So how does one learn this shaman magic?" I said.

A volley of artillery fire erupted in the distance again. Maxine checked her watch absently. "Better get going," she said, "they'll be needing me in surgery. I'll tell you more in the car."

CHAPTER TWO

Escape from Manzimwe

From the diary of Jessica Vale, July 30

*Oh my god! My family is so racist. I must have been adopted.
I asked Mom if Natanzi could come and stay for the last week
of holidays and she said NO. Her reason is because of all the
family here for Granpa Stan's funeral, but that's just another
excuse on top of all the excuses before. One more person
wouldn't make any difference in the homestead. It's because
she's black.*

*I wish Dad were more like Uncle Mark. He's so nice to all
the servants and us kids. He doesn't think he's better than
everyone. I don't know why the adults laugh at him behind his
back – just because he's different. I pray to God nothing
happens to him in Manzimwe. We can hear the bombs
exploding from here.*

From the journal of Martin Vale, July 30

*I still have to look it up, but 87 tons an acre from section 6 –
I'm sure that's a record for the Irrigation Scheme. Must have
a drink with section manager at club when things get back to
normal.*

Bloody nuisance all this fighting. Makes Dad's memorial even harder on all concerned. But in the end it might be the best thing if the army sorts the Rebels out once and for all. I'm not sure that it was a good thing letting Mark go up to Manzimwe today, tooth infection or no. If anything can go wrong for anyone, it's him. He's never been one to make anything work. I'd be really worried right now if I hadn't sent Chollo with him.

***

When we crawled back out into the bright light of day, we could see thick plumes of black smoke rising in the direction of Manzimwe. We didn't say anything to each other but Maxine and I both knew that this was not a good sign. We scrambled down the hill as fast as we could.

David was not waiting for us beside the boom gate at the other side of the plateau. The Range Rover was standing at the foot of the slope, its engine revving urgently. Though I was still physically and emotionally numb, the euphoria of the painkiller had worn off and, logically, I knew that the driver's eagerness to leave was confirmation that all was not well back in town.

As soon as Maxine and I were seated, David put his foot down hard on the accelerator and we sped off across the grassy plateau. The ndotsi with the Kalashnikov rifle was making his way to open the boom gate for us. David did not bother accommodating the pretense. He swerved around the gate and, before we knew it, we were bumping along the goat track at the edge of the escarpment. Chollo held his shotgun at the ready with the barrel poking out of the window.

It did not take long for the grave look on Maxine's face to be replaced by her usual air of cheeriness, as if our problems lay behind us and not where we were heading.

"So, what did you think of our *Mona Lisa*?" she beamed with positive expectation.

"You're full of surprises," I acknowledged. "That was incredible."

Maxine smiled knowingly and looked out over the escarpment as she chose her words. "That knowledge," she said finally, "is part of the heritage of these people, the Lapedi. Not the rock art; that's particular to the San. But the essence of shamanism – the healing culture, the wisdom, the connection with the Divine – that's what I'm talking about. You know these people, Mark, how special they are, what beautiful people they are. They deserve this heritage; they deserve the wisdom and peace and harmony they're capable of.

"Not so long ago, it was central to their culture. Now it's almost extinct. It's been usurped by self-serving politics and superstitious mumbo jumbo. You know how it is. Between the witch doctor caste and the political caste, the people of the Republic are being sucked dry.

"For a long time now, President Selele and his cronies have been concentrating their power. First they nationalized foreign-owned industries, then they invaded white-owned farms, and now they just take whatever they want. No one can say anything about it because they control all of the media.

"It's so true that power corrupts, and absolute power corrupts absolutely. Anyone else with any power, anyone who could be a threat to the oligarchy, started disappearing. You know all this stuff; it's old news. But hardly anyone knows that Selele's biggest fear is the shamans."

"You mean *sangomas*?" I said. "The witch doctors?"

"No, the shamans," Maxine insisted, "the underground lineage of the ancient faith."

"You make it sound so arcane, Max," I objected in spite of feeling a mild surge of fascination.

"Well, it's the truth, Mark," said Maxine. "There were those still holding the torch, keeping the flame alive. Selele's fear was that, as his people became more oppressed, they would turn back to the old faith, and by so doing find their substance again, rediscover their power. And, of course, he also feared the shamans directly; he feared they might use a higher-grade magic against him than his own sangomas could counter. So he had the old wizards hunted down. They've been smelled out and killed.

"Of course, all the white folk applauded very loudly; they thought it very commendable of Selele to clamp down on the scourge of voodoo. Only it wasn't the voodoo priests he was after. It was the true spiritual custodians he was knocking off. Now they've all but disappeared."

"That's very sad to hear," I said, genuinely despairing that the metaphysical tradition I had become excited about might have already died out. "So they're all wiped out, huh?"

Maxine gazed across the escarpment again. "All but one," she said wistfully. She looked at me sideways. "You know about my partner, Roger, don't you? Well, he's been secretly investigating the shaman genocide for six months now. We've heard reports that there's one left, and apparently the goons are onto him; they know where he's hiding. Our latest intelligence suggests that they are preparing to execute him."

"That's heavy." I shook my head gravely.

"We need your help," Maxine said.

"What?" I said, startled by her bluntness. "How can *I* help?"

"The last shaman is hiding in the Meluti Swamps. Roger wants to go into the Delta and find him."

"And then what?"

"Take him out through Portuguese Territory, into exile."

"Are you serious?"

"Of course I am, Mark." Maxine turned in her seat to face me, allowing me to read her guileless expression. "No matter who wins this war, they'll want to kill the last shaman. No one will tolerate the freedom, the hope, and especially the power he holds out. But if we can keep him safe in exile, he can keep the faith alive and be a symbol to the people, like Nelson Mandela was in South Africa."

"You want me to go into the Swamps and help Roger find him?" I shook my head incredulously.

"Yes."

So this was the supposed prisoner of conscience Maxine

and her man were planning to rescue. "Max," I said as diplomatically as I could, "I can't help you, I'm sorry. I'm not meant to be here. I've got to get out of the Republic before the war becomes full blown. I've got to get back to my family overseas. If it weren't for my father's memorial, I wouldn't even be in the country."

Maxine smiled a forgiving smile. "Do you think it's just a coincidence that we met again in these circumstances?" she said.

"What do you mean?" I said, blinking against the muddling effect of the Demerol comedown.

"Well," said Maxine in a kindly voice, "you being so lost right now, looking for the wisdom to know yourself, and me and Roger looking for a man who holds the key to what you're looking for." She touched my arm. "This is your chance, Mark. You have to know your path when it opens up for you. Don't blow your opportunity."

If I hadn't been drugged, I might have been more evasive; as it was, I gave it to Maxine as straight as I could. "As usual, Max, you have me at a disadvantage," I said. "I hate to say no to you after all you've done for me. And there's nothing I would love more than to meet someone who could teach me about this shamanism stuff. Believe me, I'd give anything. But the Meluti Swamps, Max! It's a total no-go zone. And, with all the shit going on in the Republic now, it's suicide. It's just too dangerous."

Maxine flinched at the word "suicide." I immediately regretted saying it. I wondered whether I had reminded her of Pat Elliot. I certainly had a vivid memory of the time I had escorted Maxine to a country club dance shortly after she had broken up with the young farmer. That night Pat shot himself with a double-barrel shotgun. He had pulled both triggers with his big toe. Maxine had assured me that his suicide was unconnected with our date. Whatever really happened, I didn't expect I'd ever find out. I still felt bad about Pat. He was a great guy, and one of the finest polo players the colonies had ever produced. I assumed Maxine's pain would be deeper than mine, even.

Whatever her feelings, she brushed them aside and turned to face me squarely again. "Mark, haven't you ever stood for something bigger than yourself?" The ever-happy glow had drained from her face, but a fire began to blaze in her eyes as she spoke. "This is not about you or about me; this is about something much bigger. You saw that painting; you felt its power. This is about keeping humanity alive in the world, never mind the Republic. You talk painfully about the ultimate secret of magic eluding you, about your yearning for the power to make choices with integrity. What do you suppose I'm talking about? The only difference is, I'm not relating it to individualistic enrichment or fulfillment. My concern is for the well-being of society.

"As long as humans maintain their connection to spirit, they remain the noblest of creatures. Their actions take into consideration all that they are a part of and everything they are connected to – individuals, the community, nature and the environment are all uplifted by whatever is done in harmony with spirit.

"Once there was a time – around here, anyway – that no matter how high your station in life, there wasn't a single decision you made that wasn't tested against the will of a power higher than yourself. Whether it was a treaty with foreigners or the naming of your child or the clearing of a piece of forest to farm on, the ancestors had to be consulted. Any action separate from this process was considered an evil deed, because it did not intuitively anticipate the overall benefit to the collective good.

"Now, all over the world – and especially here in the Republic – spiritual principles have been totally abandoned. There is a wanton disregard of the highest good. A love of power has replaced the value of creating an empowered and functional society. Politicians, churchmen and the corporate elite have kept the human race in a condition no better than slavery. Rather than enthusing the population to build a thriving, purposeful society within a lovingly cared-for ecosystem, these so-called leaders exploit the population in the cause of their own self-aggrandizement. Their hollow agendas have created hollow societies that are coming apart at the seams. What we're seeing all over the world is your Hitler Effect – the appalling consequences of clever schemers who have no heart, no soul, no wisdom. The foundations of blind self-interest are too flimsy to hold up a functional and sustainable system of any kind, let alone facilitate the complex organization of a diverse collection of individuals occupying a fragile environment.

"As you of all people will appreciate, Mark, whether as individuals or as a society, we're meant to get our energy from a higher source. We both know that. It even says that in your book, *The Magician's Way*. What's missing in your own self-empowerment model, by the sound of it, and here in the Republic, is the same thing – the practical connection to that higher wisdom. Well, right here is your chance to serve society and at the same time claim the antidote that will allow you and all who learn from you to practice magic without the accompanying negative side effect. The last shaman holds the key to the very element that can transform human beings from vulgar automatons to inspired creators. Surely finding this living treasure and ensuring his survival is a calling that no person of good faith can refuse.

"You grew up beside the Swamps, Mark. You grew up speaking Lapedi; you know the ropes. And you have a vested interest in finding our man. You're the only person I know who can lead this mission." Fearing that her argument wasn't persuasive enough already, Maxine hurriedly added, "I have some money stashed overseas, a little legacy. It's all I've got left. You can have it."

I squeezed my eyes closed a couple of times to prevent my mind from reeling out of control. There was no escaping the logic that I was a natural ally in Maxine and her fiancé's ambitious plan, but I couldn't help suspecting that the logic was in fact an artfully constructed trap that I had walked into like a dumb bird following a trail of seed.

"Max," I said, squirming in my seat, "believe me, I'm very excited about what you have shown me back there in the cave. I've dreamed of the existence of that kind of potential for years now, and I would do anything to discover it for myself – and share it with society, for that matter. But right now I think we've got other things to worry about." I nodded at the great black cloud hanging over Manzimwe.

The mood in the car grew more and more tense the closer we got to the main road leading into town. Chollo began sniffing heavily, as if he were trying to work out what he could smell. Whatever it was, it couldn't have been good. As we swung onto the bitumen road, he quickly jacked out the cartridges from his shotgun and then reloaded it, satisfying himself that the pump action was working smoothly and that the magazine was fully loaded. He pulled another dozen cartridges from his ammunition belts and laid them out on the dashboard.

For a town that had not yet seen any fighting between enemy forces, Manzimwe was in an appalling state. On the outskirts, we drove into a pall of thick, black smog choking the squatter shanties lining the way into town. Each scene we passed unfolded like a grainy black-and-white movie. Images and actions jerked in and out of focus as oily clouds of smoke from burning tires wafted across the road. All the way along, disheveled natives, whose faces had the mournful fatalistic look of those who have nothing left to lose, were packed like sardines into buses and trucks crawling out of town to who knows where.

Everyone and everything moved with the same defeated listlessness. Here and there shacks were on fire. A toddler stumbled through a pile of garbage, hand in mouth, crying for its missing mother. Within sight of the toddler, a trio of soldiers were dragging a young female – her clothing already half ripped off – into a dusty alleyway.

"How can they do this to their own people?" cried Maxine.

"She is Chitswa, madam," mumbled David apologetically. "Same tribe as the Fighters."

Close to the center of town, two corpses lay in the middle of the road, their heads and shoulders charred by burning tire necklaces. A bloodied Indian shopkeeper was herding his horrified family into a vintage pickup truck loaded with what was left of their worldly possessions. The doors and windows to his shop were smashed in; all of the stock had been looted. Chollo pointed his shotgun at anyone who so much as looked in our direction.

"My god," Maxine grimaced, "this is just awful."

I was surprised by Maxine's reaction, considering what a veteran of indigenous turmoil she was. "Maybe she's just human," I thought, "or maybe it's an indication of how bad this situation is." Personally, I was sickened to my stomach by what we saw, and dismayed that my psyche had been so exposed to the virus of human beastliness. This was why I had left Africa in the first place – so I'd never get caught up in something like this. I knew for sure that I had to get out of the Republic immediately, at whatever cost.

"Can you believe," Maxine went on, looking around bewilderedly, "this was a sleepy little town when we drove through a couple of hours ago? Who would have believed that things could turn so quickly? The line at the border obviously isn't holding."

As we arrived back at the Manzimwe Mission Hospital, an army helicopter with black smoke billowing from its tail propeller crash-landed on the grassless lawn close to the front entrance, blowing up a tornado of dust and litter. Two antique jet fighter-bombers lumbered across the sky like wounded ducks. When the screech of their engines had died down, we could hear artillery shells whistling through the air above us and exploding just out of sight. A gaggle of distraught nurses, their uniforms splattered with blood, came running over to the Range Rover. They began wailing pitifully and pummeling the car in anguish.

Maxine looked about her in consternation and then put her window down. "What is it?" she yelled. "Sisters, why aren't you at your stations?"

Sister Sarafina's mournful face appeared at Maxine's window. "Siba anda kabala vella," she moaned in Lapedi, the gist of which I understood to be something about dying from grief. She opened Maxine's door and flung her arms around her boss. "Oh, Dr. Carlyle, I'm sorry," she cried into Maxine's bosom, "Mr. Stratton, he is late."

"What?" exclaimed Maxine, aghast.

"Yes," Sister Sarafina lifted her face slowly. A torrent of tears streamed from her bloodshot eyes. "He was shot." She collapsed back into Maxine's chest and sobbed uncontrollably.

"Where is he?" Maxine whispered, staring ahead blankly.

A face at my window startled me by saying, "He's in the mortuary, madam. Dr. Kanda just took him there now-now."

Maxine continued to stare numbly ahead. Though her face was blank, I could see the cogs turning in her mind. "What's up?" I asked dumbly, eager to resolve the tension.

Finally she turned to me and, in a chillingly calm voice, said, "It was nice seeing you again, Mark. You must excuse me. I have to go now."

I grabbed her arm. "Wait, Max," I gasped. "What do you mean? You can't stay here; everything's gone to shit. We've got to leave. Now!"

Maxine actually managed a smile, and though it was thin, it seemed full of pity for me. "I can't go anywhere," she shrugged, "I'm a doctor. War has broken out. My duty is here." She pushed Sister Sarafina gently off her and climbed out of the car.

"Max," I called after her in panic, "is there anything I can do for you?" For all my mixed feelings about her, I suddenly realized that I couldn't bear losing Maxine.

She looked back at me with her trembling smile. "If you can wait ten minutes, there might be something," she said, slamming her door shut. She disappeared behind the car and then reappeared on my side, walking purposefully toward the hospital entrance. Halfway across the gravel driveway she turned, shouting to the distraught nurses following her, "Sisters, get these wounded men out of the helicopter. Come on!" She clapped her hands urgently while walking backward a few steps. Then she turned again to trot into the building.

There was a deafening explosion nearby. I looked around to see what was left of the mission bell tower crumbling amidst a cloud of dust. Chollo turned to look at me. He made a face and shook his head, as if to say, "What are we doing?"

"I don't know," I replied vaguely in English, shrugging my shoulders.

"We go," he snarled back in Lapedi, slapping his seat for emphasis. "We go now." His door swung open and he began to get out.

"We're just waiting for the doctor," I called after him, hoping my accentuation of the word "doctor" would convey the whole sentence. Not for the first time in my life, I felt like everyone but me knew exactly what to do. I climbed out of Maxine's car and followed Chollo over to our own Land Rover.

Maxine was gone a lot longer than ten minutes. I was just trying to make up my mind whether I should go look for her or simply drive off, when she appeared from the hospital with David and a middle-aged African gentleman in tow. I noted with interest that both Maxine and David were carrying travelling bags. As they reached us, the stranger planted himself between Maxine and me.

"Good afternoon, sir," he said in a thick accent. "I understand you are returning to the Irrigation Scheme."

The name tag on the man's bloodstained coat identified him as Dr. Moses Kanda. He was short and thickset, and though his gray hair and beard and steel-framed glasses gave him a scholarly appearance, he looked as strong as an ox.

"That's right, Doctor," I said, curious as to why his added weight was called for in whatever discussion we were about to have.

"I am the hospital administrator," he said pointedly.

"Okay," I swallowed uncomfortably, "is there anything I can do for you?"

"As a matter of fact, there is," the doctor looked me squarely in the face. "You can give Dr. Carlyle and her driver a lift, please. They are on their way to the Meluti."

"The Meluti?" My curiosity had been answered.

"Mr. Stratton is dead," Dr. Kanda snapped. "His body was found on the side of the road miles from the fighting. His hands were tied behind his back and he was shot in the head at close range. How do you say? Point-blank."

"I see," I swallowed again, captivated by the doctor's unblinking eyes.

"Dr. Carlyle is not safe anywhere," he said. "Her only hope is in the Meluti with the last shaman who is there."

Maxine stepped forward and put an arm around the administrator. "Thank you, Dr. Kanda," she said, "I'm sure Mr. Vale will be willing to take me as far as the Irrigation Scheme."

"Willing" was a good choice of words, because I was not happy about the situation. Getting home was going to be rough enough without transporting a marked woman. "She'll be safe with us, Doctor," I said. "But what about you? Will you be okay here?" I didn't honestly expect that he or anyone would be remotely okay once the Fighters arrived.

"Our fate is in the hands of the gods," he shrugged. "Until they decide, we have plenty of work to do."

Maxine and David climbed into the backseat of the Land Rover, clutching their rucksacks. I glanced back at Maxine to make sure she was ready. The gravity of her situation was etched deeply into her face. It was drained of all the vitality and energy that normally kept her radiant aura in place. As she absently ran a hand through her hair, she frowned, trying to block out the bitter sentiments confronting her.

I felt a heartrending sadness for my childhood friend, who I knew had now lost everything of personal value there was for her to lose. First, she had lost her father to a hunting accident when she was not much more than a toddler; then, before she graduated from college, her mother had been taken by cancer; after that, her only brother had been killed vainly defending the family ranch against the government-incited farm invasions; now it was Roger Stratton, her soul mate and ally in her unending war against the abusers of power. And in between these main pillars of her heart were the dozens of other comrades who had been taken away from her – deported, killed or silenced by fear. As someone who had just lost his father, I could imagine something of what it was like to be so utterly alone.

"Sit tight, Max," I said. "I'm going to get us out of here in one piece."

Maxine may not have heard me. She didn't say anything. Chollo, who was sitting beside me in the front passenger seat, motioned with his arm for me to get going. "*Tuma, tuma,*" he grunted impatiently. "Go, go."

The atmosphere in the Land Rover was tense; not a word was spoken between us once we got moving. No one was under any illusion about getting out of Manzimwe without incident, and each of us strained to be on guard against whatever unpleasant surprise was about to hit us. Halfway into town, the trouble we had all anticipated reared its ugly head.

Three little demons appeared suddenly in the road before us – young boys in garish wigs of purple, green and yellow, respectively; their faces painted in hideous death masks; and grim fetishes tied about their necks. All were dressed in ragged camouflage fatigues and brandished Kalashnikov assault rifles that seemed absurdly oversized in their hands. The pit of my stomach turned hollow. These were Children's Brigade soldiers, the psychically crazed vanguard of the Rebel army. They waved us down with the impudence of herd boys culling out an ox for slaughter.

"Okay," I said between gritted teeth as I brought our vehicle to a standstill, "everyone stay calm." To Chollo I began to say, "No shooting unless…"

The boy soldiers rushed forward, all three of them leveling their guns on me. I heard Chollo's door swing open, and before I knew it, he had jumped out onto the road, using the open door as a shield. Three blasts erupted in quick succession and the little demons crumpled to the ground, their faces contorted in thwarted despair. In an instant Chollo was back in his seat, stuffing fresh cartridges into the magazine of his smoking shotgun.

Two of the boys were riddled with buckshot holes in their chests and lay motionless on the gravel. The third, the last one to fall, had taken his blast in the hip and lower abdomen and was now feebly raising himself into a shooting position. I revved the Land Rover to maximum and dropped the clutch. Even above the roar of the over-exerted engine I heard the boy's startled scream, followed by a loud crack as the bull bar smacked his yellow-wigged head. There were two kidney-jarring thumps as the right-side wheels crushed his body into the gravel. Then we were off, racing away from the wasted pups of war who might so easily have been the death of us.

In the rearview mirror I saw Maxine looking anxiously back in the direction of the hospital. I wondered if she shared the image that was in my mind of an angry swarm of little demons ravaging the sanctuary of the Manzimwe Mission. David laid his hands on Maxine's head and turned it to face back in the direction we were driving.

"Well, Chollo," I sighed heavily, speaking in English, "I was going to say, no shooting unless we didn't have any other choice."

"Eh," Chollo grunted distractedly, stabbing his forefinger at the road ahead. "Tuma, tuma."

CHAPTER THREE

The Last Supper

Seen from the air, the Vale family estate looked like a giant green fruit split in two lying on a tablecloth of khaki savannah. Huge sections of verdant sugarcane fields and citrus groves were crisscrossed by veins of service roads and irrigation canals, while seed-like clusters of cottages accommodating the two thousand African workers and their families were spread symmetrically across the two green circumferences. More or less in the middle of the northern half of the farm stood a hundred-acre compound surrounded by a ten-foot-high mesh fence crowned by a roll of razor wire. This was where the fifty or so expatriate managers and technical supervisors lived with their families in a style well beyond what they would have been accustomed to in their European homelands. Each expat – as the permanent ex-colonial residents called them – occupied a large air-conditioned homestead-style house set within an acre of manicured gardens, all cared for by company-issue house servants and gardeners. With their own segregated country club and shopping facilities located safely inside the executive enclave, patrolled day and night by armed security guards with attack dogs, the expats lived a life totally sheltered from the grim realities of the Republic.

My family deigned not to live in the normally safe

confines of the executive enclave. As the founders of the estate, they had chosen to live in the original homestead built by my grandfather on the southern bank of the great river that split the farm in two. This choice was based on several reasons. Partly it was nostalgia – no one could find it in their hearts to move. Partly it was a deliberate attempt to set themselves apart from the itinerant Europeans whom they viewed with a thinly disguised disdain. But mostly, they did not feel the need to be protected.

For my family, Africa held no mystique; there was no hidden danger lurking in the shadows. Over the generations, they had transformed their district from virgin bush land teaming with wild animals into a civilized mecca of modern industry. Four columns of caramel smoke rose reassuringly every day from the sugar mills of the area. Everywhere the unfailing sound of machinery clanked as tractors plowed fields and big trucks hauled hundred-ton loads of cane off for milling and trains pulled into railway sidings to take on loads of raw sugar, citrus, and canned fruit.

All this clockwork stability was the culmination of generations of hard work. It had been a massive task for my grandfather to persuade colonial authorities to consider the establishment of an irrigation scheme in what was originally one of the most remote and inaccessible territories in the land. Soil from over three hundred thousand acres of land had to be sampled, dam sites found, survey lines cut through the thick scrub, roads and railway lines brought in, investors found and persuaded. And for all that, the biggest task had been to convert the local population from an illiterate tribe of subsistence farmers and hunters into a skilled workforce.

This latter task had been achieved by starting at a grass-roots level. My grandparents and parents had worked hard to get in with their prospective employees. They had learned their language, studied their customs and involved them-selves in tribal life. Before long they had become indispens-able to the local community, called on to shoot rogue lions and crocodiles, dispense basic medicines, and settle clan disputes. Next we were improving their livestock by crossing our heavier-set bulls with their lean, hardy cows, acting for them in their dealings with colonial authorities and teaching their children to read and write. At the time of Independence, not only was the Irrigation Scheme the biggest employer in the country, but over half of the Republic's civil service also owed their education to my family. So it was no wonder that the Vales behaved like horsemen who had no fear of the horses they had broken in. Well, maybe there was something my family feared as much as the next person – the Meluti Swamps.

"You can't go there," said my oldest brother, shaking his head emphatically. Martin had the reputation of being "an imposing man" and it was easy to see why. Built like a brick shithouse, as the colonials used to say, he had a hard sundried countenance with dark-brown eyes burning fiercely from sockets set deep in his skull. With his big, blunt forehead, large, shapeless nose and full beard, he resembled an unfinished woodcarving. Staring at him then, it struck me that he looked just like the man I once believed I would grow into: all knowing, decisive and unassailable – just like my father.

"Let me tell you about the Meluti, boy." Martin leaned back in the swivel chair behind his study desk. His home office always struck me as an antidote to the stately elegance of the homestead. Other than shambolic piles of paperwork on the desktop, a couple of plastic chairs, and two faded photos on the walls – a framed picture of President Selele in field marshal regalia and an aerial shot of the estate – the room was bare; there wasn't even a rug on the concrete floor.

"Marty, I'm not going," I protested. "I know all about the Meluti."

"You don't know anything about the Meluti." Martin pointed a letter opener at me as if he were aiming to throw it. His biceps bulged brutishly out of undersized shirtsleeves. "You've been away for nearly twenty years. You don't know, man, that place is hexed."

"It's a bad place, I know, Marty. Jesus!" Martin was fond of being an authority on every subject. I was hoping to concede his superior knowledge on the Meluti before he got too carried away.

"No, you don't know." Martin sat forward, leaning his elbows on a jumble of paperwork. "Did you know that one of the biggest copper deposits in the world is sitting right there?" Martin pointed the letter opener over my right shoulder. "Also, one of the biggest coal seams in the whole of Africa. For all we know, there's oil in there, too. Those riparian forests are the most exotic and valuable hardwoods on the planet. That's five thousand square miles of the most fertile soil on Earth. The place should be wall-to-wall sugar cane and cotton fields – mines – towns. So why hasn't it been developed? Why is it just a swamp crawling with deadly creatures? It's a Venus flytrap, that place. You go in there and you get swallowed up; something eats you."

I didn't want to contradict Martin, lest it provoke him into a full-fledged diatribe, but the Meluti Swamps are no longer swamps, really. They are a massive delta formed by the Muchocho River being trapped in a valley between two mountain ranges. The Muchocho, on whose banks the Vale homestead stood, spills into the Meluti Valley through a canyon in the Lesoti Mountains – the Stanley Gorge – and then finds its way through a web of waterways meandering between thousands of low-lying islands, until it eventually escapes into Portuguese Territory via another canyon in the second range nearly one hundred miles northeast of the Stanley Gorge. It used to be that in the rainy season the water level would rise to flood most of the islands. Now, though, a series of hydroelectricity and irrigation dams curbs the seasonal deluge upriver and the waterways flow constantly at their old winter levels.

"Malaria," I shrugged. "Everyone knows that."

"Malaria?" Martin scoffed. "Do you believe that rubbish? That's what people tell themselves so they can sleep at night. No, man, people live out there: tribesmen, poachers, smugglers, mercenaries. The reason that the Meluti is still a swamp is because there's something evil out there that defies the rule of law. The police and army don't go near the place. Even when the Rebels thought they'd use it as a safe haven, they got their ass kicked. They didn't last a season out there. They ran back to Portuguese Territory so fast they left half their equipment behind. There're monkeys out there in the forests carrying bazookas now."

"So what's out there that modern armies can't deal with?" I ventured.

"I'm telling you," said Martin, "it's a God-forsaken place, ruled by evil spirits. There have been stories about strange goings-on in the swamps for a long time, but now there's something out there that's seriously bad news. In the old days going into the Meluti was a rite of passage, a testing of the self against the elements. Now, though, whatever is out there doesn't just bash you up or kill you, even – it catches you by the soul like a crocodile and drags you down into its lair to rot.

"No normal person goes in or out of the swamps anymore. Men come out of there completely deranged, babbling about all sorts of horrors they have witnessed. Do you know that psychiatrists from all over the world come here to study this phenomenon? Meluti Syndrome, they call it – an unexplainable, permanent, chronic state of psychosis.

"We had one of these shrinks staying right here in our house," Martin stabbed the desk with his letter opener. "A fellow from Harvard University in America. He crapped on about 'suggested states' and 'psychological susceptibility' and stuff. But let me tell you, I've seen some of these swamp zombies, and you see them and you know something has happened. It's not just their imagination; they're not hypno-tized or something. By their faces you can tell they've had a good look into hell and they can't get that image out of their mind.

"You know, Uncle Jack most probably had a touch of Meluti Madness. He's sort of okay now, but he was quite screwed up for a long time...years. He swore he was attacked by a creature with antelope legs and a lion's head. Can you believe that? Our own uncle carrying on like a spooked native! Now he denies that he ever said it...or saw it. He gets very touchy if anyone raises the subject."

"I didn't know that," I said.

"There's a lot you don't know; this is what I'm telling you," Martin rested his case, sitting back in his chair again with an air of satisfaction. "Maxine should know better, though. She's a doctor; she's a local. Never mind the Madness, those guys there in the Swamps, they're about the only unconquered tribe in history. They regard their domain as sovereign territory. They only have one punishment for trespassers." An ugly grimace contorted his face as he drew his letter opener across his throat.

"Don't worry, I'm not going, Marty," I laughed wearily in exasperation. "Just getting out of Manzimwe was enough adventure to last me a lifetime." I was still haunted by the sound of the bull bar cracking the child-soldier's skull.

"Getting out of Manzimwe!" Martin scoffed. "Oh, please! Running over a few *umfaans* is nothing. We're talking serious stuff now, and I don't trust you when it comes to this broad."

"Broad?" I chuckled again. "You sound like someone in a fifties movie."

"Broad, chick, woman – whatever word you uppity cosmopolitan people like to use," Martin shrugged. "She's just bad news, especially when it comes to you. You spent half your life besotted by her and then when you finally work out that you can't have her, you run away and live halfway around the world."

"That's crap," I objected.

"Is it?" said Martin. "I'm not so sure. That's not what it looked like to us."

"You want to know why I left?" I blurted out, feeling the hot flush of anger on my face. "I could see the writing on the wall. I knew the Republic was going to go to the dogs, just like every other country in Africa. And look at this place now. If the folks had sold this place before Independence, we'd all be worth millions. Now you can't get two cents for the estate. Only Somalia has a worse sovereign risk rating than the Republic. Instead of speculating about my motives for going, you should maybe have been asking yourselves why you bloody well stayed."

"What, and just give up?" Martin bristled. "Just let this place go to ruin? Let Granpa Cecil's and Dad's legacy go to waste? Turn our backs on thousands of workers and their families? You don't understand. The day we leave, the whole Irrigation Scheme will fall apart, not just the estate. You don't know anything, that's what I'm telling you. You don't know what's right, man."

"No, I don't," I said. "I don't know what's right. But how do you know? What makes you so sure that you're so right about everything?"

"You do what's there in front of you," Martin shrugged. "You play the cards you're dealt. You don't run away."

"Playing cards is a good analogy," I came back heatedly, "because even in cards you have to know when to hold and when to fold. When do you stick at a marriage and when do you decide it's over? How do you know if the best thing for the people of the Republic is giving them a job today or letting the country fail so that the people can learn to take responsibility for themselves tomorrow? Do you get on the first plane out of here so you can see your children again, or do you go into the Meluti to look for a man who might have the answers? What's the best bet, huh? Which choice has the highest value?"

"So you *are* thinking of going into the Meluti!" Martin cried.

"No, I'm not," I said quickly, "but there's a part of me that is sorely tempted. You know, I saw creatures just like Uncle Jack described in the cave Max took me to."

"The *Mona Lisa of Africa*?" Martin snorted. "Do you believe that bull? It's a bloody hoax, if you ask me. More like Maxine is the Don Quixote of Africa. And come to think of it, who's that *Muntu* traveling with her? What's he up to?"

"David, her driver? What do you mean, 'What's he up to?'"

"Why would any native give up everything, including his family ties, which are more important to him than his own blood, to follow a loopy European woman on such an insanely dangerous and improbable mission?"

"I don't know, loyalty maybe?"

"Loyalty? You see, that just shows how naïve and ignorant you are. With these people that kind of loyalty only develops over ages, where families, not just individuals, have looked after each other for generations."

There was a short, confident wrap on the door, followed by a lilting "knock, knock" before my mother swept into the room. She was wearing a crisp khaki safari suit with gauze vents at the knees and elbows. In her hands was a pith helmet with a canary-yellow paisley scarf tied around the brim.

"What are you boys fighting about?" she enquired in a disapproving tone.

"We're not fighting, Mom," Martin reassured her as we both rose hastily to our feet. "I'm just making sure your baby son here doesn't get any crazy ideas about taking his doctor friend into the Meluti."

For someone in her mid-sixties, Cynthia Vale had a face that would have looked fifteen years younger had it not been for the mannishly cut gray hair that she steadfastly refused to color. Unlike Martin's blunt looks, my mother's features were finely chiseled, with high cheekbones, a thin blade-like nose, thin lips and a small square chin. Her sharp features lent her gray-blue eyes a cold, piercing quality that commanded respect. Precisely applied bright-red lipstick and matching nail polish accentuated her air of superiority.

"How is Maxine?" I said.

Before she could reply, a male servant at the still-open door announced himself with a timid cough. He was dressed in a collarless white linen shirt with green piping and shorts in the same style. His feet were bare. "Your tea, madam," he said, while his eyes begged for guidance as to what he should do with the tray trembling in his hands.

"Just put it down here," Mother waved her hat at the desk.

The servant didn't move. His eyes raked the desk in panic.

"Oh, for God's sake, Martin," Mother sighed, "clear a

space for him, will you? Otherwise, he'll be standing there all day."

Mother poured her own tea. "You asked about Maxine?" she said as she stirred her teaspoon of sugar. "She's fast asleep. But I'm afraid things are not going well on other fronts." Both her voice and demeanor became very grave.

"What's happened?" said Martin. "Has Manzimwe fallen?"

"No, not yet," said Mother, "but fighting has broken out right in the Capital. Insurgents have attacked the international airport. Three jetliners have been blown up on the runway. All flights in and out of the country are suspended."

I felt my heart sink. "So, I'm stuck here," I said, collapsing back into my chair.

Martin looked equally stunned. "Fighting? In the Capital?"

Mother motioned for him to sit down and took a seat beside me, holding a teacup in one hand and a saucer in the other. "It's much worse than anyone predicted," she said. "We really have to be prepared for the worst. This might be the end of the Republic."

"Oh my god," I groaned, burying my head in my hands.

"Don't worry, man," said Martin sternly. "We'll get you and the women and children out on a charter plane from our airstrip."

"No, Martin," Mother shook her head, "the whole country is a no-fly zone. If a crop duster takes off, it will be shot down."

No one spoke for a minute. I sat there contemplating the horrific situation I was caught up in. It was a grim irony, I thought, that in the end I was, after all, meeting the fate I had fled from nearly twenty years before. Silently I cursed my father's bad timing.

"Well," I said, breaking the silence, "maybe it's for the best that I can't go. You'll need me when the fighting reaches here."

I didn't sound very convincing, least of all to myself. The thought of my reunion with my children being delayed for an indeterminate period of time was awful enough to contemplate, never mind the prospect of never seeing them again.

"No," Mother shook her head absently, "we can't fight our way out of this. Besides, you have your own family now that needs you." She looked at Martin and then at me meaningfully, preparing us for her pronouncement. "The best way out of here for you, Mark, is the Meluti Swamps. You should go with Maxine."

"What?" cried Martin incredulously. "Have you lost your marbles, Mom? That's impossible; it's a death sentence."

"We might all be dead tomorrow," said Mother. "If Mark can get through the Swamps and into Portuguese Territory, he'll live to see his family again." She put her cup down on its saucer and held up her free hand to stop Martin from interrupting her. "The thing we've all forgotten is that when Granpa Cecil arrived in these parts it was a much wilder place than it is now, though that's hard to believe. And yet, he didn't only survive, he singlehandedly tamed and developed this district."

"But nobody tamed the Meluti, Ma," Martin objected. "Not even Granpa."

"No," Mother allowed, "but everyone said that he couldn't achieve what he did. There were those who said he wouldn't survive his first summer out here."

"I don't know, Ma," I said, beginning to resent my mother for deciding my fate for me. "I'm not sure that I want to take my chances in the Meluti."

"I'm not trying to get rid of you, Mark," said Mother. "You chose your own path a long time ago when you decided to go and live overseas. For better or worse, that's where you belong – not here. If you could fly out of here today, you would, and you would have my blessing. Now the Meluti is your only way home.

"I understand that you're scared. But you won't have to contend with anything that explorers from time immemorial didn't have to contend with. Think about Burton in the Forbidden Cities of the East, unarmed, alone. And Marco

Polo, and Dr. Livingstone and Lewis and Clark. Think of these solitary men forging across continents full of barbarians and savages, armed with what? Swords? Guns? Don't be silly. Character! The force of their character! Sooner or later every man has to find his substance and impose himself on life or resign himself to a life of insignificance. This is a time when we must all dig deep or be obliterated."

She took a sip of tea, savored the taste and then took another sip. "Well," she said, as if these matters were occurring to her for the first time, "I have things to attend to and I suppose you boys have plans to make. Mark will want to leave before the Rebels get here."

Martin and I stood again as she got up and put her cup down. "Don't worry about the tray; one of the boys will get it."

I followed Mother to the door and, with a leaden heart, watched her stride purposefully down the covered pathway back to the main house. The family hunting dogs picked themselves up off the lawn to follow the mistress of the house. With a whistle, I invited them over for a pat. They looked anxiously backward and forward between me and my mother, and after looking back at me apologetically, trotted to catch up with the person who in their eyes had taken over from my father as leader of the pack.

It was the middle of aloe season and everywhere I looked there was a profusion of flaming orange-red flowers. I was struck by how much the grounds around the homestead resembled my mother's cultivated image: the trimmed lawns, the well-trained creepers, and the exotic shade trees collared by neat flowerbeds. Meanwhile, at the bottom of the garden, behind a sturdy electric fence, a pod of about fifteen hippos lay contentedly on a sandbank beside the dark, greasy waters swirling inexorably toward the wildest place on Earth.

***

Dinner that evening was a tense affair. In honor of Maxine's and my departure early the following morning, Mother had formally invited the entire family to dine with her in the main house. As with all formal dinners presided over by any of the older Vale generations, the dress code was dinner jackets and black tie for the men and evening gowns or cocktail dresses for the ladies. Anyone under sixteen could wear whatever they liked because they ate separately in an adjoining room where they were out of earshot of the serious matters being discussed at the grown-ups' table.

At seven o'clock on the dot, fourteen impeccably groomed adults filed out of the surrounding houses and guest pavilions and made their way through the bountiful gardens to Mother's parlor for pre-dinner cocktails. Maxine arrived a couple of minutes late with one of my female cousins who had loaned her a short black dress and a pair of high heels for the occasion. Refreshed from her late-afternoon sleep, she was once again a vision of beauty and grace, needing only the touch of her lipstick and eye shadow to transform her cherubic good looks into a sultry radiance.

Looking around at the collection of urbane, presentable dinner guests, I wondered what our display of charm and sophistication counted for now. All the talk was of war. "It's all on in Manzimwe now, what? I wonder if the army will be able to hold the Rebels there," mused an uncle, his face twitching nervously.

"Huh," snorted a cousin, "a whole regiment of those drunken Muntus couldn't even stop one charging buffalo. What chance do you give them against amphetamine-crazed suicide brigades?"

"They were saying on *BBC World News* that the French and English are calling an emergency session of the UN Security Council," said a sister-in-law, doing her best to soothe everyone's frayed emotions.

"Jesus Christ," laughed her husband in disgust, "those bloody Frogs and Poms are about as useless as tits on a bull. By the time they get their act together, the whole bloody Republic will be burned to the ground." My brother Oliver was a few years older than me and a couple of years younger than Martin. He looked much like Martin would have without his beard. He wore a drooping mustache that matched the dark bags sagging beneath his flashing eyes. It was obvious that he had begun drinking long before the accepted colonial starting time of sunset.

Encouraged by the harrumphs of agreement, Oliver held the floor. "You know who's crapping themselves more than anyone now? The bloody expats. Now they've got something to worry about other than the next costume ball or their ranking on the tennis ladder. They'll be on their hands and knees praying that the Rebels don't get hold of them. Let's see how high and mighty they are about Selele now. They'd kiss his backside if he drove up tomorrow at the head of a regiment of soldiers."

Someone nudged me in the back. I turned around. It was Uncle Jack, standing by himself, listening to the chatter with a forlorn detachment. He leaned forward and said quietly in my ear, "I'd kiss Selele's arse, too. Wouldn't you?" He raised his glass and winked. I assumed he was alluding to me being forced by the war to brave the Meluti Swamps.

"You bet," I said, grimacing at the queasy churning in my stomach.

The strained bravado-laced conversation darted this way and that like a herd of antelope trying to evade a pack of Cape Hunting Dogs. Was it such a foregone conclusion that the Rebels would overrun the country? Why hadn't anyone seen it coming? How long before they arrived at our door? Was there an outside chance of foreign intervention? What would become of us in the worst-case scenario? And what about the best-case scenario?

Hopes were raised and dashed between every sip of gin and tonic until Mother swept into the lounge, resplendent in a long, dark, wine-colored velvet dress, with three layers of black pearls choking her throat, black pearl earrings, and her hair glistening like a halo in the mellow chandelier lighting.

"I'm sorry to keep you all waiting," she apologized.

"Matters to attend to." She surveyed the faces staring at her expectantly. "Well, what are we waiting for? Let's eat."

"Ladies first" was still a practical convention in the Vale world. The women led the men into the dining room and waited with a well-rehearsed poise for their chairs to be pulled out by their male dinner partners. As soon as we were all seated, Mother rang a little silver bell for silence. Everyone looked at her dutifully. She rewarded our attention with a gracious smile.

"Now listen here, my dears," she said melodiously, "before we eat, I just want to say that I have asked you all together again tonight because tomorrow morning my son Mark will be taking off to escort his old friend, Dr. Maxine Carlyle here, on an expedition into the Meluti Swamps. Heaven knows what the future will bring, and who knows if and when we'll all be together again." Mother's voice began to quaver. She forced a smile to maintain composure and then continued in a strong voice, "So let's not have any talk of war tonight, and let us be grateful for each other and the privileges that are ours for the time being."

A resounding response of "Hear, hear!" echoed around the table. Mother rang her silver bell again and two waiters dressed in white uniforms with dark-green sashes and matching fezzes began serving an entree of sweetened pork belly topped with crackling of roast duck.

As the last plate was laid on the table, Mother called to one of the staff. "Simeon, a moment please."

"Yes, Madam Cynthia." Simeon sidled up beside her.

"Who set the table for tonight?"

"I think it was Freda, madam." Simeon shifted his weight nervously. His eyes darted about apprehensively.

"Well, you should teach her properly to do the knives and forks. Look here, you see how she's put the big ones on the outside and the small ones on the inside?"

"Sorry, madam, I tell her many times, but she not understand." Simeon clucked and shook his head in sympathetic annoyance.

"Well, maybe she isn't ready to work in the main house

yet. I'll talk to Philemon about her."

"I think madam is wise."

Mother paid the servant no more attention. Once it became obvious to him that his presence was no longer required, he shuffled away from the table surreptitiously.

"Thanks, Simeon," I called after him.

No one else seemed to be affected by the humiliating exchange between mistress and servant – not even Maxine. With the war out of bounds, the dinner guests seized voraciously on my impending mission as the topic of discussion. Most of the women appeared to be ignorant of the plan and wanted to know more: Where were we going? Why on Earth would we go there? Was it a worthwhile exercise considering the risks and the dubious, far-fetched goal of the mission? The men were unanimously at one with the women in expressing their skepticism about our chances. That we were going in winter outside of the malaria season was the sole upside anyone was prepared to concede. Only Mother and Martin remained silent on the subject.

"Uncle Jack," said Oliver, "what do you think about looking for shamans in the Swamps?" He held up his hands and curled each one's index and middle fingers to signal quotation marks as he emphasized the word "shamans." His innocent tone was belied by a lingering smirk.

"You only need one bullet in the Meluti," said Uncle Jack without looking up from his plate, "and that's for yourself." Looking at him then, it was the first time I noticed that he wasn't with us. His face was consumed by a deep melancholy. I could see what Martin had been talking about – he was in hell.

"That's enough now," Mother cut in. "I can't believe I'm hearing this nonsense. For goodness sake, if Stan were still alive and he decided to go into the Swamps, no one would question him for a minute. Well, Mark is a Vale. Remember? We're all Vales. Maxine excepted, of course...but you're still one of us, dear."

"Yes," coughed Oliver jovially, "we're starting to sound like a bunch of expats."

Mother took advantage of the responding chuckles to introduce some cheer to the occasion. "Alright, my dears," she chimed forgivingly, "you have a choice of two courses tonight: pheasant cooked in clay or barbequed cane rat."

"What about some of both?" bellowed Oliver, apparently oblivious to the mischief he had caused.

"Or both," Mother shrugged magnanimously.

"And Martin," Oliver carried on, "what about the claret? Has it breathed enough or must we die of thirst?"

Cane rat is a delicacy in the sugar-growing regions of Africa. The uninitiated Westerner is predictably disgusted by the thought of eating rat, not appreciating that the cane rat is a large, tailless rodent that has more in common with a suckling pig than its domestic namesake. Their original habitat was marshlands, and when sugar cane was introduced in their territory, they quickly chose eating sweet cane roots over their bland staple of papyrus and reeds. The meat tastes sublime, comparable to nothing else on Earth, covered in a thin rind of fat that roasts into a heavenly crackling. My helping – the first in many years – was sensational. I passed on the pheasant, not being a fan of the stringy, dry flesh or the embedded tooth-cracking lead shotgun pellets. Everyone sat silently for the moment, relishing the sumptuous feast. All that could be heard was the clink of cutlery along with groans of appreciation. I was glad for the pleasant distraction.

Suddenly there was the chime of someone tapping a wine glass. It was Maxine. She coughed self-consciously and gave us a demure smile. "Well," she said, "I want to thank you all for your kindness. It has been a shocking time for me. I don't want to distress you further, but attending to the causalities at Manzimwe has been absolutely horrific. My entire career did not prepare me for these last few days. And then to have my fiancé..." her voice wavered slightly and then found its mettle again, "to lose my fiancé so suddenly, so brutally."

The discomfort of her audience was palpable, but Maxine was undeterred. "I don't know if I'd still be alive if

Mark hadn't gotten me out today. Now here I am, needing your help again, asking you to lend me your son – your brother – your nephew – your cousin, to guide me through the badlands of Africa. I must seem so ungrateful, so self-indulgent, though I assure you I am not. I appreciate your support; I can't tell you how much. And I know that I impose on you in your time of mourning. I'm truly sorry for your loss."

There was a mad rush to assure Maxine that no one harbored any ill will toward her. Only Maxine and I, who sat on Mother's left and right, were close enough to hear her mumble, "And yours, too."

"I beg your pardon, Cynthia, what was that?" Maxine stiffened, sensing my mother's comment to be loaded.

"I said, and yours, too." Mother fixed Maxine with her penetrating gaze. "Of course, you have lost a loved one today, and so tragically, my dear. But I was not referring to Roger. I meant Stan. He was your loss, too."

"He was the nation's loss, I know," said Maxine, taken aback, "but what do you mean, Cynthia?"

Mother gave Maxine a weary smile that forgave her ignorance. "Stan promised your mother on her deathbed that he would take care of you. So he did, until his dying day. You look shocked, my dear, and no wonder. But, you see, all the times you've run afoul of the government, Stan was there to save you. When they wanted to execute you, Stan managed to persuade them to cool you off with some jail time. When they wanted to jail you, he'd suggest a demotion or a transfer to a more harmless post. When they wanted to sack you, Stan would send a haunch of venison to the offended party. And don't think it didn't cost him. Oh, he paid all right: money, favors, compromises, loss of face. But that was Stan – a promise was a promise."

"I had no idea," mumbled Maxine, shaking her head in astonishment.

"No," retorted Mother, "we seldom recognize the powers facilitating our fate. But now your guardian angel is dead, Maxine. That is why Stan's passing is as much your loss as ours. He kept you alive to play out your anarchistic fantasies, even while you painted him as a mercenary doing deals with the devil to secure his wealth and property."

"Don't say that," Maxine protested. "Stan and I had our political differences, but I've had nothing but respect and affection for the Vale name."

"And I you, my dear," sighed Mother, "which is why it saddens me to be the one to tell you that your privileges in the Republic have expired. Roger would never have been killed while Stan was alive, believe me. It would be a pity if all of your agitating amounted to nothing. I truly pray that you find your shaman – as improbable as that is – so you can have something to show for your crusade. But with or without him, you must go into exile. Your death will not serve any purpose."

The assembled company's embarrassment for Maxine could not be contained any longer. A chorus of dissent erupted around the table. Martin's stout wife cried out above the din, "Cynthia, how could you? Why could you not have shared this with Maxine in private? What's come over you, for God's sake?"

My mother was unmoved by the outcry. She stared everyone into silence before lashing out with great venom. "I'll tell you why, Fiona. It's because this doesn't only concern Maxine; it concerns all of you. You've all been living in a child's paradise, indulging your pet ideals and hobbies, while grown men toiled to keep your playground safe. You all have to wake up – not just Maxine. Our world is changing, and you're each responsible for what you make of it now."

As everyone, the older members of the family included, looked shamefacedly down at their plates, Maxine stepped coolly into the breach. "Thank you, Cynthia," she said, her eyes sparkling with exaggerated affection, "thank you for your honesty. I know you mean no offense. In fact, you do us all a great service, especially me. Granted, it is a shock to find out that for all these years I have not been sustained by my own power. It is actually more devastating than everything I have encountered in the last days put together. To think I've been a child playing make-believe games, imagining I was making a difference." Maxine laughed, shaking her head in disbelief. "Now, thanks to you, the bubble has burst. And while it is extremely daunting, it is at the same time just as liberating. I'm free to live my own life now."

Maxine gazed evenly at Mother and said, "That's what you mean, isn't it, Mrs. Vale?"

"Precisely, my dear," said Mother peevishly, not happy for Maxine to escape her invective entirely unmortified. "And please don't start calling me 'Mrs. Vale'; we're all family here."

If nothing else had suggested it, I would have known the dinner was in my honor when the dessert turned out to be my favorite: French pancakes – a stack of thin crepes cooked lightly on one side with icing sugar and cinnamon dusted over each moist layer. My enjoyment of the delectable treat was marred by the return of a dull throb at the back of my jaw, which escalated into a sharp pain when I chewed. I could not finish my helping. My hands began to tremble and sweat ran down from my temples.

Knowing that Maxine and I had to rise well before dawn to set out on our journey into the Swamps, I decided that I had best excuse myself so that I could get a good night's rest. I made a short farewell speech, thanking everyone – in particular Martin and Mother – for their love and support, and wished them the best of luck with whatever they had to face.

"So, I hope you will not think that I am running away," I said in conclusion, my voice catching just as Mother's and Maxine's had, "and I hope that we will all be together soon in more cheerful circumstances."

"Bloody typical," Oliver called out in mock disapproval, "always the one to go on a fishing trip when there's work to be done. Nothing has changed." As the chortles from around the table subsided, he dropped his facetious mask and put on a grave face. "No, but seriously, Mark," he said, "we all salute you. It would be bad form to let one of our own women head off into the Swamps alone. Just make sure you get back to your family in one piece."

Martin stood up and raised his glass. "To Max and Mark, everyone. Bon voyage."

"Max and Mark," the family chanted. "Bon voyage." I noticed some of the women turn away to wipe their tears.

***

As I escorted Maxine to her pavilion, we encountered three separate pairs of armed security guards along the way. None displayed the usual warm Lapedi civility, a sure sign that something serious was about to go down. We sat for a short time in front of a dying fire in the guest wing lounge, going over the plans for the following day. When we were done, I apologized for my family's behavior.

"Oh, don't be silly, Mark," Maxine cried, fixing me with a reassuring smile. "I'm grateful for their help, even if they don't believe in what I'm doing – even if they're just getting rid of me. I'm the one who should apologize. I feel guilty that they're packing you off as my escort."

"No," I insisted, "I'm so ashamed of them. My mom is so arrogant; they're all such racists. I mean, the fact that David couldn't stay here and had to sleep in the native compound… this is why I left Africa. You can't reason with them. They're so stuck in their colonial mentality."

Maxine didn't share my concerns; she was absorbed by her own preoccupations. "What about that bombshell Cynthia dropped?" She shook her head as if trying to throw off a bad dream. "But she really did do me a favor, you know? Now I know so clearly where I stand. All those years I thought I was invincible, that I was getting away with my activism because I was getting through to Selele's cronies. I actually believed I was holding them to their conscience. God, how naïve I was." She smacked the palm of her hand against her forehead and shook her head again.

She sat dazed as realization upon realization hit her like a hundred-car pileup. I tried to think what it must be like for her to have the meaning of her life gutted over dinner – to end the day with no family, no home, no citizenship. Most of all, though, I thought of how Maxine's experience demonstrated how little any of us knew what was really going on in our lives.

No doubt my empathy for Maxine's situation was influenced by my own condition. I was sick from the exhaustion of a long, harrowing day, run down by the toxicity of my abscess and paralyzed by the fear of what I had to do to get home. I felt as though I was being sucked into a pitiless vortex against my will, and that what was best for me – what I wanted – had so little power that it was not even worth considering. The only thing I could do for myself was try to make my friend feel better.

"Hey, Max," I said as soothingly as I was able, "don't be so hard on yourself. You've done a lot of good; you've healed a lot of people. It wasn't your job to save the Republic."

As I reflected on Maxine's merits, a devastating thought occurred to me. "If anyone's the screw-up here, it's me," I confessed. "My family pretends that I'm escorting you through the Swamps, but really they're using you to get me out. They don't believe I'm capable enough to make it on my own. Don't be fooled by the 'He's a Vale' talk. They don't fool me."

"No, screw them," said Maxine, surfacing from her reverie, evidently unconsoled. "Screw them," she repeated with added conviction. "I'm just getting started. They're not going to defeat me."

"Started with what?" I ventured. I wasn't sure whom she meant by "them."

"Changing this country, liberating the people, overthrowing the government."

"Well, that might be accomplished for you in the coming days, anyway."

"I'm not just talking about Selele," Maxine sneered. "I'm talking about all of them, the Rebels included. All the megalomaniacs – get rid of the bloody lot, I say. Bring back the rule of law, the will of the people. Give the people their spirit back. It's their country."

"Max," I cried in dismay, "you're crazy. You can't single-handedly change the destiny of a country. This is much bigger than you. Come on, let's get some sleep. You're just in reaction now. Your motivation is all wrong."

"No, no," Maxine insisted. "Listen to me, Mark. This is just like in *The Magician's Way* – like that scene in the Bull Market Pub. You see, there are all these destructive energies: the dictator and his goons, the bloodthirsty Rebel army, the hostile swamps full of demons and crocodiles – and all we're conditioned to think about is surviving them. The real danger here is that we have no vision beyond coping with whatever comes at us. If that happens we're just victims, refugees on the run. Victims have no power, though; they just get crushed. And even if we make it through the Swamps alive, what then? What's changed in us? What's changed in our world? Didn't you hear what Cynthia said? We're responsible for the world we're going to create now."

Maxine's eyes gleamed, willing me to appreciate what she was saying. "We have to go for something greater than just escaping. We have to believe there's something else out there in the Meluti – a force for good, a power that can stand up to the malevolent shadow that is lengthening over this land. That's got to be our mission: to find that benevolent force, engage it, enlist it – before the country is completely overtaken by darkness."

"The last shaman?" I said, moved by her argument. It made more sense than anything I had heard or considered in a long time.

"Yes, the last shaman." She rewarded my keenness with a bright smile. "Looking for him mustn't just be a pretext for us slipping out of the Republic. We must actually find him."

I was flushed by a sudden burst of enthusiasm. "You're right, Max. Why should we act like lambs being dragged to the slaughter, eh? We'll do it. We'll find your man."

"Brilliant, Mark, that's the spirit," Maxine beamed. "I know how wary you are of making choices lately, but we really have nothing to lose with this one. We must choose it with all our hearts. Intention is everything; it's what took the shaman through the crack in the wall into the Other World, and it's what will carry us to our end result, too."

"This is it," I thought, feeling myself shiver with excitement. What lay ahead of us was the ultimate test of magic: were my desperate circumstances an immutable reality that could only end in tragedy, or could I set an intention and trust some unfathomable force to come in and navigate everything to a satisfactory conclusion for me and my loved ones?

More than that, I was about to find out whether I had it in me to stand tall in life and shape it to my will. I was stirred by the prospect of finding within myself the character that had helped my forebears tame the wilds of Africa. Something in me had changed. I was suddenly electrified by the realization that I was doing something that I had up until now dismissed as outside the realm of possibility – I was daring to go after the secret that would transform me from stumbling, half-wise, would-be magician to masterful adept.

I was amazed at how powerful I felt after making a positive choice about going into the Swamps. At the same time, I could also feel the exhaustion underlying my newfound enthusiasm. Knowing that we were going to need all our wits about us from the word "go" in the morning, my biggest worry now was that I was over-tired and in too much pain to go to sleep. I pushed myself out of my seat.

"Well," I said, "we better get some shut-eye. Big day tomorrow."

Maxine held the back of her hand to her mouth and yawned. She stood up with exaggerated weariness, a silent comment on what a big day she had been through.

"Goodnight hug?" she smiled warmly.

We held each other for a long time. Though her embrace was diffident to begin with, at some point Maxine's demeanor changed; she let herself fully sink into my arms. I could sense her reluctance to let go of me. The thought that I could take her then and there was emboldened by her warm breath on my neck and her hand brushing the hair on my nape. She casually adjusted her body so that it locked more snugly into mine. If ever I had received a signal from a woman that she wanted me, this was it. There was no modesty in her embrace; I could feel her body stirring with passion. And yet, even though I had lusted after Maxine for all of my life, and in spite of my aching loneliness and desperate longing for the warmth of another human being, and even considering that this might be my last night on Earth, I did not have it in me to take up her unspoken offer. Things were complicated enough without me going to bed with a woman whose fiancé's body was hardly cold.

Sensing my reluctance, Maxine disengaged from me. She stood back, keeping her hands on my shoulders. Her eyes searched mine. "You're very sweaty," she said. "Are you alright?"

"My tooth's hurting," I groaned. "I hope I can sleep okay tonight."

"I better give you something. Why don't you go get into bed and I'll be over with my medicine bag in a minute?"

Outside, the night air was perfumed by the scent of flowering Queen of the Night cacti. As I walked to my bungalow, I bumped into a group of guards who took no interest in my appearance. They were mesmerized by three bright lights drifting earthward on the horizon.

"What is it?" I asked conversationally. I could tell that they were flares.

"Witches," replied one of the guards without taking his eyes off the lights. "There are many in the sky tonight."

I saw no point in disabusing the guards of their ignorance. I simply requested that one of their number escort Maxine to my pavilion. As I moved on, I imagined that I could hear thunder in the distance. When I stopped again to listen, I could definitely hear the muffled sounds of cannon fire from up on the Lesoti plateau. It was a depressing reminder of the fighting that would sooner or later spill over into the Irrigation Scheme and consume my family. While the thought saddened me, I was grateful that I was going out to confront my fate rather than waiting for it to creep up on me at its own convenience.

Maxine wasn't far behind me. I had hardly undressed and climbed into bed when she let herself into my bedroom and pulled up a chair beside me.

"Did you manage to speak to your children?" she asked conversationally while popping a thermometer in my mouth.

"No service," I mumbled. "Can't get through."

"Okay, don't speak," she hushed me, picking up my wrist to feel my pulse.

For me, there has always been something blissfully therapeutic about surrendering to the care of a medical practitioner. Maxine's presence was especially soothing. As I lay there in the peaceful silence, I noticed all of my hopes and fears stand down and slip back into the shadows of my consciousness.

Maxine let go of my wrist and took the thermometer out of my mouth. "Well, you do have a fever, but don't worry, I'll give you something for that...and the pain."

She stuck a syringe needle into a little bottle and drew its contents into the syringe. "Okay, just make a fist for me and pump it a few times. We want to bring this vein up." Her fingers tapped the crook of my arm.

"An intravenous injection?" I balked. "You sure it's not too strong? We need to be up in a few hours."

"Don't worry, I know what I'm doing."

I closed my eyes as Maxine inserted the needle into my vein. Once the stinging passed I opened my eyes again. A small plume of blood rushed into the syringe barrel. In the same instant that Maxine depressed the plunger, I tasted a rush of gas in the back of my mouth and a warm, dreamy glow washed over me.

The euphoric sensation didn't last long. I began sliding into a dark void. When I came to, I was hiding in thick undergrowth along the banks of the Muchocho River. An ancient tribe of aborigines was beating the bushes to drive me out of cover. One of the primitive hunters chased me into a house, where my daughter was taking a shower.

"Why are you showering with your clothes on?" I said, mystified.

"So the Easter Bunny doesn't see me nudie," she said.

"How's the Easter Bunny going to see you?"

"He's always watching to see if I'm good. You told me."

"There's no Easter Bunny, sweetie."

"Then how come you have a rhino's head?" She pointed to a full-length mirror, which reflected the image of a creature with antelope legs, a human torso and a rhino's head. I tried desperately to pull the head off my shoulders. Exhausted by my effort, I stopped and looked in the mirror again. Blood was running from the rhino's nostrils.

CHAPTER FOUR

Passage into Another World

Optimism is often the last resort of those pushed beyond the point of no return. There were most probably times, usually after a few drinks, that I might have given people the impression that I was something of a Meluti expert, though the truth was far from that. I had only ever gone into the Swamps twice when I was a teenager, and then only by airplane. Both times, my father had flown my brothers and me there in his single-propeller Cessna for a weekend of fishing. We had landed on a grass airstrip servicing a lodge situated on one of the biggest islands in the heart of the Delta. I remember us catching some spectacular tiger fish and Meluti pike, but that did not necessitate us travelling beyond the channels surrounding the hotel. We never met a single person native to the territory. The little toe I had dipped in the Meluti had revealed nothing of its nature to me. I had not even heard the local dialect spoken. For that matter, my regular Lapedi was rustier than the *Titanic*. The notion that I was in any way qualified to lead an expedition through the marshes and jungles of the Delta to find a shaman in hiding was totally ludicrous.

Yet, since committing myself fully to the undertaking, there was something about the crazy mission that stirred my heart. Living in civilization had always clashed with me, whereas wilderness always seemed to console me. I might have been awkward and out of place in the subtle and restrained atmosphere of Western society, and wary of the raw, unfiltered passions of African culture, but in the pristine wilds of Africa I always felt a deep sense of ease – a sense that I was held, that I belonged and knew my way around. Now that I had embraced my mission, I looked forward to it, if not with relish, certainly with a vague hope that I was heading into a world that my own nature and spirit could relate to.

Our plan was that Maxine and I, accompanied by Chollo and David, would launch a tin fishing boat onto the Muchocho River just upstream from the Stanley Gorge and then ride the mile-long section of rapids into Lake Stanley, the great expanse of water that lay on the far side of the gorge. Once we had made it onto the lake, we could then pull an outboard motor from one of the watertight holds, fix it to the back of the boat and motor across to Mlumu Village, the semi-tame settlement that for many years had served as a gateway into the Swamps.

Beyond that there was no plan; we would have to play it by ear. In peaceful times we could have driven all the way to Lake Stanley on the road that cut into the southern wall of the gorge. Now, though, the pass was cordoned off by a small garrison of soldiers with orders to shoot anyone trying to sneak in or out of the Meluti.

Once the decision had been made for me to go, Martin and I had readied the boat and packed it with the essential provisions my party would have to rely on. There was not much: one pump-action shotgun, one hunting rifle, a pistol, ammunition, a change of clothes each, a plastic tub of medical supplies, including antibiotics and painkillers for my bad tooth, a couple of collapsible fishing rods, sleeping bags, flashlights, batteries, and matches. That was it.

At Martin's insistence, we were not carrying any food or

money. "Look," he had reasoned as we sighted in the hunting rifle at the bottom of the garden, "extra baggage will just slow you down. You're going to have to live off the land sooner or later, no matter what. As for money, there's nothing you can buy with it in the Meluti, but someone will kill you for it. The success of your mission depends on you being able to be of use to the natives. If the moment you arrive there it's not obvious how you can help them, you're not going to go any further than Mlumu – you'll be stuck there for the rest of the war as their prisoners…if they don't kill you."

Sensing my despondency, Martin had slapped me on the back and laughed. "Don't worry, little brother, I have something that will tip the odds in your favor."

His secret weapon turned out to be a bottle of port swaddled in ample layers of bubble wrap. "The headman of the village, Veeti, loves this stuff," he told me as he stowed the bottle carefully in one of the boat's fishing compartments. "He's a real rogue, mind you. A couple of years ago we caught him and some of his crew trying to drive a herd of our cattle through the Stanley Gorge. But with him being our easterly neighbor, we like to keep him on side. A bottle of this stuff every Christmas seems to do the trick. His people only give us enough trouble to keep up their self-respect. A Christmas bottle in July will buy you enough time not to get your throat cut straightaway. Just make sure you give it to him when he's on his own. He'll hate you if he has to share it."

On waking the following day, I was extremely happy to find that the ill effects of my tooth infection had disappeared overnight. There was no ache or swelling in my gum; my head was cool and clear. I was very thankful for Maxine's healing touch, though my gratitude did not have any time to linger, due to the unpleasant surprise I had to contend with the moment I got out of bed.

Having had no reason, up until then, to get up before sunrise, I had forgotten how cold it was in the dark hours of winter mornings. Maxine, David and I wore the olive-green fleecy jackets of the Vale Estate security guards' uniform over our khakis to keep ourselves from freezing. When we arrived at the trackers' compound deep in the bush to pick him up, Chollo waved away with disgust the offer of a jacket for himself. All he had on was a sleeveless woolen knit pullover and a faded Java-print sarong covered by a jackal skin *bejuga*, the local name for a loincloth. His feet were bare, and in his hands he carried everything he was bringing on the trip: an *assegai* – a short stabbing spear – and a battle axe fashioned from a sharpened strip of metal wrapped around the top of a stout stick.

My heart lit up at the sight of his stern countenance in the Land Rover's headlights. If there was anyone I would have chosen to accompany me on a foray into darkest Africa, it was Chollo, who had agreed to go with us as far as Portuguese Territory. He was the son of Leechwe, an old-school tracker who used to work on the cattle and game section of the estate. For reasons known only to himself, Chollo, who was more or less the same age as me, had refused an education, preferring instead to spend his formative years running wild in the bush. There was nothing he had not learned from his father about the tracker's trade. In the old days, we used to pay him a few shillings to find us wild honey or catch parrots with birdlime. When the ancestors had come to guide Leechwe home, Chollo had taken his job.

The very qualities that I usually found disturbing about Chollo now comforted me. He did not understand a single word of English, even though Africans are very gifted at languages and will pick up a smattering of vocabulary just from overhearing the odd conversation. Chollo must have actively avoided taking anything in. It was as if his only concern in life were hunting things down, and anything that did not further this focus was of no value to him – something to be resisted, like the common cold. His face, which happened to be blacker than the average Lapedi's skin tone, showed no sign of having been moderated by any culture whatsoever, African or Western. In many ways, Chollo reminded me of a hunting dog – an animal that understood no language; that needed no affection, no comfort; who lived only for the opportunity to fulfill the characteristics of its breed.

Concerned by the lurid purple color of his jersey, I asked Chollo, through Martin, whether he did not have a more camouflaged alternative. I did not understand his curt reply. "He says that he wants to be very obvious," Martin translated. "I don't think he wants to give the impression that he's hiding from anyone. Very sensible, if you ask me."

Chollo spoke quietly for a few moments to a woman wrapped in a thick blanket. She nodded her head in mournful acquiescence at whatever was being said. Though she could only be in her thirties, the woman was withered and frail, as if bush life had already sucked from her what she had to give over a lifetime. Chollo handed her a tight role of bills, which she took with the same hand she used to wipe a tear from her cheek. Then he smiled at each of the bare-skinned children, who took in the departure scene with bewildered expressions, patted the smallest ones on the head and climbed into the front passenger seat of the Land Rover.

Half an hour later we arrived at the natural slipway situated on the border of the Vale Estate game section, about a mile upriver from the Stanley Gorge. The first hint of a red aura glowed faintly above the Lesoti Mountains. The bush around us echoed with a cacophony of barking and grunting and crowing and chirping as every living creature made whatever noise it could to shake off the cold. The freezing temperature numbed my nervous anticipation of the one-mile gauntlet of rapids we were about to run.

Martin was unusually taciturn. There was no emotional farewell, no fond words of goodbye or stern warnings or advice. He ordered us into the tin fishing boat and then reversed it into the river. I unhitched the boat from its trailer and we began drifting slowly away from the bank. I shivered with dread, feeling myself slipping from the known universe that had, up until that moment, cradled me for all of my life. As we each took up a paddle to face the boat downstream, Martin emerged from the Land Rover and stood at the water's edge, watching us float into the current of the river. Once the boat caught the current and we started to race downstream, he finally called out, "Take care of yourselves. Tell Veeti I see him."

Seconds later there was nothing we could see of Martin or his vehicle, other than the taillights glowing like the ruby eyes of some monster lying in the shadows of the giant wild fig tree that hung over the slipway. Our attention turned quickly to the roar of the rapids ahead of us. We used what little time we had to practice controlling the boat with our paddles and adjusting our eyes to the dim light. After we negotiated a few patches of whitewater, I was at least confident that everyone could follow my commands. David's attitude and capability was especially impressive. He responded to each of my orders with a cheerful "Yes, Boss" and spirited action in support of whatever maneuver we were attempting.

Our paddling drills counted for nothing, though. As soon as we began approaching the gorge where the first serious rapids loomed, Chollo pointed ahead at the bank on our side of the river.

"Masotcha!" he called out over his shoulder from his position on the prow. Soldiers!

With my heart racing, I strained my eyes to make out what he could see in the gloomy light. About a hundred and fifty yards below our position I detected a long line of silhouetted figures filing down the bank to the water's edge. It was a platoon of soldiers coming down to the river for their morning ablutions.

"What are we going to do?" Maxine whispered urgently.

I had to think fast. In a few moments we would be bobbing right past their noses. If we tried to navigate the boat to the bank before we reached them, we would surely end up close to the soldiers, and under the circumstances, none of us could afford to be taken into custody, least of all Maxine. If, on the other hand, we tried to drift by them, we would just as certainly be cut down in a hail of machine-gun fire.

"Okay," I shouted, "lay your paddles down. Now!"

As the other three let their paddles fall to the floor of the boat, I dug mine into the water with every ounce of my strength, sending the boat into a one hundred and eighty degree turn. Then I threw my paddle down, too.

We went down the first big water chute tailfirst. All we could do was hang grimly to the side railing as the boat was swept into the rapids in an uncontrollable spin. Maxine let out a panicked shriek when the boat suddenly dropped away again down the second chute. I glanced desperately at the riverbank through my sodden fringe. Soldiers along the river's edge began jumping to their feet excitedly. We had been spotted. I, too, began screaming hysterically. The others quickly realized what my game was. They began calling out with me to the soldiers, "Help! Help! We're going to die. Throw us a rope."

With the boat being smashed from rock to rock, and constantly threatening to capsize in the broiling torrent, it was not a difficult act to put on. For their part, the bewildered soldiers watched us drift by them in absolute astonishment. The few who had had the presence to reach for their guns, now held their weapons lamely with the barrels pointing down. The platoon officer, followed by a couple of his men, skipped helplessly along the bank from rock to rock, trying to keep pace with us. He gesticulated frantically with his pistol in the direction of the gorge, presumably warning us of the peril we were being swept into. After a short distance the going got too rough for him to keep up. He stood on a big boulder, holding his hands to his head in despair. Bullets began to throw up splashes of water around the boat as some of the soldiers fired a few parting shots at us. Seconds later, we fell below their line of sight.

Rafting through the gorge itself was even more frightening than riding the preceding rapids. The entire greasy Muchocho River funneled into a deep channel only about twenty-five yards wide, creating a long, continuous chute of foaming water that propelled us along at a heart-stopping rate. We sat with our paddles in hand, in the vain hope that we could use them to prevent our craft from being wrecked against the rock walls ominously crowding us on either side. In the dim light the cliffs of the canyon seemed to rise up forever; there was no telling where they ended and the sky began. Nor was there any light coming from the end of the gorge; it looked as though we were heading into a solid wall of basalt.

Maxine pointed to the dark walls and yelled out over the roar of the water, "Just like going through the shaman's portal...the crack in the wall."

The thrill in her voice resonated through my body. "Let's hope we have an astral cord to guide us back out again," I shouted back. I chose not to voice my concern about what demons might be waiting for us on the other side.

Just as I was beginning to assume that we might get through to Lake Stanley without being dashed to bits, the rapids ceased to roar – and began to thunder. What lay ahead of us in the final stage of the canyon, as it widened to meet the lake's entrance, was a series of rough, shallow rapids and small waterfalls. Our boat began to scrape over rocks again. We were dragged sideways down a big chute and swamped with water as one side of the boat dipped precariously into the frothing pool below.

Our progress became more and more difficult over the next two or three hundred yards, until we were upended by a large cataract next to the edge of the lake. All four of us went flying through the air and crashed into the icy water, rushing toward the next waterfall. Winded by the impact of the fall and the freezing-cold water, I flailed about in panic, trying desperately to keep my head up as I was dragged relentlessly toward the edge.

Before I knew it, I was airborne again. I hit the water beneath with such an impact, it might as well have been concrete. The force of the cascade drove my body deep underwater. Try as I might to surface or swim away from the cascade, the crashing water kept me helplessly submerged. Realizing I was no match for the thundering water, I let my body go limp while I tried to recall anything I might have been taught about this eventuality. At that moment I felt myself being dragged into a violent underwater current. My first reaction was to panic again, but then it suddenly occurred to me that I was saved. I was being sucked into a whirlpool. I surrendered to the spiraling current, allowing it to pull me deeper into the water. Then, just as I thought my lungs were going to burst, I suddenly popped out on the surface a good fifteen yards away from the waterfall.

The first thing I noticed when I surfaced was our boat floating right side up in an infinite expanse of calm water. We were in the lake. The boat was only as far away again as the waterfall, though I feared that I would not be able to reach it. My waterlogged boots and fleecy jacket weighed heavily and my body was beginning to cramp. I fully expected, with every feeble kick and stroke, to seize up and sink down into the seemingly leaden water. To my relief, I made it to the boat and summoned my last reserves of strength to drag myself aboard. I sat on the floor, propped up against one of the aluminum benches, and looked around for the others. All three of my companions floundered in the water surrounding the boat, gasping loudly on account of the cold and their exhaustion.

The unnerving thought that their noisy splashing was very likely to attract crocodiles gave me the adrenalin boost I needed to help them aboard. Once everyone was safely on the boat, Chollo became very vocal about something that had happened to him in the water.

"What's the problem, Chollo?" I asked him through chattering teeth.

"Get the guns out," he said frantically. "There's a *Tokoloshe* in the water."

"What?" I said in astonishment. I had often heard Africans refer to the dwarf-like water demon in mythical terms, but never to suggest an actual encounter with one.

"There's a Tokoloshe in the water," Chollo cried again. "After I landed in the lake, someone tried to hold me down under the water."

"But that happened to me, too," I tried to placate his

superstitious mind. "That's the big water falling; it pushes you down."

"Not true," Chollo shook his head contemptuously. "This was a man. I could feel his body and hands." He pointed at David. "He was with me. He can tell you."

I turned to David. He showed no sign of anything other than being freezing cold. "I don't see nothing," he said in English. "I just help him when he comes to the top."

"Can we discuss this some other time?" gasped Maxine. "We'll all end up with pneumonia if we don't get warm." She sat curled up on a bench, shivering in great spasms.

I opened one of the holds and pulled out the shotgun and a box of cartridges. Chollo snatched them from me with a satisfied grunt. After loading the gun, he positioned himself on the bow and peered into the water, searching for some sign of the evil water spirit he believed was lurking beneath the dark-indigo surface.

From the same hold I pulled out our sleeping bags, which we unzipped and wrapped around ourselves like blankets. I absently checked my watch to see if it was still working. It occurred to me that it had been only twenty minutes since Martin had launched us on our journey – and already we had been shot at, almost drowned, and now we were practically freezing to death.

Next I should have hauled out the outboard motor and fixed it to the back of the boat, but I felt too numb and weary to perform the task. With everyone's teeth rattling so violently, I guessed that, like me, they must be frozen to the marrow. I decided that the port I had brought along to butter up the headman of Mlumu Village could serve a more immediate life-saving purpose. I looked into the compartment Martin had stashed it in, praying that it was still in one piece. Sure enough, the miracle of bubble wrap had prevailed. I tore at the packaging with trembling hands. When finally the bottle was liberated, I pulled out the corkscrew that had been stowed with it and worked feverishly at pulling the cork out. I took a few generous swigs of the sweet, fortified wine, then passed it to Maxine.

The bottle only lasted two rounds before it was empty. Still, it did the trick. A warm fire burned in my solar plexus and radiated outward through my body in pleasurable waves. Almost instantly the excruciating brain freeze behind my eyes subsided, replaced by an exhilarating buzz. Not wanting to leave any trace of the port, I held the empty bottle under the surface of the lake until it had filled with water, and let it sink.

Brimming with a cheerful confidence, I hauled out the little twenty-horsepower outboard motor and attached it to the stern. After connecting the motor to its gas tank and priming it, I switched on the choke and pulled on the starter rope. My confidence had been justified. The motor spluttered to life, raising a hearty cheer from Maxine and David. Chollo was still preoccupied with his Tokoloshe.

Operating the steering handle of the engine, I drove the boat around in circles looking for our paddles. Another cheer rose into the air when we found the last one. We were like a winning team who, toward the end of some contest, are so high on victory that they relish even the smallest gain, taking everything as a sign of their invincibility. Each of us was flushed with the success of outwitting the soldiers and surviving the rapids, not to mention the efficacious effect of the port. With a cavalier hand I swung the boat around to face Mlumu Island and opened the throttle to full speed. The bow of the boat kicked up, sending the others sprawling. They all laughed cheerfully at each other as they sat back on their seats and gripped more tightly on the side railing.

Plowing across the water to our destination, we were greeted by the most magnificent panorama. The sky above the mountains on our starboard side glowed like a cosmic cocktail. A heavy band of crimson sediment hung over the black ranges, and above that red layer the atmosphere was washed in a diffuse purple light. Low wisps of gentian violet clouds floated across the lake, which now shimmered with the same mauve sheen. A flock of white egrets sailed in a V formation ahead of us, following the same route out into the swamps as they had every day for thousands and thousands of years. Their ghostly presence opened my mind to a transcendent timelessness, a feeling that I was in another world where nothing ever changed, but flowed consistently within some divinely engineered rhythm.

Never before had I experienced such a clearly delineated frontier, such a marked crossing from one terrain into another – especially psychologically. It was as if a gate had bolted shut on the life I used to live upstream of the Stanley Gorge. Something inside of me told me that I had popped out in a dimension where the alienated, self-gratifying struggle to rise above and stand over existence would not be smiled upon by the pre-existing order of things.

As we began closing in on Mlumu Island, I asked Chollo to take out the other guns and load them. He dismissed my command by pulling a sour face and shaking his head emphatically in the negative. "What's the matter?" I called to him, affronted by his insubordination.

"No guns," said Chollo flatly, jacking the cartridges out of the shotgun. He put the gun and ammunition back in the hold I had retrieved them from.

I noticed David's eyes darting between Chollo and me. He was clearly distressed by the tension between us. "They have too many guns," he offered quickly. An appeasing smile spread across his face.

David's intercession irritated rather than mollified me. I glanced at him, trying to figure out what it was about him that did not sit well with me. He was a pleasant-looking man with light-brown skin and fine features. He was roughly the same size as me, though in much better condition. While he appeared much younger than me, I knew that African men often retained their youthful looks much longer than Europeans, which made me guess that he was about the same age as Chollo and me – somewhere in his mid to late thirties. There was nothing overweening about him, nor was he subservient. He could look me in the eye without the need for defiance. Nothing about his appearance spoke against him. Moreover, his actions so far should have recommended him. The kindness and loyalty David always showed Maxine was touching, his willingness to pull his weight in every situation faultless. Yet there was still something about him that bugged me. I did not like the thought that it might be his closeness to Maxine that grated on me.

I put my annoyance aside and focused back on our approach to Mlumu Village, which was now close enough for us to make out some of its dwellings and signs of life around them. It appeared as though a large crowd was gathered on the shore in front of the first line of huts. I kept an apprehensive eye on the silhouetted mob for some sign of their mood, wondering whether a large reception committee was a good thing or not. No indication was forthcoming. The villagers stood motionless on their clay beach watching our arrival. A fleet of *mokoros* – dugout canoes – pulled halfway out of the water, fringed the shoreline.

"Eh! Eh! Eh!" Chollo suddenly exclaimed. He rattled off a string of incomprehensible words, finishing with an emphatic "Eish!" Usually this expression anticipated something painful, though I couldn't tell whether that was his inference now. Maxine and I exchanged perplexed glances and peered intently at the shore to fathom the reason for Chollo's excitement.

"Oh my god," Maxine said in amazement as we drew closer to the beach.

David turned to look at me in consternation. "You must go back, Boss," he cried urgently, his eyes beseeching me. He used his free hand to make frantic turning circles.

I steered the boat parallel to the gray beach, letting the engine idle so that I could judge the situation for myself. It was indeed a strange sight to behold. The crowd on the shore, which was now less than a hundred yards away, consisted mainly of a large group of youths wearing nothing but white paint from head to toe. Perched on their heads were what looked like white pots. Standing among the youngsters were a number of men dressed in animal hides, predominantly leopard and cheetah skins. The sun had not risen yet, but even from a distance I could see that their heads were splendidly adorned with brightly colored parrot feathers. Unlike the youths, who were unarmed, the men carried assegais and fighting sticks. There were no guns in sight.

"What are you going to do?" whispered Maxine anxiously.

I surveyed the spectacle on the beach, trying to decide. If we wanted to go into the Delta, there was no way around Mlumu Village – we would get nowhere without the goodwill and services of its inhabitants.

"What do you think, Chollo?" I checked with my scout.

Without taking his eyes off the shore, Chollo casually waved for me to go in. As he did so, two elders walked toward each other from opposite ends of the crowd and conferred briefly. The less regally dressed of the two seemed to do most of the talking. After their short discussion, he walked down to the edge of the water and beckoned us ashore. On his command, a bunch of youths rushed into the shallows to move some of the mokoros out of the way for us. Chollo waved impatiently at the beach again.

"Looks alright," I said to Maxine and David, still not one hundred percent convinced.

I turned the boat again and pointed it toward the gap in the mokoros. As the nose of our craft touched bottom, I killed the motor and tilted the propeller out of the water. A group of youths leaped eagerly forward to drag the boat halfway onto the beach, creating a great pandemonium with their loud shouting and ululating. Their rambunctiousness was more than a little unsettling, calling to mind the violence with which tribesmen often treat captured animals. At close range the cream ochre smeared across their faces gave them a macabre, soulless appearance that conspired with their behavior to create an impression of savage hostility.

Undaunted, Chollo stood up on the prow and, clutching his sleeping bag around his neck with one hand and his assegai and fighting stick with the other, hailed the headman of the village, "Yes, Veeti, father of Mlumu, we see you."

The crowd parted as the two elders who had invited us ashore walked up to the boat. They stood looking us over, as they would have a bull at a cattle yard sale. Finally, the regally attired one looked up at Chollo and greeted him listlessly.

"Yes, son, we see you, too," he said. "Is that Vale's son?" he asked absently without looking at me.

"Eh," Chollo confirmed, "he is the late master's youngest son."

Still not looking at me, Veeti spoke again in his mild monotone. "Yes, we are very sad to hear of the great man's passing. We are all suffering with his family."

The headman was tall and thin. Except for his ceremonial garb, which looked somehow ill-fitting on him, he was an exceptionally unimposing individual. His hair was not yet gray, but dull and lifeless, matching his washed-out, glassy eyes.

"And this female, is she the doctor?" Veeti said, looking directly at Maxine.

"Yes, Chief," Maxine spoke for herself, "I am Dr. Carlyle of the Manzimwe Mission." She hesitated a moment. "How did you know I am a doctor?"

Veeti seemed taken aback by the question. "We have been waiting all night for you," he said as if we were late for an appointment.

The headman's crony stepped forward. He was exactly the opposite of Veeti in looks and manner. Short and portly, he had a wide, chubby face that was framed by a wispy beard and an incongruous pair of horn-rimmed spectacles. "Yes, children of our people, we see you," his voice boomed. Even though he was modestly attired in a plain buckskin bejuga, he nevertheless projected a charismatic energy. He reminded me of a great stage actor whose presence alone creates awe and anticipation, as if he has the ability to create a vacuum in others that the audience craves for him to animate with his expression.

"I am Dumani," he continued after a contrived pause, addressing not just us perched trepidatiously on the boat, but the whole gathering. "We all thank you for answering our call so quickly. The headman's daughter will be late before long." He stuck his chest out proudly and regarded us with his head tilted slightly to one side.

"What's wrong with her?" Maxine asked the man who called himself Dumani.

"She is asleep," he said, "she cannot wake up." Then in perfect English he said, "By all appearances, I would say that she is in a coma." Murmurs of astonishment rippled through the crowd. The natives were obviously just as taken aback as I was to hear their fellow tribesman speak in the Queen's tongue.

Maxine's brow furrowed thoughtfully. "For how long?" she continued to talk in Lapedi.

"Since yesterday evening," said Dumani.

"What happened to her?" said Maxine. No one replied. "Was she hurt, or bitten by something? Has she been sick before, maybe?"

Dumani looked at Veeti to see whether he had any information to offer. The headman shook his head apologetically. "She has been in good health. But then yesterday she began passing out at intervals. Last evening she just fell down." He let his spear and fighting stick fall to the ground lamely. "Like that."

"From then, they could not revive her," Dumani offered.

"Alright," said Maxine decisively, "take me to her right away. David, bring the medicine bag, please."

With that, she and David were off, led by Veeti and Dumani through the extraordinary throng of males into the village. Chollo and I stayed on the boat. I used the opportunity to change into my dry set of clothes, much to the amusement of the ochre-daubed youths who had been staring at me in open-mouthed amazement. Chollo laughed good-naturedly with the boys, trading quips with them concerning the inadequacy and unattractiveness of the white man's appendage.

"Okay, fellows," I shouted mirthfully, "that's enough. You know the water is very cold today. It makes things small." I pinched my thumb and forefinger together to indicate shrinkage. Everyone in the crowd laughed uproariously. Faces looked about to check that those around them were enjoying the moment as much as they were.

"You want fire?" one of the elders smiled at me.

"I will be very thankful," I said.

We were soon sitting beside a fire that the villagers had relocated to the beach. I was relieved that the people of the Meluti were just as easily charmed by humor as the average citizen of the Republic. I was also encouraged that the plight of Veeti's daughter might be the perfect chance for us to be useful to the village. Whether or not we could live up to expectations remained to be seen.

After an appropriate amount of banter, I asked the males gathered around us what ritual they were all made up for. They looked around for the most senior among them, and when the old man realized that all eyes were on him, he smiled timidly and mouthed "*didakta*" very slowly, as if communicating with a deaf man.

"Didakta?" I repeated.

"Eh," he grinned, well pleased with my comprehension, "didakta."

"And what's didakta?" I frowned.

The smile vanished from the elder's face as he realized that the single word did not in fact explain anything to me, and that he would have to be more forthcoming.

"When boys want to become men," he said finally, "they must go off into the bush for this many nights," he flashed his ten fingers at me twice, "and survive on their own. This is didakta."

The expression of unresolved anticipation on the boys' faces told me that the old man was, for whatever reason, holding back from telling me everything. Not wanting to intrude on the initiation more than I already had, I let him off the hook by looking around dubiously and saying, "Thank you, father, but surely this lot are not ready to be men."

Though Lapedi males will not think twice about killing anyone who insults them, they do love a good ribbing – especially one delivered with irony. A chorus of good-humored dissent rose up from the crowd. Many of the youths challenged me to stand in front of them and repeat my comment, though they could not contain their laughter.

At this point Maxine returned with David and Dumani. The crowd hushed and moved back to give her room beside the fire. She did not say anything immediately, but stood in silent contemplation, holding her hands out to soak up the warmth of the flames. Once she felt thawed to her satisfaction, she spoke.

"Oh, what a sweet little girl she is," Maxine winced sadly. "The good news is," her tone became optimistic, "I'm certain I know what the problem is. She has an extradural hemorrhage on the right side of her head."

Maxine's words had an effect on me that was opposite to her tone. "What's an extra...something hemorrhage?" I said, feeling my hopes getting ready to bolt.

"The poor thing must have taken a knock to her temple," said Maxine, "which lacerated the middle meningeal artery, causing bleeding in the extradural space. Basically, she has a blood clot between her skull and brain, with an ever-increasing buildup of pressure on the brain. That pressure is what caused her to pass out intermittently and eventually lapse into a coma. Soon it will kill her."

I bit my lip to stop myself from giving the crowd any sign of my fading optimism.

"If we can take the pressure off the brain, we can save her," Maxine continued, deep in thought. "The question is, how?"

"How do you normally take the pressure off one of these epidural hemorrhages?" I asked her.

"Extradural," she corrected me. "We usually make an emergency burr-hole in the skull to let the blood out of the extradural cavity. But that involves using a surgical drill."

"Brain surgery!" I thought bitterly. It seemed as though our chance to be of use to the villagers was not one we would be thankful for, after all. I looked about me with a forced smile. The natives stared at Maxine and me with unreserved fascination. For virtually all of them, it was the first conversation they had heard in English. From the expressions on their faces, it was obvious they were waiting with bated breath to discover what magic we planned to conjure up for the occasion. There was not a shadow of a doubt in their minds that we would meet their expectations. The goodwill they had extended us was based on their assumption that our express purpose for being there was to save the head-man's daughter.

"Is there no other way?" I urged Maxine, not very hopeful of an inspired answer.

"No, it's the only way," Maxine assured me. "I can't think of anything we could possibly use, though."

"I think you have something," Dumani interjected, also speaking in English.

"What's that?" I snapped in surprise.

"Something you brought along with you," Dumani offered, "that you now believe you have no need of. What could that be?" He spoke in a low monotone, not wanting the villagers to know he was assuming a leading role in our deliberations.

"What could that be?" I thought aloud. "The port...no... the corkscrew!"

Dumani's face remained impassive. He did not look up from the fire. "Perfect, is it not, Dr. Carlyle?" he said in the same quietly detached voice.

Maxine was aghast at the idea. "We can't drill into her head with a corkscrew," she objected. "Anything could happen. It could crack her skull, or break off in the bone. The thought of it is just too horrible to contemplate."

"Remain calm, Doctor," Dumani cautioned her through gritted teeth. Then, in his natural voice, he said, "If we do nothing, is there any hope for her?"

"Not really," Maxine conceded.

"So it seems you have no option, Doctor," Dumani said. "If you do nothing, the girl will die. That would be a tragedy in itself. She shows great promise. The whole village is working and saving to help her become the first villager to go to school. She is their light and their soul that they hope to send out into the wide world. Right now their hopes are high that you are here to save her. God forbid those hopes are dashed. You will be blamed for her death. And no doubt you have seen what happens when the Lapedi mob's mood turns angry."

Maxine swallowed nervously. Her eyes bulged slightly as her mind boggled at our predicament. "Okay, let's try the corkscrew," she said vaguely, still lost in thought.

I climbed into the boat to fetch the corkscrew. It was the type with two arms that rise up as the screw turns in the cork, though I did not pay it any mind in that moment, not thinking that I would be the one who was going to have to use it as an improvised medical device. I was more preoccupied with puzzling over how Dumani fitted into the current picture. What was someone who spoke and understood English so fluently doing in the Swamps dressed in a buckskin loincloth? And how did he guess that we had something with us – something we thought we didn't need anymore – that we could use as a substitute for a medical drill? I jumped back down from the boat to rejoin him and Maxine. I held out the corkscrew for Maxine.

"No," said Dumani emphatically, "the person who performs the operation must be both strong and fierce of heart. Dr. Carlyle has the skill and the determination, but not the strength. You must do it, Mr. Vale." To my astonishment, he even laughed. "You look like someone who has had plenty of experience with corkscrews."

"He's right," Maxine agreed, "this has to be done smoothly and cleanly. It can't be botched."

There was no arguing, I knew. As unprepared as I felt for the task, deep down inside I was the only person I trusted with the makeshift procedure. If there was only going to be one shot at getting it right, I wanted to be the one taking that shot. Being in control, though, was hardly any consolation. I thought back ruefully to the days when, as a trainee magician, my mentors had set me the comparatively lame tasks of sticking straws through potatoes and getting pretty girls to sit on my lap. How I had sweated over those challenges, as if they had been a matter of life and death, when all that had been at stake was my pride. It was a strange thing to dwell on, but I was suddenly filled with regret at how frivolous the hang-ups and worries of my life had been compared to this moment, in which several lives literally did hang in the balance. My mind, I realized with some bitterness, had no ability to distinguish between a threat to my pride and a threat to my life.

I left the boat in David and Chollo's care and followed Maxine and Dumani into the village with about as much enthusiasm as a condemned man digging his own grave. The sun had risen, though it was still hidden by the jungle on the eastern flank of the village. The tribal initiates, who in the dimmer light and jovial atmosphere had come across as wholesome apparitions, now struck me as drab and hideous. In the brighter light of day, streaks of gray and brown mud tarnished the white ochre smeared roughly and unevenly across their bodies. They had the look about them of decomposing corpses, their bloodshot eyes and featureless faces void of any empathy or grace. I shuddered at the mental image of myself fleeing through the tangled forest after an unsuccessful operation, with a swarm of these adolescent demons hot on my heels.

***

Mlumu Village consisted of a wall of mud huts built in three or four indistinct rows along the shore of Lake Stanley, with as many dwellings again clustered along some dirt avenues heading into the forest. Generally, the village seemed in good order: its thatched roofs were all well maintained, the interlocking rectangle motifs on the rich-brown adobe walls glowed in vibrant primary colors, and the wide pathways and courtyards were swept into an obsessive state of cleanliness. In other circumstances, my heart would no doubt have delighted in the organic charm of the traditional hamlet. Now, though, I appreciated none of the quaintness of the place, other than to recognize the signs of a cohesive and well-ordered society. I hardly paid any attention to the blue-balled, red-bummed monkeys scattering in front of us.

Nor was I even curious about something I saw out of the corner of my eye that might have been a leopard melting into the shadows at the edge of the forest.

Veeti's compound was located at the junction between the back row of foreshore dwellings and the central forest avenue. It was ringed by a neat wall of sturdy poles, with a semicircle of half a dozen huts backing against the wall. In the middle of the *boma* stood a thatch-and-pole gazebo, surrounded by a horde of villagers craning to see into the shelter. The crowd was made up almost entirely of women, all wearing only Java-print sarongs fastened around their waists. My eyes blinked at the stirring sight of a flotilla of breasts bobbing above a sea of paisley.

A loud murmur of approval greeted our arrival. From the smiles and waves and cheers, it was evident that this was some kind of morbid entertainment for the women, in which Maxine and I were a surprise star attraction. Maxine wasted no time in shooing the spectators away.

"Okay, people, clear out," she shouted. "Only doctors and next of kin. Go on, out of the boma now! The girl will be late if you do not leave straightaway."

The villagers filed out of the compound reluctantly, some half-heartedly pleading to stay on, while others wished us well or admonished us to take care. As the crowd thinned, I could make out a small limp body lying on a tattered foam mattress under the gazebo. Veeti helped a haggard-faced woman shuffle over to us.

"Hauw, we thank you big time, white people," she called out in a strong, clear voice at odds with her frail demeanor. Her head shook from side to side forlornly to underscore her sincerity. As she came closer, she looked up at me and gave a muted cry of awe. "Eh, it is the descendent of the old man Vale, praise the ancestors." She poked her right hand out of the blanket draped around her and offered it to me. "I am the wife of Veeti – the girl's mother."

"Young Vale will be doing the business," Dumani informed the parents.

"My grandfather pissed in old man Vale's eyes to save

them from cobra spit," the woman mused. "Now the grandson returns to save our child. It is how the ancestors make things go."

Veeti ushered Maxine and me onto the pole deck. As I knelt beside the girl, my misgivings about the operation intensified a hundredfold. Though her parents were not able to tell us her age, I guessed that she was around seven or eight years old. The idea of twisting the corkscrew into her skull sickened and terrified me. Looking up from the angelic face, I tried to give myself a sense of certainty by testing Maxine's resolve. "Are you sure it's a dural what-you-ma-call-it hemorrhage? To me, she just looks like she's sleeping peacefully."

"Absolutely," said Maxine. "Feel her right temple. Can you feel that bump there? The bruising is hard to see beneath her hair." She pried the girl's right eye open. "See the dilated pupil? That's caused by the pressure on the nerve of the eye muscle as it goes around the skull, okay? Now jab her with the corkscrew on her left arm. No, harder. That's it. See how she doesn't move. Now jab her right arm. There, see how her face twitches. The side of her body opposite the head bruise is paralyzed. I'm telling you, we're dealing with a meningeal hematoma. She must have had a good knock to the head and then carried on as if nothing were wrong – till she started fainting."

"Okay," I sighed, "let's do it."

First Maxine shaved the girl's temple with a razor from her medical bag and then dabbed the area with disinfected cotton balls. While she sterilized the corkscrew, I closed my eyes and hyperventilated in the hope of steadying my trembling hands. I would have killed for a few swigs of port right then. My concern for what would happen to me and my companions if things went badly was trivial compared to my fear of what harm I could do to this fragile, helpless child who, but for the grace of God, might have been my own daughter.

"I'm going to support her head while you drill," said Maxine, handing the corkscrew back to me. "Dumani, can you hold her body in case she goes into spasm? And please ask Veeti and Mamma to stay back."

Every word she uttered raised my anxiety levels. "So, how far do I have to go in?" I asked her nervously.

"Just so much," she held her thumb and forefinger a fraction of an inch apart. She licked her lips and wiped away the sweat on her brow with her forearm. As she took the girl's skull in her hands, a stern look of resolve came over her. "Time to get out of your swing circle, Mark," she said.

Those words were the exact encouragement I needed. They alluded to the central theme of both my book and magic training, which revealed how people could get out of their own way and allow their super-conscious ability to take charge of whatever they attempted. My introduction to magic, and what had inspired me to write *The Magician's Way,* was a mind-blowing golf lesson in which the golf pro had demonstrated, beyond any doubt, that we can achieve unbelievably great results in everything we undertake simply by being more focused on the end result than on what we believe it takes to achieve the outcome – as long as we take action. In half an hour, using this "trick of the mind," as my instructor had called it, I had gone from a bumbling hacker suicidally frustrated with my swing, to landing the ball exactly where I chose without even worrying about how I hit it. That lesson, and countless instances since, had proved to me that we are endowed with a creative nature that is fully equipped with the innate skill to achieve absolutely any undertaking.

I took a moment to acknowledge all the doubts assailing me and let them be. Then I visualized the corkscrew drilling cleanly through the girl's skull into the blood clot. Once I imagined my desired end result, a reasonable calm came over me, accompanied by a certainty, not that the procedure would work, but that it was at least possible.

Holding my vision firmly in mind, I put the corkscrew to the girl's head and started screwing it into her skull. The point of the spiral bit sliced easily through the skin, but to my dismay it began slipping on the bone. I closed my eyes, the better to focus on my vision. Doing so also helped me ignore the blood leaking from the lacerated skin. My heart skipped as I felt the corkscrew take purchase and begin burrowing into the bone. Though my breathing accelerated and my heart pounded heavily against my chest, I did not allow my excitement to affect my focus. I kept pushing on the corkscrew with the same force, but now turned it more carefully, waiting for any sense that the skull had been penetrated. Soon there was a feeling of less resistance. I suspected I might be through the bone.

"I think I'm there," I said hesitantly.

"Okay," Maxine said, "just unscrew it gently. We'll see if there's a discharge."

I did as she ordered. I was horrified to see a little fountain of blood squirt from the side of the child's head. "Oh, no," I gasped.

"No, that's good," Maxine laughed. "See, it's already stopped. Phew, I think we've done it." She pressed a wad of cotton gauze against the hole. "Mamma," she called, "please bring the boiling water now. We must clean her."

"Hauw, is it over?" the mother asked in disbelief.

"It is over," said Dumani. He relaxed his hold on the girl and straightened up. "Do as the doctor says and bring some water."

CHAPTER FIVE

The Myth of
The Last Shaman

I was dying to share my spectacular achievement with someone. Only, out in the Swamps there was no one capable of appreciating the feat. When I explained the successful procedure to Chollo and David, they made a show of being impressed and even enrolled a few bystanders into being suitably amazed, but I knew they were putting on an act for the sake of politeness. The truth was that they expected nothing less of the son of Vale, a white man working in league with a medical doctor.

Maxine was attending to a long queue of villagers wanting the kudos of having been treated by a Western physician. Considering there was not much she could have done for anyone with any serious ailment, it was fortunate that, mostly, they just wanted to harangue her with their medical war stories. David had been called to help keep order in the line. Without anyone for me to bounce off of, it didn't take long for the elation I had felt after the operation to evaporate. While in one sense I was glad that we had secured our entry into the swamps, I was overwhelmed by the thought of what it would take to fulfill our mission, given what we had gone through in just the first couple of hours into it. Having just witnessed a mother and father's anguish over their imperiled child, I was starkly reminded of the jeopardy my own family in the Irrigation Scheme was facing. I wondered if there was any chance for them or me.

I took a seat in the fishing boat with Chollo and watched the goings-on along the shore. Pairs of men wearing nothing but bejugas pushed their mokoros into the water and, standing upright like gondoliers, poled their dugouts through the shallows, setting out on their foraging expeditions in the Delta. Young women waded waist-deep on the other side of a reed bed, dragging a fine-meshed fishing net. They slapped the lake surface with sticks to scare away crocodiles, while they laughed and chattered incessantly to keep up their nerve.

"Here he is," I heard Dumani's voice booming jovially behind me, "the big brain surgeon." When I turned to look his way he clapped his hands together in delight, crying out, "Wasn't that something! You are a wizard with a corkscrew."

I gave him a weak smile, not sure that he wasn't making fun of me.

"Interesting what perils some people must face every day to feed themselves and defend their territory from man and beast," he said, nodding at the people out in the lake. "Here in front, the return isn't very good. Just little minnows." He held out his forefingers, two inches apart.

By now he was standing very close to me. I could see his cunning thought process glinting in his magnified eyes. "You and I should go out fishing," he said as if the idea had occurred to him spontaneously.

"Sure," I said, "when would you like to go?"

"Right now," he nodded. "No time like the present. We can make a contribution to tonight's feast."

His insistence that we go alone, without Chollo, made me nervous. I pictured myself floating facedown among the reeds while Dumani sped through the Delta channels in my boat at full throttle. As it was, though, sooner or later I was going to have to broach the subject of our intentions for being in the Meluti. Dumani seemed like the most appropriate person to have that conversation with. The private excursion he proposed seemed like the perfect opportunity.

I navigated the boat slowly away from the village so that our wake didn't rock the men in their precarious dugouts. Once we were out in deep waters, I pushed the boat as fast as it would go toward the eastern side of the lake as Dumani had directed me. Not a word was spoken between us the whole way. The ride was a welcome diversion from the many dilemmas tormenting me. All I wanted to do was lap up the spectacular world around me, without missing a single drop.

Mauve mountains at the far end of the lake lay like petrified dragons in a distant world of their own. Ten-thousand-strong flocks of flamingos floated across the mirror-flat, icy blue waters like pink cloud shadows. Formations of spur-wing and Egyptian geese sailed calmly over us, as squadrons of whistler ducks darted and weaved around them. An emerald band of papyrus choked the shallows of the islands' shorelines, while the banks behind were covered in dry, bronze winter grass. Perched in the high gray branches of dead trees, the distinctive forms of fish eagles looked imperiously down on their kingdoms. We passed herds of buffalo, in their thousands, stampeding down to water like flows of black lava. Huge pods of hippo lay half submerged, attended by oxpeckers and tickbirds picking parasites from their heads. Fawn-colored Lechwe, a specially adapted swamp antelope, lunged through the reeds, either in play or to dart away from predators hidden from our eyes. It was the most breathtaking scene I had ever witnessed.

After we had travelled several miles, Dumani waved his left hand urgently, indicating for me to head to shore. He guided me into a channel that narrowed to a tight canal just a little wider than the boat. I slowed the craft down to a crawl as we passed under low, overhanging mangrove branches. Finch-sized kingfishers with rust-colored bodies and turquoise rumps flitted through the dappled light from bough to bough, leading us deeper into the waterway.

Just as I was beginning to get a bad feeling about my

guide's choice of fishing location, we broke out of the claustrophobic vegetation into a wide, placid stretch of water. There wasn't much reed or papyrus along the banks, a sign that the water here was very deep. Beyond the tall palm trees lining the banks, the vegetation thinned into sparse parkland carpeted by well-grazed grass. Inland, we could see herds of grazing zebra and antelope.

Dumani motioned for me to cut the engine. "This is a good place," he said.

As the boat drifted idly downstream in the sluggish current, I began preparing the fishing rods. I first rigged up a rod for Dumani. Knowing that tiger fish were cannibals, I selected a lure resembling a tiger fish fingerling and attached it to a short steel trace, essential for preventing the freshwater game fish from biting through the nylon fishing line with their ferocious fang-like teeth.

Dumani didn't have a clue about fishing. Even after I spent some time patiently teaching him the art of casting and retrieving a lure, he still managed to make a meal of things, casting backward, getting his line in a tangle or slapping the water in front of him with his unreleased lure. Though I was annoyed that his bumbling would scare off the famously shy African fighting fish, Dumani himself appeared to be thoroughly enjoying himself.

"So, who are you?" I said, trying to sound casual. "I mean, how do you fit in...in Mlumu?"

I was intensely conscious of the paradise we were floating through. I took in the single red feather planted in Dumani's frizzy hair, which was from the wing of a purple-crested Lourie bird – appreciating what an eloquent statement it made about his inherent belonging to this part of the world.

"Ha ha ha," he laughed heartily, shaking his head in the negative. "No, no, no," he waved an admonishing finger at me, "that is not the question. The question is: who are you?"

"Mark Vale..." I began to answer.

"No, go away, man," he said in Lapedi, and then resumed in English. "It's not my question; it's your own question.

Who are you? That is what you want to find out. That is what you are doing here."

"Actually," I said, somewhat confounded and affronted, "we're looking for a shaman. It's said that he is the last one of his kind. You might be aware that civil war is raging across the Republic. Some people think that he can do something, not just about the war, but about the mess this country is in."

Dumani's hearty laughter peeled out across the water, confirming my regret that my petulant rejoinder might have sounded a little absurd. "The last shaman?" he cried mirthfully. "The last shaman? Oh, dear." He wiped the tears from his eyes and shook his head in disbelief. "No offense, but you settlers are pretty dumb."

"How's that?" I murmured, feeling very dumb.

"The last shaman is a Lapedi myth!" Dumani exclaimed. "It's an old legend about how the people's magical connection to the Soul of the World is always dying; how each person is the last chance to save that connection and bring it back to life. It's saying that unless each one of us takes responsibility for our spiritual heritage, it will die."

"Are you saying that the person we're looking for doesn't exist?" I said, feeling my heart sink.

"You know, your culture is the first in history that needs to comprehend everything in literal terms," said Dumani as he fumbled with a tangled bunch of line. "That is why you come out here looking for a ready-made hero. All other cultures have always understood everything metaphorically. We see the literal not as an absolute, just as a possibility."

"I don't understand," I said.

"Well," Dumani said, "it's like your Jesus Christ – we Lapedi totally accept that he walked on water, maybe literally, maybe as an analogy of his unlimited potential. Neither interpretation exists exclusive of the other." He focused on reeling in the untangled line and then cocked the rod over his shoulder. "So the last shaman is a myth, but there is equally a chance that the savior you're looking for exists. My bet is that you won't find him until you look inside yourself!"

"How could *I* ever be a symbol to the people?" I frowned.

"I'm just a white man."

"Ha-ha! Did you see that?" Dumani cried after a half-reasonable cast. Only when I had acknowledged his effort did he go on. "No one who becomes an expression of greatness ever sets out to be that. You don't have to do anything more than face your own demons and take care of your personal purpose."

"Demons and purpose?" my brow furrowed again.

"What brought you out here," Dumani said, "is your eternal dilemma that you have no wisdom, that you don't know anything for yourself – that, and the safety of your family. These are your demons. When a man takes care of his own demons, he takes care of the demons of the world. When he starts with the demons of the world, he accomplishes nothing other than feeding his own demons."

I had just made my first cast. As I listened to Dumani, my hand automatically stopped grinding my reel. My lure sank to the bottom of the deep channel. "How do you know what my demons are?" I asked, dumbfounded.

"Ha ha ha," he cackled. "Out here in the Meluti we know everything." He sang out the word "everything." His eyes twinkled with merriment.

"What's your secret?"

"We don't identify with what our senses tell us. We identify with our connection to everything through all time and space." Dumani gave his rod a sharp flick of the wrist and his lure went flying upstream to splash a very respectable distance away. "By Jove," he laughed, parodying a posh English accent, "I think I'm getting the hang of this."

"Is it something I can learn?" I asked hopefully.

"Sure, on day one." His hand worked his reel at exactly the right speed. "In a few days, you'll be flying."

"Seriously?"

"I'm very serious," he said. "I don't joke about these things. Never." He peered at me over his glasses. "Were you always so fluent in Lapedi?"

"Fluent?" It hadn't even occurred to me that since I had arrived in the Meluti I had been doing a remarkable job of understanding and speaking the local language.

"You see, before, you could hardly catch one word in a sentence; now already you talk like a native again. Out here in the Meluti, there's nothing holding you back. Don't look so startled; you'll soon get used to it." Dumani watched his lure intently as it fishtailed up to the side of the boat. After he had lifted it out of the water and reeled it to within a foot of the tip of his rod, he spoke again. "You are sick, isn't it?"

"I had a tooth infection, but I'm fine now," I shrugged dismissively.

"Yah, but lucky for you, who you are back where you came from is still very sick. Sickness can take the mind where minds don't like to go."

We sat in silence as I tried to fathom the meaning of his cryptic statements. After a while he spoke quietly out of the corner of his mouth: "Can you see an animal behind me, in between the trees?"

"The baboon?" I said. "I've been watching him follow us since we came into the channel. He seems interested in us. Typical baboon curiosity, eh?"

"If that is a baboon, where are the other baboons?" Dumani kept his voice down.

"Nearby, most probably," I found myself whispering.

"If there were other baboons, we would see them or hear them. That is not a baboon."

"What is it?"

"A spy."

"What spy?" Though his assertion was ridiculous, I couldn't help but feel a twinge of eerie trepidation.

"There are many spies out here," said Dumani. "Government spies, Rebel spies, outlaw spies, spirit spies, spies for other villages or medicine men. Point your fishing rod at him and see what happens."

I aimed my fishing rod at the baboon. It took no notice of me. Sitting back on its haunches, it held something up to the light before popping the thing in its mouth.

"Now get a gun out and point it," said Dumani.

I opened one of the holds and pulled out the rifle. When

I looked about for the baboon it was still sitting back on its haunches, scratching its belly and cocking an ear at the different sounds of the bush. I raised the rifle to my shoulder and looked down the barrel. In my sights there was no longer a baboon sitting there but a tribesman crouched on one knee aiming an AK-47 rifle right back at me. I froze in shock. I had not thought to load my gun and now I was in a Mexican standoff holding an empty weapon.

"Ah," cried Dumani, "it's only Sibongila. He's a scout from Mlumu. He likes to get about as a baboon."

As I lowered my gun, the man in the bush did the same. "I see you, Dumani," he waved, getting to his feet.

"Yes, Sibongila," Dumani called out, "what are the signs?"

"Nothing special," the man shouted back, "but after tonight when the boys leave the village, it will be a different story."

The scout waved farewell before turning and walking away. I stood staring dumbly after him.

"You look like you have seen a ghost," Dumani laughed.

It seemed to take an eternity before I could respond. "If I'd seen a ghost, I think I'd be okay," I said, "but I've just seen a baboon turn into a man."

"This is only the beginning," Dumani said. "You will see and do many strange things in the days to come – far stranger than shape-changing. Just don't try to square things with your preconceived notions of reality. If you accept everything as a metaphor, and as literal at the same time, you'll do just fine."

"Are you saying I can learn to change shape like that scout?" My mind reeled in astonishment while my heart did cartwheels.

"Sure you can," said Dumani, laying on his most encouraging tone. "If I tell you where to land your next cast and you catch a fish, will you accept that as proof?"

"Okay," I said. My belly fluttered anxiously as I prepared to cast. The last thing I wanted was proof that I couldn't do what Dumani said I could.

"If you can land your lure right next to that dead tree lying in the water, that's where a big tiger fish is prowling," he said. "If you drop in just beside the outer branches, he can't resist."

Once Dumani had identified my target for me, my nervousness eased. My confidence in my own natural ability was riding high since the successful operation on Veeti's daughter. I had no problem applying the "trick of the mind" to an activity I was quite competent at. I mentally allowed that our lures hadn't had so much as a bump in all the time we had been fishing. Then, I visualized my lure splashing a foot away from the snag. Still in my imagination, I saw a massive swirl in the water right where I had cast, as a prize tiger fish lunged at the lure. With my vision in mind, I took action. Holding my rod in one hand, I tilted it back over my shoulder and snapped it forward with a sharp flick of the wrist.

The length was good, but the second I released the lure I knew I'd given my rod a nervous jerk to the right. "No, no, no!" I squirmed as my line arched straight toward the branches sticking out of the water. Sure enough, the line wrapped around an outer branch, leaving the lure swaying back and forth a few inches above the water. I let out a groan of despair. Hoping against hope, I reeled in the slack and pulled on the line to test if the branch, which was about as thick as the butt of my rod, might break. All that happened was the line tightened around the branch, lifting the lure a few more inches above the water.

Dumani's clucking and shaking his head disparagingly didn't ease my disappointment. I pulled the line again as hard as I felt I could without breaking it. The branch bent toward me and then swayed back again, sending the lure swinging in a glittering arc. My shoulders slumped in defeat. Then, suddenly, there was a great splash and flash of orange as a whopping great tiger fish rose out of the water to sink its teeth into the dangling lure.

"Hauw! Hauw! Hauw!" Dumani shouted.

The fish thrashed about in a blur of orange, trying to

shake the treble hook out of its mouth. The tension on the line wasn't going to let that happen. My fear was that the line would break – it was a monster of a fish. To my great surprise – and delight – the branch snapped and the fish charged out into the channel, stripping line from my reel at an incredible speed as it tail-walked across the water.

Pound for pound, tiger fish are the strongest freshwater fish in the world, and they put every ounce of energy into their initial run. My reel was nearly out of line by the time the fish ran out of steam. After that, I was able to reel it in without too much opposition. But when I brought it close to the boat, the sight of its opponent gave the flashing monster the will to dive down into the deep water in a succession of ferocious tugs. I held on to my rod with grim determination, not confident that I could prevent it being jerked out of my hands. Just when I thought the line could not bear the strain any longer, the fish tired again and I was able to bring it back to the surface with only the occasional, and short-lived, spurt of resistance.

"Praise the ancestors!" Dumani marveled as I brought the brute alongside. He leaned out and, grabbing the fish by the tail, reefed it on board. It was a magnificent specimen, weighing in at easily ten pounds, with vibrant orange and black stripes on the back, a silver belly and a grizzly tangle of crooked teeth sticking out of its mouth.

"Well, that's proof, isn't it?" said Dumani amiably. "We can start your training tonight."

My heart was beating furiously, coursing adrenalin through every inch of my body. The glorious setting, the primal activity, evidence of supernatural phenomenon, Dumani's proof – it all made me jump out of my skin with excitement. Yet in the back of my mind there was still a cautionary voice telling me that I had already done some training in magic before and it hadn't all been beer and skittles, to say the least.

"Best we keep things between us," Dumani said as though stating the obvious. "Secret business, eh?"

"Sure," I said vacantly. "Why?"

"Because one of your number is a traitor," he said.

"Traitor?" I cried out in alarm. "Who?"

"That's not how it works," said Dumani. "My job is to teach you about you. When you know you, you can work out the rest. Otherwise, I take your power away, not so? But I'll tell you this," he paused, as he often did, for dramatic effect, "your traitor is the one that does not belong."

Martin's misgivings about David came back to me, but I dismissed the thought along with Dumani's riddle. Neither was appealing to my pumped-up state of mind. As long as the fish were biting, I could forget about the rest of the world.

***

By the time we got back to Mlumu Village it was sunset. In the washed-out light, the distant mountains took on a surreal appearance, looking more than ever to be in a mystical faraway world of their own. The green, bronze, and gray layers of the Meluti waterfront burned with an incandescent glow. As the sun began to sink, the sky became a luminous orange backdrop to marmalade rind–like clouds hanging above the western horizon.

On our return, we saw even more birds than we had going out in the morning. Great flocks of egrets and ibis flew above us, making their way back to their roosts beyond the Stanley Gorge. Bloated fish eagles flapped laboriously from one hunting perch to another, letting off piercing cries, as if to lament the effort they were forced to make. Seemingly held aloft by something other than the law of physics, wild geese glided impossible distances over the water. Endless formations of duck harried us as they raced up and down the foreshore searching for suitable bays to cozy up in overnight. When I suggested to Dumani that I could also make a contribution to the evening's feast with my shotgun, he shook his head good-naturedly and called out over the drone of the boat engine, "In the Meluti we only use guns for self-defense, not to make an unfair advantage over the animals. That would mean the end of our world."

When we beached our craft, it was evident that late

afternoon was the social time of day for the villagers. Men disembarked from their mokoros carrying trophies of cane rat, wild fowl, and strings of fish joined together by reeds threaded through their gills. Children, wearing nothing other than a string of beads around their necks, splashed about in the shallows, actively ignoring the old folks' warnings about the dangers of crocodiles at dusk. Nubile girls promenaded along the beach hand in hand, doing their best to attract attention by laughing loudly at each other's jokes. A pack of mangy dogs yapped at the heels of some boys running after a battered soccer ball. The thin blue-gray smoke of fish-smoking fires hung over the glossy red water of the outer lake, and the air was filled with the exuberant sounds of people celebrating the end of another day in paradise.

Maxine was sitting on an overturned mokoro with David and Chollo on either side of her. She seemed to be in good spirits, smiling at the cheerful activity around her and waving enthusiastically to Dumani and me as we motored in. I had been worried that Maxine might be put out by my leaving her stranded with the village hypochondriacs while I spent the day fishing, but on the contrary, she turned out to be as impressed with our catch and happy for me as everyone else was.

"Eh, eh, eh," Chollo's eyes opened wide in amazement. "Hey, everyone," he called out, "come and see what my boss has brought back. He is a hunter of the highest order."

Though David made a show of cheering our catch, there was now, to my mind, something disingenuous about his manner. His eyes flicked continually to Maxine and Chollo, as if he were looking to them for cues on how to respond. He sidled self-consciously up to the boat, hoisted a couple of big perch by the gills and smiled at me ingratiatingly. "Very big," he said without much conviction.

"What do you think?" Dumani addressed Maxine proudly. "Not bad, eh!" Gesticulating to Chollo and David, he snapped: "You two, see that the fish are divided among the people equally."

The villagers crowded eagerly around the boat for their share. Judging by their excitement, it was not every day that they encountered such an abundant catch.

Once the last fish had been handed out, and the boat pulled onto the beach, we carried our things up to an empty hut near Veeti's compound that had been designated for the four of us to sleep in. It was a dark, dank earthen-floored space, void of any furnishings or decorations, that didn't inspire one to spend any time there, other than to sleep. After we had stashed everything away and laid out our sleeping bags on the reed mats provided for us, I happily accepted Maxine's invitation to go for a walk along the beach in the last of the evening light. As we set off down one of the avenues leading back to the lake, Maxine skipped beside me with girlish exuberance, holding on to my arm with both of her hands.

"What an incredible day, huh?" she sang breathlessly. I was happy to see a beatific smile brightening her face.

"Very successful," I agreed, reflecting on the auspicious start to our mission. "How's the girl doing?"

"Oh, she's doing fine," Maxine gushed. "Her name is Yapile. She's such a little trooper. I didn't want to worry you unnecessarily, but the chances of her dying or being left permanently brain-damaged were very high. But she's already talking coherently. She'll be running around in no time. It's rare to see someone bounce back from an extradural hemorrhage so quickly. Let's keep our fingers crossed."

"What's wrong with Veeti?" I said. "He doesn't seem right."

"Well, he'd be exhausted from his all-night vigil. But you're right, there's something else. If you ask me, he's clinically depressed."

"Depression?" I exclaimed. "How can anyone be depressed out here?"

"Well, it might be physiological rather than environmental."

"Strange," I said, "but not the strangest thing I've seen out here. Would you believe me if I told you that I saw a baboon turn into a man while we were fishing?"

"What do you mean?" Maxine laughed. "How can a baboon turn into a man? Your eyes must have been playing tricks on you."

"No, I'm telling you, it was a regular baboon following us down the river. Then, when I pointed my gun at it, it suddenly changed into one of the village scouts with a submachine gun – right in front of my eyes. One minute it's a baboon; next it's a man. Have you ever heard of anything like that?"

"Not among the Lapedi. I've never heard of them being associated with shape-shifting. Are you sure you guys weren't smoking funny stuff out there?" Maxine's fingers dug into my arm playfully.

"You don't believe me, do you?" I said. "What are you so happy about, anyway? Why do I feel like you have something to tell me?"

Maxine stopped and waited for me to turn around and look at her. She glanced about conspiratorially. "I think we've found the last shaman," she whispered breathlessly.

"What?" I shook my head in astonishment. "Who? Where?"

"Your fishing buddy, Dumani," she said, squeezing my arm to signal that we should keep moving. "It took me a while to figure out, but finally it clicked."

"Figure what out?"

"If it hadn't been for Dumani, I might not have diagnosed the girl's hematoma. He knew exactly where the problem was. When I was examining the girl, he asked me enough leading questions that I suspect he could have performed the operation himself."

"How does that make him *the* last shaman?"

"It all fell into place with something David reminded me of. President Selele had a younger brother, Cedric, whom he sent off to study medicine in England. The brother came back a doctor, but not of medicine – he had a PhD in philosophy. Selele was so furious at his brother's deceit that he ordered him killed. Cedric managed to escape, though, and he's never been heard of since. It's so obvious when you think about it. Where is someone who doesn't want to be found going to hide? Out here, of course."

Though I was intrigued by Maxine's theory, I was far from convinced. Hearing David's name associated with the hypothesis made it even more suspect, considering the uneasy feeling I was beginning to have about him. "But Max," I said, "just because Dumani has some medical knowledge, it doesn't make him *the* last shaman. How does it even prove that he's Selele's brother?"

"Add it up, Mark," said Maxine. "You think a guy as erudite and sophisticated as Dumani just fell out of the sky? It's him."

"Look, Max," I said hesitantly, not wanting to disillusion her, "I know some things that you don't. I've had this conversation with Dumani himself. He told me not to repeat it, so don't let on that you heard anything from me. There is no actual last shaman – it's a tribal myth."

I went on to tell her everything Dumani had told me about the myth of the last shaman. "This might not be about us finding a savior for the Republic," I said in conclusion, "this might be about our own personal empowerment."

"Are you kidding?" Maxine retorted. "The very fact that he's volunteered to give you some shaman training means that he's a shaman, doesn't it? And not just any shaman, mind you. He might be one of the most exceptional mystics that ever walked the earth. Think about it: a man born into a voodoo culture with a fascination and talent for native magic, who amplifies his knowledge by studying everything from comparative religion to the origins of Occidental Alchemy and quantum physics.

"You and I might learn some snippets from him, but how could we ever compare with him? How could we ever match his life experience or learning? How could anyone? There is no one like him. I don't care if he denies it; he is the last shaman. No one is better qualified as a cultural icon than him in the cause against his brother's tyranny."

"Think about it logically, though," I said, raising my

final objection. "Just statistically, what are the chances that we would find the last shaman the minute we arrive in the Meluti? If this guy is in hiding, why would he let us find him so easily?"

"Synchronicity!" Maxine chimed blithely. "It's the law of attraction." Her tone turned a touch sanctimonious. "You, of all people, shouldn't be surprised that we've bumped into him so quickly. The minute we made our intention to find him, forces beyond our understanding began arranging for our paths to cross. And who says he's letting us find him? Taking you out fishing on your own was a preemptive strike. He's obviously trying to shake us off the scent."

"Okay," I said, moved by the force of Maxine's argument, "but even if we get him to admit or accept that he is the last shaman, how are we going to convince him to go into exile with us?"

"There you go again." Maxine nudged me playfully in the ribs. "You're a disgrace to magic, asking how! But don't worry, we don't have to do anything. They'll be coming for him any moment now. Unless he wants to die, he'll have no choice but to come with us."

The light faded quickly once the sun had set. It was now almost completely dark. The beach was practically deserted save a few stragglers finishing some final preparations for the feast. Giant fruit bats flapped stealthily over us in the twilight. The muffled sound of thunder rolled across the water and lightning flashed dimly in the southeastern sky.

I wondered how Maxine could so quickly get over her fiancé's assassination the day before, to the point where she could laugh and smile about the outcomes of our day and look forward with relish to getting mixed up in the trouble she anticipated was coming our way. To be fair to her, though, I had to concede that I myself hadn't given matters outside the Meluti much thought, either. We were in another world, so close and yet so far from the one we had come from.

It dawned on me that the rumbles and flashes were not thunder and lightning after all; an artillery duel was raging on the Lesoti plateau. As far as I was concerned, it was a good sign that the war was still in full swing. It meant my family most probably had not yet fallen prey to the Rebel onslaught. But in that moment, thoughts of my family's safety didn't distress me as much as the frustration I felt at being convinced only by what others convinced me of.

CHAPTER SIX

Stranger in a Strange World

From the journal of Martin Vale, July 31

No time to write tonight. Sounds like Armageddon out there. I don't know if it's my imagination, but the fighting sounds louder and closer every minute. We have to do something to get the women and children to safety. I can't bear to think what their fate will be once the Rebels break through. As for Mark, poor bugger, got a bad feeling. Not happy to think his life is in the hands of a fruitcake like Maxine Carlyle.

***

A big, round, yellow moon hung low in the sky, casting a shimmering silver-gold path across Lake Stanley. A circle of massive bonfires lit up the foreshore like a stadium under lights. An orchestra of talking drums marshaled the village for the feast. The villagers filed into the fire-lit circle dancing and ululating, the men wearing ceremonial skins and the women dressed in their finest Java-print sarongs and beads. It was a spectacle to stir the hardest heart. Veeti sat dismally unmoved on a wooden stool at the center of a warriors-only section, waiting for the crowd to settle. On the other side of the circle I could see Maxine waving to me from where she sat with the headman's wives.

Veeti leaned over and spoke in Dumani's ear. Dumani in turn leaned toward me and, after a pensive pause, said, "The headman asks me to thank you again for answering his call. He is very much obliged."

"It's my honor," I spoke directly to Veeti in Lapedi, touching my hands to my elbow and head in the native salute of respect. To Dumani I muttered, "Why does he think we answered some call? You know that we are here on business of our own."

"Last night was supposed to be didakta," Dumani explained, "the night we see off the boys coming of age. But the sangoma of the village told Veeti that his daughter was in great peril and there was nothing she could do for the girl. That is when he suspended didakta to take the sacred medicine and follow guidance from the ancestors. In his vision he saw a doctor brought here by the son of Vale, whom the ancestors had contacted to help him with his daughter.

"You see, we live in our own worlds. In Veeti's world, you are an instrument of his destiny come to save his daughter. In your world, his daughter is an instrument of your destiny, helping you have a reason to be useful to Veeti. That is how the gods weave the game of life. From their perspective, everything is connected."

"I think I get it," I said. "And what exactly is didakta?"

"Didakta?" Dumani cackled, happy for the opportunity to be an authority on the subject. "It's what we talked about before. Didakta is the final rite in the whole initiation of the last shaman. The young men are painted white to wash away their childhood personalities and they are crowned with bark pillbox hats that symbolize their super-conscious mental capacity. Then we send them into the bush for twenty days to survive on nothing but their wits. They may take nothing with them. No one can help them in these three weeks, and if they are caught by any of the villagers they are beaten within an inch of their life."

"Wow," I grimaced judgmentally, "that sounds harsh."

"In the old days, when didakta was still the custom in the Republic, the missionaries made a lot of noise about how barbaric it was," said Dumani contemplatively, "but to us, it is barbaric not to bring up your children to know who they really are and how to conduct their true natures in the world. Didakta is a spiritual analogy that teaches the boys that for their spirit to survive, they have to be fierce." He snatched at the air with his hand. "You have to take it like this. No one will give it to you."

Dumani stopped for a moment to acknowledge the warriors around us listening with fascination to our unintelligible conversation. Turning back to me, he said, "Don't think it's only one way – the elders beating on the youths. The initiates are at war with the village also, like hyenas living in the shadows, waiting to grab what they can. Everyone has to look sharp at the time of didakta."

The crowd was almost settled. Only a few men and women picked their way through the crowd to sit next to friends or relatives. Some old crones worked the inner fringe of the circle, dancing suggestively while blowing on tin whistles and pumping fighting sticks up and down in the air. Their buffoonery was rewarded with loud staccato whistles, the Lapedi equivalent of the wolf whistle. I began to feel a wary sense of anticipation. No one had shared with me the program for the night's events, nor had Dumani let on what form my first teaching with him would take.

As the drumming subsided to a hushed rhythm being played on a single *djembe*, a deep growl started up from inside the village. The drumming stopped altogether. The old crones hurried back to their seats. The noise grew louder. It sounded like a chainsaw biting into wood. A male leopard was making its way through the village down to the foreshore.

Despite my being surrounded by a company of warriors, the ferocious growls gave me a hollow feeling in my stomach. A chorus of good-natured laughter erupted around me. It took me a moment to realize that the natives were laughing at the look of apprehension on my face.

Every villager's head followed the sound of the leopard as it circled the gathering, their eyes now also widening with anticipation. As it stalked around behind where I was sitting, I had the feeling that it was seeking out someone in particular, and that it had taken note of my presence, as if it knew from the smell of my fear that I was the vulnerable member of the group.

After it had passed me, the leopard went quiet. A deadly silence fell over the gathering. All ears listened intently for any sign of the beast's location. Suddenly a roar erupted not far from where Maxine sat. A path opened up in the circle as startled women scrambled to get out of the way. The leopard tore into the ring, spitting and screeching like a banshee. It ran around in a blur, lunging and clawing wildly at the front row of villagers. I was afraid to watch what damage the giant cat would inflict, and even more afraid of what would happen if it came for me. No one seemed to be doing anything to prevent it from running amok.

Far from being afraid of the leopard, the villagers took great delight in its antics. Those who had been the target of its feints and swipes laughed and jeered at the leopard as it moved on from them, while the crowd whistled and cheered their appreciation. The creature was not far away from me when it stood up on its back legs and teetered around to face in my direction. My eyes blinked at its fearsome howl, and when they opened again there was no leopard before me, but rather a shriveled old woman dressed in leopard skins. I was utterly amazed. No human could have made those noises, and although the woman wore a leopard-skin skirt and leopard-skin cape, complete with a leopard's face on top of her head, I was absolutely certain it had been a real big-cat thrashing about in the ring.

The old crone let out a blood-curdling screech and pointed a withered finger at me. Her eyes burned with fierce animosity. Something told me that this was the local witch doctor and that we had made her lose face by healing Veeti's daughter with white man's medicine. She was here to get back at me.

Still crying out, she raised a trembling hand to the heavens. Her eyes rolled back in her head. Her body shook so violently that the clusters of shells tied around her wrists and ankles sounded like a set of rapids in the Muchocho. I swallowed nervously, thinking I would rather have faced a real leopard than this witch's wrath. Finally she looked back at me and began yelling in a dialect I did not understand. When she was done ranting, she waved her finger from Dumani to me, signaling him to interpret her words.

"The *ndotsikatsi* – the lady sorcerer – says that there was a lord of the realm who died. He had three sons. The eldest one took over his father's lands, the middle son took his seat on the high council and the youngest one became a fish eagle." I was surprised to hear Dumani using such a deferential tone.

"Thank you, mother, for the blessing of your words," I stammered.

"Go away, young man," the witch waved dismissively, using common Lapedi. "It is a curse, not a blessing." I definitely got the feeling that she didn't like me.

She turned away and began haranguing the group in the Meluti dialect. Dumani nudged me in the ribs. "This is a good time to go and smoke the medicine," he whispered. "Soon they will begin feasting. It's not good to take the medicine on a full stomach."

I wanted to ask Dumani what medicine he was talking about. After all, I thought I deserved a say in what he had planned for me, but my tongue was tied by a shameful sense of not belonging. I was very much deflated by the ndotsikatsi's treatment. To think that I was totally at the mercy of the judgments and discretion of people to whom I meant nothing left me crushed. I was a stranger in a very strange world.

With some members of the gathering beginning to get up to help with dishing out the feast, it was easy for us to slip away without appearing rude. We passed by makeshift tabletops fashioned from poles lashed together and covered in banana leaves. Spread out over the leaves was a smorgasbord of smoked fish and flame-roasted meats. Between each table was a heap of more banana leaves for the villagers to use as plates. There was no cutlery. My stomach grumbled at the appetizing aroma of the traditionally prepared food. The sight of whole char-grilled cane rats was particularly torturous.

Even though, thanks to the full moon, it was nearly as bright as day, the main thoroughfares of the village were marked by lines of burning torches. Dumani led me down one of the jungle pathways beyond the village. The forest around us glistened like a silver wonder world. A short way along the path, we came across a small hut built among the trees. It was nothing more than a platform of bamboo poles nailed to some tree trunks about three feet off the ground with a palm-leaf roof and animal hides stretched across three sides. The side facing the path was open.

"Let's sit up in here," said Dumani. "The demons of the jungle like this place. Lots of nature around us."

I followed him onto the platform without saying anything. The enchanted ambience of the moonlit jungle lifted my spirits, filling me with wonder at what magic was about to unfold for me. The realization that I was about to be introduced to the supernatural forces at large in the Meluti gave me goose bumps. I could feel my palms sweaty with a half-dreaded, half-eager expectation.

Dumani surprised me by lighting an oil lamp. I had not expected such a modern convenience in so primitive a setting. In the lamplight I could see that the hide walls had been decorated with intricate etchings of various birds and animals. The most popular motif appeared to be guinea fowls. "Who does these?" I said, thankful for having something mundane to talk about.

"The village women," said Dumani, taking off a woven grass shoulder bag and emptying its contents in front of him. "They paint it with vegetable dye. Not bad, is it?"

"What about that leopard woman?" I said, feeling my tongue loosening. "I thought she was a real leopard there for a while."

"Of course she was," Dumani said archly. "A human

can't make those noises. And didn't you see with your own eyes a leopard there? In the jungle she lives as a leopard, and when she comes to the village she turns back into a person."

"How do they do it?" I said. "That baboon scout and the leopard witch?"

"Before you can know that," he said, "there are other things you must see first." He held up a marijuana head the size of a large banana. "You smoke this stuff?"

"I have," I grimaced. "It just makes me paranoid."

"Not this one," he laughed. "Anyway, this is just a taxi for the magic dust."

"Magic dust?"

"Yes, magic dust," said Dumani, grinding the ganja up in a small bowl with his fingers. "We get it from the bark of the acacia trees where we were fishing today." He began to laugh quietly. "The people here say that the aliens planted them."

"Aliens?"

"Yes, when you smoke the magic dust, they come out of the ethers." Dumani tapped a dull-colored powder from a tiny bottle into the bowl and began mixing it into the crushed-up ganja. "Now, remember what I told you this morning, eh? It is very important that you accept everything you perceive. This medicine is going to push up your whole subconscious reality into your self-conscious awareness. When you deny things self-consciously you don't feel any consequences, but it causes subconscious pain. With the dust you feel everything self-consciously."

I gulped. Remembering Martin's vivid lecture on Meluti Madness, I wondered whether I was up to the psychological rigors Dumani was alluding to.

He began packing the ganja and magic dust mix into a conical clay pipe. Plucking a leaf off a branch that poked into the hut, he rolled it up tightly to make a filter for the chillum. "Here you go," he said, handing me the pipe. I wrapped my hand around the chillum and held it to my lips. Dumani lit a match. As he held it up to the pipe, the flame reflected in his glasses so that he looked like a demon with eyes of fire.

"Suck hard," he urged me. "Suck, suck. Breathe in. Now hold it. That's it. Good man."

I managed a few big draws on the burning pipe before I started coughing hysterically. Dumani took the pipe back from me and took a big drag. As he sucked on the pipe, the smoldering mix lit up so fiercely I expected the pipe to burst into flames. When he finally exhaled, he let two plumes of smoke stream from his nose, and then blew out a massive cloud from his mouth that fogged up the whole hut. "There's still some more for you," he croaked, choking back a cough of his own as the last wisps of spent smoke trailed from his lips.

We smoked another pipe and sat cross-legged, staring at the gleaming silver vegetation across the path. The beauty of the jungle was breathtaking; it looked like a giant underwater garden submerged in an ocean of moonlight.

At first I didn't feel anything more than a mild elation accompanied by a drunk-like lack of inhibition. I asked Dumani a question that I had, up until then, been uncomfortable broaching with him: "Are you Cedric Selele?"

"Yes," he said.

I could think of a few more logical questions that followed his admission, but that one word told me unequivocally that all the things I would usually want to understand counted for nothing in this moment. I had a sense that an outer layer of who I was had been peeled away, and that the being that existed on the layer at which I now rested was governed by a completely different set of reference points.

"You want to know why I'm teaching you, don't you?" Dumani said.

"Yes," I said.

"I don't know why. I just know that I must. It is our way. We know what, then we find out why later. Your way is to know why first. But if you don't start, you usually never know why."

I heard Dumani as loudly and clearly as I had all day. Only, his lips did not move. My own mouth was shut tight. Our conversation was happening entirely telepathically. I had to brace myself to stop from swooning in astonishment.

The lamplight stopped flickering. Everything grew still. No leaves rustled, no fronds swayed, nothing glinted or shined. The lamp flame had crystallized into a luminous pyramid. Dumani sat petrified, not breathing or blinking. Everything was frozen – even time.

I could hear the jingling of a thousand miniature sleigh bells coming from the direction of the village. It sounded like a colony of swamp frogs on the march through the forest. When the exquisite noise had completely surrounded me and was beginning to send me into raptures of delight, it suddenly stopped, at which point a dwarf materialized on the path that made its way by the front of the hut. He was a leathery little man covered in scales. His oversized head was full of lumps, and a serrated ridge ran from above each eye to the back of his skull, giving him a slightly reptilian appearance. I found him at once scary and unthreatening, and even funny in an endearing way.

The little man spoke in a series of grunts and guttural hisses. I tried to say something in Lapedi. No words came out. The dwarf pointed to his throat and grunted. I took his signal to mean that I should grunt the words. I tried to force my words from the back of my throat. Nothing intelligible resulted. But it felt good, so I began making guttural sounds for the pleasure of it. As I did so, the dwarf started grunting again – and this time I could understand him. We were speaking the same language now.

"I am the Tokoloshe of the backwaters behind this village," was what he was saying.

I responded with a few amiable grunts, which, once I had emitted them, I realized meant, "You look like an honorable person."

"It was I who saved your man at the waterfall today. My cousin wanted his bile for a potion he's working on."

"Okay, many thanks. You're a good person."

"Hah! As if good has anything to do with it. When your people clear the forests and drain the swamps, you think that is good. Meanwhile, many lives are lost and spirits left homeless. And then, when we express our nature, you say that we are bad and must be driven away. But when our actions coincide with your self-interest, you say that we are good. Oh ho, then you are full of praise."

"Then why did you save Chollo?"

"Because you are here to save our world from the blindness of your kind."

"I don't think so. But I am looking for someone who can save the Republic, and maybe give me the master key to magic." I was enjoying making outlandish sounds with my throat. It occurred to me that this might be somewhat like the pleasurable sensation cats feel when they are stroked. Any noise I chose to make always managed to express exactly what I had on my mind.

"Your kind have all gone to sleep to why you are here," the Tokoloshe grunted. "You think you are awake, when really you are sleepwalking through life."

"That's all very well for you to say, but I can't see what I can do for your world."

"No, because you see with what your five senses can see now and what your five senses have seen before. We would not be talking now if it were up to them."

"How do I know I'm not dreaming now?"

"Tomorrow you will learn that your fishing rods have been stolen from your boat. If you ask a man called Mumuletu, he will bring them back to you. Now I must be on my way. I have business with some crocodiles over yonder."

The Tokoloshe vanished before my eyes. Right away the swamp frogs started up their enchanted chiming around the hut again. To my disappointment, the sound began to fade as it moved down the path away from the village. Everything else jumped back to life: the candlelight flickered, shadows moved, moonlight shimmered through the trees. Dumani rocked back laughing.

"You missed a Tokoloshe right here," he cackled. "I tried to wake you but you were frozen. My god, man, what a sight. You can spend a lifetime in the Swamps and never see one."

"No, I saw it," I said. "You were the one who was frozen.

I was talking to it."

"Go away, man," said Dumani, unable to stop himself giggling hysterically. "You see that, how he can freeze everything and make you think you are the only one he's talking to. What a specimen he was, and so ugly, too."

Another fit of hysterics convulsed Dumani. I began laughing, too. Not only was the sight of Dumani rolling on the floor in convulsions funny to me, his uninhibited opinion of the Tokoloshe freed my suppressed inclination to laugh at it to its face. Soon I was laughing so hard my sides split.

"Hey, hey." I came around to Dumani shaking me. "Now the sadness is coming." A spasm of pain swept across his face. "Remember," he groaned, "existence is counting on you to accept your pain. Be strong, my friend." He fell back to the floor weeping. "Be strong," he whimpered.

To say that I was astonished would be a massive understatement. Never in my life had I experienced such a sudden and intense change of mood. One second I was laughing with self-assured abandon, and the next I was waiting with dread to be annihilated by every conceivable peril in the universe. A wave of insecurity flowed through me like a rushing tide. Out of the hollow pit of my being crawled the paranoid realization that I might be the traitor Dumani had warned me about. Everyone I could think of belonged to something, whether that was a place or people or even ideals, while I was like a jellyfish at sea with no prospect of finding anything to anchor me. The more I tried to push the thought out of my mind, the more it consumed me.

"Go away, please go away," I groaned. The faces of the leopard woman and Veeti and Chollo and Maxine and my mother and almost everyone I knew loomed in my mind, condemning me for not having a binding association with anything in life. There was no limit to the depth of my shame; it was flogging me to death. The only thing I could do to make my pain half bearable was admit to myself that I could be...no, I *was* the traitor, a lost soul.

Someone began to stroke my arm gently. Each caress

sent a soothing wave through my emotional being. I opened a teary eye to see who it was. There was nobody. I closed my eyes again. Now I could see her, a young nubile Lapedi girl sitting beside me, smiling compassionately. When she spoke, her words and manner filled me with a deep compassion for myself.

"Look at my bare breasts heaving on my chest," the girl said softly, "do they not fill you with desire? Are they not something to behold and appreciate? Do they not waken you to the beauty that stands behind all things? Do not my lips fill you with hunger to be drowned in my body and reunited with the mother of all things? Do you see me dance? Do you see how the drums move my hips, grinding me against the rhythm of life? Do you see my deep passions marrying me to life? Do you see the ecstasy of my unbridled sadness and joy, my pleasure and pain?

"This is my raw nature. This is what defines me as native in your eyes. And you are a colonial boy, supposed to be the opposite of me. The most important aim in your life is to not be like me, to remain civilized. That is why you deny your sexuality, your rhythm and your song. You hide from your impulses and your feelings in case they reveal something native about you. You pretend that you do not know, but really you're afraid to know what you want.

"You can cry now for the banishment you have suffered. Weep for the fraud that you have become. Let yourself mourn for the rejection of yourself and the truth you have evaded, the lies you have lived. It was all done by yourself, though you did not know it."

I listened spellbound to the girl's revelations. By the time she was finished, I felt sickened by a profound sense of violation, as if I had been duped by an extraordinarily treacherous conspiracy. I was physically nauseated. It was all I could do to hang my head over the bamboo platform before I started vomiting. Once I had purged myself physically, my emotional pain was replaced by a sweet relief.

"Man, this is good dust," said Dumani, wiping his mouth with the back of his hand and pulling a sour face. His glasses had come off and his myopic eyes were blurred with tears. "That tree I got this stuff from is a lion, I'm telling you." He stared at his hand with intense curiosity.

For a brief moment I imagined I was completely straight again. I checked in with my brain to see how it was functioning and it seemed to be more lucid than it had ever been. The illusion of sobriety did not last long, though. When I looked out at the jungle, it was writhing and convulsing like the innards of some gigantic beast. I tried to contain the sensory overload by confining my gaze to the inside of the hut. It was still too much. Objects warped in and out of shape. The size of everything became ludicrously distorted. Caterpillars of fur crawled around every edge and outline. Most disconcerting of all, the animals in the hide motifs began leaping across or flying off the walls.

I closed my eyes to escape the insane psychedelic disturbance. Another flush of relief washed over me. Now, waves of euphoria pulsed through me. What followed is almost indescribable, because it didn't happen in any linear sequence, but all in one beginning-less and endless moment. My consciousness opened up to include the universe and then other universes. Galaxies and solar systems floated through my mind. Yet this vision was not being apprehended by my conventional mind alone. Each and every one of the trillions of cells in my body contained the same images and perceived them with the same transcendent awareness. Reams and reams of information pertaining to everything that could possibly be known scrolled out of every cell in the form of symbolic code. Featureless human forms of pure light came out of the ethers to commune with me and then went diving like porpoises between the universes and dimensions to appear in one world as a subatomic particle or in another world as a sage. A sublime energy radiated through this world of worlds – an energy that I understood to be God, the creative force underlying everything that humans could ever possibly conceive of existing. And yet, at the same time as I was in awe of this infinite divinity, I perceived that it was a very minor deity in the total scheme of things.

Although no boundary existed between me and every-thing else through all time and space, there was still, para-doxically, a powerful sense of myself in my consciousness. The day-to-day self-perceptions responsible for keeping my identity intact hovered about impotently, as sentimentally fascinating and irrelevant as a ruined city of antiquity. I had towered into a fabulously charismatic being of infinite creativity and omniscience. There was no arrogance in this experience of me. I jubilantly appreciated myself as a glori-ous speck of cosmic dust.

How long I lay there tripping with my eyes closed I could not tell. It felt at once like a second and a lifetime. I imagined I could hear Dumani having a conversation with one or more other persons. I risked opening my eyes to see who was there. The repulsive contractions and contortions of the environment had settled down. Now my surroundings were delineated into geometric facets, as if contained within an atmospheric diamond. Right before us, on the path, stood four initiates wearing nothing but their white pillbox hats. In the moonlight, their white painted bodies glowed lumi-nescent, giving them the exact appearance of the dimen-sion-hopping light beings I had seen in my magic dust–inspired imagination. They exuded a magnificent aura of power. I had the distinct impression that they stood fully in who they were and what they had to do. They felt to me the freest of all wild creatures, having been completely excused of needing permission to be exactly who they were.

As the youths waved Dumani farewell and started down the path, following in the invisible footsteps of the Tokolos-he, a feeling of disappointment came over me that the effect of the magic dust was beginning to wear off and I would soon lose my exquisite sense of omnipotence. As if in response to my sentiment, Dumani said, "The boys are leaving the village now. The ancestors will begin working on them. Many strange forces will start coming together now. It is best we get back to the village. But it was a good night, no? Wasn't that Tokoloshe something?" He tried to laugh, but he didn't have the energy. He let out an exhausted sigh instead.

"Sir, sir." It was David timidly shaking my feet through my sleeping bag.

"What is it?" I groaned, worried that Maxine's sidekick would only disturb my sleep-in on account of bad news.

"Sir, someone took the things from the boat," he said apologetically.

"What things? Didn't we bring everything with us?"

"But the gas and the fishing rods were locked in the cupboard of the boat. Someone, he break the locks and take the things."

I noted that David's English was beginning to deteriorate since being in the Meluti. He avoided my eyes when I looked at him. Had my conversation with the Tokoloshe not come back to me I would have suspected him of being the guilty party.

"Okay, David," I said. "I want you to find a man named Mumuletu and give him a message from me. Tell him that Master Vale was visited by a Tokoloshe last night, who told him that Mumuletu knows who stole our things and that Mumuletu can save this person from a lot of trouble if he persuades them to give our things back – through Mumuletu, of course."

"Hauw!" David looked up at me, his eyes wide with surprise. "You met a Tokoloshe last night?" He laughed, shaking his head with feigned credulity. After a pause he said, "I think it's better if I can tell him what trouble this person can be in."

"Tell him that the Tokoloshes are looking for the bile of a guilty man to use in a potion they are making."

David's eyes widened again and the color of his skin paled a shade. "I think he will definitely help us," he said. It occurred to me that there was every chance that David was somehow complicit in the theft after all.

Once David had gone, I lay on my back with my head resting on my folded arms, trying to order the thoughts in my groggy brain. Losing our gas would not be the end of the world. With the waterways of the Meluti being progressively reduced into narrow, reed-choked channels, motoring our way through the swamps was not a feasible option. But if we wanted to move stealthily, as well as avoid the ire of the natives for hunting with guns, then our survival depended on us catching fish. For some reason, though, I was confident that the fishing rods were going to turn up.

I was just beginning to turn my thoughts to the phenomenal experience of the night before when a sarong came flying through the door and landed on my face. "Come on, lazy bones," Maxine's chirpy voice cried out. "Bath time."

I pulled the sarong from my face. Maxine was squatting just outside the hut, tousling her damp hair with another sarong. After a series of vigorous rubs, she smoothed her hair back with her hands and regarded me with a fresh-faced smile.

"A bath?" I said, not too keen at the thought of dipping my body in the cold lake.

"It's the most amazing bath I've ever had," Maxine gushed. "Come with me."

I climbed out of my sleeping bag and wrapped the faded cotton sarong around my waist. As I stepped into the glaring light of day, Chollo waved to me from under a nearby tree, where he sat watching our hut with the shotgun resting across his lap. I tramped after Maxine in my unlaced boots, holding my sarong at the hip with one hand and my khakis under the arm with the other. A growing throng of children followed us, calling out to whoever could hear to come and see the funny undressed white man.

When we reached the most westerly pathway into the forest, Maxine shooed the kids away with the promise of some white people's storytelling later in the day. We followed the path for a few hundred yards to a small clearing beside a crystal-clear inlet.

"Tah-dah!" Maxine sang, gesturing theatrically to a pair of porcelain-coated bathtubs raised off the ground by big, flat rocks. A fire was smoldering beneath one of them. "These are the village laundry tubs. If you don't mind using my bath water, you're in for a treat."

"Just what the doctor ordered," I said. "Thanks, Max,

you're a legend." When she sat down on a big washing stone between the two baths, I added, "You planning on sticking around?"

"It's okay, Mark, I *am* a doctor. I have seen it all before," she laughed. "With you always disappearing on your secret men's business, it's the only chance I get to talk to you."

The boiling-hot water scalded my skin as I climbed into the tub, but once I was fully submerged the temperature became blissfully bearable. I lay back with a satisfied groan, savoring the warmth soaking through to my bones. All tension evaporated from my body and mind. I became present to nothing but my surroundings. The liquid calls of a golden oriole resonated through the forest. Bright flashes of crimson in the upper branches accompanied raucous calls of "gwala-gwala," as purple-crested Lourie birds made way for an invasion of monkeys moving into the trees around us. Velvet black butterflies with phosphorescent green markings on wings the size of my hands flapped languidly on strings of dappled purple-and-orange orchid flowers.

"It's not secret men's business," I sighed. "You should join us. Last night we did some amazing psychotropic medicine. I don't think I'll ever be the same again." I had a smug sense of being permanently immunized against emotional vulnerability.

"Don't worry," said Maxine, "I don't feel left out. There's enough action going on around here. You should have seen the dancing last night. It was incredible. I've never seen anything like it in all my life."

Bereft of my usual tact, I said, "Tell me something, Maxine."

"What?" she came back quickly. A crease of anxiety crossed her forehead before she could smooth it away with a smile.

"The whole world has gone to shit. You've lost your whole family, all of your friends, everything. I'm about to lose my African family, and there's a good chance my kids are never going to see me again. And we're out here looking for a shaman. For what, I ask you? There's a whole world of magic unfolding out here. Yesterday I saw a man who can change himself into a baboon, and last night I met a Toko-loshe...and even God! The power and the glory that the *Mona Lisa of Africa* is a testament to – that's for us. Why would you risk your own life in search of fire that you won't use to brighten your own life?"

A look of tender piety sat on Maxine's face. "We're not the first ones to lose everything," she said. "If you had seen the things I have seen: the slaughter by the thousands...by the tens of thousands; government-sanctioned death by starvation and disease and torture; wholesale neglect and abuse – in jails and hospitals and villages. In the end, you realize that life and death itself is meaningless. One person, their whole family or their whole clan – what are they in the scheme of things? This is about keeping humanity itself alive. What good is the human race without humanity?

"It's terrific that Dumani can convince you that men can shape-shift into baboons and whatever, and that you're meeting water demons. I'd expect no less from a great shaman. That's the quality we need to fire the people's imag-ination. But I know my path, Mark. I don't need to learn anything more; I've learned all I need to know. My single purpose in life is to get Dumani safely into exile. That's his value: an educated, erudite man who can galvanize his people back home and inspire active support internationally. That's how it's done nowadays. No matter what you and I pick up from Dumani, neither of us is cut out to be another Dalai Lama."

Maxine sat leaning forward with her forearms on her knees and her hands clasped. The top two buttons of her shirt were undone, exposing a good portion of her right breast. What the Lapedi girl in my magic dust trip had revealed about my sexuality now gave me the resolve to look without inhibition. As I did, the combination punches of Maxine's succulent, creamy physicality and the nostalgia of our lifelong association hit me hard. Maybe there was some guilt in there, too, about bringing up her unenviable life situation.

I found myself saying, "Have I ever told you that I love you, Max?"

"Not since we were about ten," she smiled.

"I wish I hadn't stopped telling you," I said. "I wonder why we didn't end up together. It makes no sense."

"I don't know," said Maxine, "life doesn't make sense sometimes. Two people fall out of a boat into a river. One gets washed up on the bank and the other gets pulled out into the current."

I knew, though. As she had just demonstrated with her persuasive little speech, Maxine had always been possessed of a mind far loftier than my own. The scale of her vision and ambition was not something I could keep up with. She was way ahead of me, far too superior. And yet, in that moment, I wondered whether our being in the Meluti together wasn't a sign that we should be with each other. I found myself thinking that if by some miracle we could spirit Dumani safely into exile, and I was instrumental in this crowning achievement of her life, then finally I might measure up to her.

I felt a sudden impulse to look up at Maxine's face. She squinted to one side without moving her head. Then her eyes glanced the other way. Her body was frozen. The forest was strangely quiet. A little further inland a guinea fowl cackled in distress; its wings beat loudly as it labored to rise above the treetops. The monkeys sat stiffly on their perches, darting their heads about nervously at the sound of their scouts' warning squawks.

Any notion I had that the magic dust might have permanently altered my neurological wiring to exclude the mundane concerns of mortality was quickly dashed. I could definitely feel something – and it was fear. My brain went into overdrive trying to anticipate what was stalking us. I immediately ruled out leopard. They rarely hunt collaboratively and there was more than one of whatever was sneaking up on us. That was obvious because the bird and monkey warnings were coming from every direction.

It was either lions or humans – though if there were

lions in the area we would have heard them roaring through the night. I shuddered to think that we might be the first victims of a didakta assault. But what could the young initiates take from us other than my boots?

The expression on Maxine's face implored me for help. I lifted a hand carefully out of the water, motioning her to stay still. Any sudden movement by us would be taken by our assailants as a signal to charge if they were beast, or open fire if they were human. A bushbuck snorted in alarm from behind a nearby thicket. Maxine and I had both stopped breathing. We could hear twigs cracking in the undergrowth. I was cursing myself for not bringing my rifle along.

Suddenly Maxine let out a squeal. I jerked up in fright as something crashed through the treetops alongside us by the creek. A monkey screeched pitifully in shock. There was an awkward flapping in the trees above us. The silhouette of a giant eagle lumbered through the canopy with its limp, long-tailed load.

"Oh my god," Maxine gasped, holding a hand to her chest.

"Isn't that a magnificent sight?" someone called out. It was Dumani, standing on the path with his hands clasped before his chest in reverent appreciation. "It's a real privilege to see a crowned eagle kill. Did you know their staple diet is small antelope? That's why that bushbuck, he was calling like that – tshwe, tshwe."

"Shit, Dumani," I laughed with relief, "you're starting to sound like a travel agent."

"I like that," said Dumani. "A travel agent, ha, ha. Most apt, because I'm here to continue the tour we started yesterday." Turning to Maxine he said, "The children tell me you have promised them some storytelling."

"That's right," said Maxine.

"Don't occupy them too long," Dumani wagged a finger at her, "otherwise, the women of Mlumu will never let you go."

Maxine got to her feet. "Dr. Selele," she said. "You are Dr. Selele, aren't you?" Dumani said nothing. The joviality drained from his face, leaving a stone-cold mask. "We need to talk, sir."

A knot formed in my stomach. It only released once I saw Dumani's face relax again. "Dr. Carlyle," he said, "I assure you, you are barking up the wrong tree. But if it's talk you want, we have all the time in the world. Why don't you join me for tea this afternoon?"

"Tea?" Maxine raised her eyebrows.

"Yes," said Dumani, "I find it most conducive to a convivial discussion. Don't look so surprised, my good woman. If we can offer you luxurious bathing facilities, why not a good cuppa?" It sounded most incongruous listening to his impeccable English spoken in a thick African accent.

CHAPTER SEVEN

Behind the Veils of Perception

D umani told me in his inscrutable way that he wanted to show me around Mlumu Island. Unsurprisingly, he insisted that I bring my rifle along for the walk. As we were leaving the hut where my companions and I were billeted, David walked up to us proudly brandishing my fishing rods.

"I have them, sir," he said cheerfully, "and I put the gas back in the boat." Though I was pleased with him, he still appeared bashful in my eyes.

"Well done, David," I said. "But you shouldn't leave the gas on the boat. Bring it up here and make sure either you or Chollo are watching our things all the time."

"You don't have to worry about your things," Dumani shook his head disapprovingly. "Nobody in the village will steal anything while you are Veeti's guests. There are spies watching all the time." He grabbed me by the elbow and turned me down the path leading toward the jungle.

"What do you mean?" I protested. "Last night someone broke into the holds on my boat and stole the fishing rods and gas."

"Yes, I know," said Dumani. "A fellow by the name of Mumuletu. He's one of the village's most trusted elders."

"Not so trustworthy now," I said.

"He did what he did under my instructions," said Dumani. "It was a test."

"A test?" I blurted. "What do you mean, a test?"

"Don't feel so insulted," Dumani said sharply. "Life is short; energy is precious. You don't know it yet but the soul's path unfolds for us, while the ego's story happens to us. You have to be able to tell the difference. Is something unfolding or is it happening?

"I knew you were looking for something, but I wasn't sure that I was the one to show you. You know the maxim 'Don't cast pearls before swine'? So I thought if you and I are meant to work together, you would find out who had your things when you took the dust. How did you know it was Mumuletu? Was it that Tokoloshe, did he tell you?"

"Yes, it was the Tokoloshe," I said deep in thought. "But how could you be sure that I would find out? Suppose we are meant to work together and I didn't find out?"

"When you work with magic, you have to be prepared to take chances," said Dumani. "This dust is powerful medicine. It opens you to the oneness of everything. I made my intention and trusted that in your oneness you would respond. All that matters is that you passed the test."

As the path we were on narrowed, he nudged me forward. "You have the gun, you should lead."

"So the dust was just a test?" I said petulantly.

"From my point of view, yes," Dumani replied, prodding me with his fighting stick to keep walking, "but from your point of view, it was a sacred lesson. You saw right through your identity to your true nature. Now you know that you are not separate from anything, that everything exists in your consciousness. Everything you see and touch and smell and remember, everything you love and hate is you. And now you know the truth: you know everything. If you knew that your things were taken and by whom, what can you not know?"

"But the Tokoloshe told me," I said. "Did we just imagine him?"

"It doesn't matter," Dumani said. "Don't waste your energy working out what's real and what isn't. Focus instead on what is true. The only thing we know for sure is that you got your fishing rods back. Now I must teach you quickly. There is not much time to save your family. The war is not going well for our side; it will be over by tomorrow."

"The war? My family?" I said, instantly uplifted by the suggestion that my family could be saved, though my hopefulness was tempered by the thought of what Herculean undertaking it might involve.

"Well, isn't that your ultimate mission in the Meluti?"

"I thought it was to take the last shaman to safety and get back to my children alive." In spite of my effort to maintain consistency, I was aware for the first time that if there was anything I could have wished for, it would have been that my family was spared the gruesome consequences of a Rebel victory – and that I didn't dare wish it for fear that it was too much to hope for.

"How would you know with your thoughts?" Dumani clucked dismissively. "Like when that eagle attacked those monkeys, you thought something was coming on the ground. Your thoughts didn't reach as far as the sky above."

As we talked we kept walking. Eventually, our path led to a waterway that we followed into the Delta. The dense jungle kept us cramped against the water's edge. Every ten paces I was startled by the sound of giant monitor lizards splashing into the water beside us. Each time it happened, I jumped back in readiness to defend myself against a crocodile. It was no consolation to my frayed nerves that I would not even hear a crocodile coming.

Dumani did nothing to settle my jitters by calling out from a good distance behind me, "Be careful along here. Anything can come at you: didakta boys, spies, crocodiles, hippos, lions, wild dogs. Even in winter the big pythons wake up from their sleep very hungry, very aggressive."

I tightened my grip on my rifle and strained my eyes and

ears for the slightest sign of danger. The splashing of the monitor lizards jolted me more than ever.

We had walked more than a mile when a clearing opened up in front of us. It was about a hundred yards long and thirty yards wide. A big herd of hippo lay submerged in the oily pool abutting the opening, their fat aubergine cow-shaped heads poking out of the water. We were halfway across the clearing when a bull elephant stepped out of the forest shadows and began complaining loudly. It waved its trunk at us and flapped its ears irritably. In a millisecond, my mind assessed and ruled out the obvious courses of action available to me. Retreating into the water was not an option; making a run for the other end of the clearing would only invite the elephant to charge; and I certainly didn't have enough gun to drop the beast – only enough to make it angrier.

"Stay still," Dumani whispered so quietly I wasn't sure whether I had imagined him speaking. "This one is crazy."

I swallowed involuntarily. I was shaking so badly I wouldn't have hit a barn door with my rifle. All I could do was stare in horror at the enraged elephant as it picked up dirt with its trunk and blew a dust cloud around itself. It pawed the ground violently with its feet, blaring loudly and thrashing its tusks from side to side. Then the elephant went quiet. It stood dead still with its ears fully stretched out. All its bluster had failed to make us disappear – now it was going to trample us. I could practically see the rage in its eyes. It charged forward at a deathly pace. In a second it covered the clearing. I prepared to die.

To my surprise, the elephant pulled up about five yards short of me. Now, as it fanned me with its colossal ears and trumpeted wildly, I was certain I was going to die. The rogue's murderous intent was clearly visible on its face. It occurred to me that at point-blank range I might be able to drop the mad beast. In as slow and even a motion as possible, I brought the butt of my rifle to my shoulder.

"Wait," called Dumani, "he's only a baby." He walked decisively out at the elephant, waving his hands in the air.

"Go on, you silly fellow, we haven't come to play games."

The big animal tripped over its own back legs in its haste to get away. It staggered back a few more paces and then trumpeted indignantly, while its trunk reached out submissively to Dumani. Now I could swear that a self-conscious affection showed on the elephant's face.

"Ha ha ha," Dumani laughed, "there you see, not so scary now. This one we call Ngomani – the lonely one. For some reason he likes the company of humans more than his own kind. It's like that with all species of animals. There's always one that wants to be friends with us. That's why we have domestic animals, I think."

Dumani looked back at me. He waved his hand irritably. "Point the gun down," he said. "He's afraid."

I wanted to lower the rifle – I could see the fear in the elephant's eyes – but I stood frozen, unable to drop my guard. Dumani had to grab the gun barrel and push it down forcefully. I slung the rifle over my shoulder to foil the overwhelming urge I felt to point it at the elephant's head again. I noticed my hands trembling violently. My breathing was shallow and quick. I blinked a few times to relax my bulging eyes back into their sockets.

"There, you see that?" said Dumani, facing the docile animal again.

"See what?" I said.

"Reality!" Dumani exclaimed, as if the answer were patently obvious. "Reality," he repeated enthusiastically. "This is a big lesson in the nature of reality."

"How so?" I blinked again.

"Aha," Dumani gave a self-satisfied cackle, "you see, when we started walking, I suggested to you the dangers of this walk. 'Walk up in front with the gun,' I said, 'there are many dangers here: spies, didakta boys, lions, crocodiles.' Our walk has been defined as a dangerous enterprise. So that is what you imagine – danger everywhere. The jungle is going to attack you. The water lizards become crocodiles. Your nerves are strung tight. Then Ngomani comes out to play with us and you imagine he is a rogue bull."

"You were the one who said he was crazy," I protested.

"I was playing along with your reality," said Dumani. "You were the one who created the reality in your mind of a wild, angry beast. That's what you saw with your own eyes. Then he even behaved according to your expectation. You see that?

"Now I tell you he's a baby, a friend of the villagers. Look at him again. He's not so big like you remember him. He's really still a little fellow. You see how insecure he is? He wants us to like him. He's not some killer monster."

As Dumani spoke, Ngomani swayed from side to side excitedly, as if inviting us to join him in a game.

"Are you saying that we see what we're looking for?" I mused.

Dumani turned and considered me with a curious look. He took a few uncertain steps toward me until his face was very close to mine. "Can I tell you a secret?" he said hesitantly. "No one in the village can know what I am about to tell you."

"Sure," I said warily.

"Well, this can't go past you," Dumani said. "Especially not to Dr. Carlyle. If anyone found out, I'd have to kill you."

"Come on, Dumani," I smiled uncomfortably.

"You think I haven't killed someone before?" Dumani's mood was suddenly provocative. His features burned with hostility and an unrestrained violence flashed in his eyes. As he stared at me menacingly, I wondered how this unhinged quality in him had escaped me until now. I swallowed nervously. Neither of us said anything. The malevolent expression on his face did all the talking. I could see his murderous nature oozing from the pores of his skin. Gruesome homicide scenes played out in my mind.

"What are you getting so upset about?" I squirmed. "I said I won't tell anyone."

"You sure?" he demanded. It occurred to me that he might be on drugs again. Spit was beginning to foam in the corners of his mouth, and his eyes were bloodshot.

Ngomani's trunk suddenly snaked over Dumani's

shoulder and began feeling around his face. Dumani held the trunk with both of his hands.

"I saved Ngomani's life," he said with deep feeling.

"That's your secret?" I sighed.

"That's not my secret entirely," said Dumani mournfully. "My secret is that I had to kill some people to save his life – poachers. It's the only time I ever took another human's life. Sometimes I wonder whether it was worth the guilt I must live with now. The rest of his herd died anyway and now he lives all alone. Imagine, a creature to whom family is even more important than to us humans, having to live with the memory of the slaughter of his whole herd."

Dumani held Ngomani's trunk away from his face with one hand and stroked it with the other. I looked at the elephant's massive head looming above Dumani. Though I could see a touching affection written on its face, there was no mistaking the deep lines of sorrow etched into it, either.

"Of course you did the right thing," I hurried to reassure Dumani. "It's not just Ngomani's herd. You stopped the slaughter of many other families, no doubt."

Dumani's eyes were moist. I noticed that they were not so bloodshot as I had just before perceived. It might have been the thick lenses of his spectacles that had magnified the red veins in the whites of his eyes. Now he looked harmless – pitiful, even. Far from appearing unstable and dangerous, Dumani now came across as someone greatly injured by the unfairness of life. I felt guilty that I had let him down by taking him for a monster. This man was a fugitive, I remembered. My intention to save him was fully restored and redoubled.

Dumani stroked one of Ngomani's tusks, which stuck out from under his armpit. "But I haven't told you the full truth," he said with a suddenly bitter expression.

"What's that?" I said, steeling myself for more of his grief.

"I have been taking advantage of this innocent animal's misfortune," said Dumani, the sorrowful vulnerability still shrouding his countenance. "When he comes of age and comes into musth, then he will seek out his kind again, and when he does he will discover that he does not belong. When that happens to an elephant, they do go crazy. The testosterone mixed with the re-ignited trauma is like dynamite. Ngomani will become very vengeful against all creatures. He will want to extinguish life wherever he sees it."

I had heard the horror stories of previously traumatized bull elephants coming into musth and the ensuing carnage that resulted. I was saddened to think that this was Ngomani's inevitable destiny. When I looked up at him, I nearly jumped back in fright. His ears were standing out and the endearing features of a moment ago were replaced by a vacant zombie-like glare, as if he were waiting for some diabolical urge to act on.

"And when he goes crazy," Dumani continued, "I will be the only one who can control him."

My shock at seeing the change on Dumani's face was even greater than from the change I had seen on Ngomani's. As my gaze shifted back to Dumani, I was horrified to see no trace of the crushed victim. Instead, I was being appraised by a sly, calculating monster. The personality being revealed to me now was scarier even than the murderer I had seen before. While there had been something mindless about the violent personality, this side of Dumani was all sinister calculation. I was dealing with a most sick individual, I realized – one who was toying with me by letting me know how far into his web I had strayed. I felt utterly helpless. Shooting him and his elephant would only get Maxine and me in more trouble, I knew. He had me. All I could do now was find out what twisted plan he had in mind for my companions and me.

"Don't look so terrified," Dumani yelled. This time I couldn't stop from leaping back a pace in fright. "I'm only playing with you."

I unslung my rifle and held it in my hands again to show Dumani that I wasn't completely impotent. "Jesus, Dumani," I complained, "what the hell are you playing at?"

"Reality!" he snorted indignantly, pushing Ngomani

back. "I'm teaching you how you create your reality. You see how when you define the jungle as a dangerous place it becomes dangerous? And when you define Ngomani as a harmless baby, do you see how he becomes a sweet little thing? Eh, white man, you see that?"

I nodded my head absently.

"Yes," Dumani went on, "when you define him as a victim, then he looks so sweet and behaves so cute. But then when you define him as a crazy rogue, he looks like a monster and behaves like one, too. Even inside yourself, you change – the pictures, the memories, the thoughts and feelings change according to the definition.

"Even how you see me, when I feed you the definition, I change...you change. I'm a killer: you see a bad person, I look like that; and you, you feel scared. Then I'm a saint and a martyr: you see a wretch without power, and you feel righteous indignation and pity; you want to save me. Then I'm a villain: you see a snake and you feel bitten already by the poison of my fangs.

"You see? You assign a definition and the reality follows. You change the definition and the reality changes – out there and in here." Dumani beat his fist against his chest.

"My god," I said, amazed. Dumani might as well have splashed me with a bucket of cold water. "So how I think or feel other people are, or how things are, is not how they actually are, but how I imagine them to be?"

"Yes," Dumani sounded delighted by my observation, "you define something, then it looks like that, then you feel like that, and next thing it's all like that, everything is happening like that – the definition comes true."

I looked at Dumani to check how I perceived him now. His face was mild, with a scholarly air about it. I felt an engagement with him, a desire for discourse with him. I smiled to myself, realizing that I was defining him as my teacher again.

"Definition is the underlying determinant of our subjective reality," said Dumani. "In the metaphysical circles I came across in my time abroad, there was a lot of power attributed to thoughts and feelings, no doubt because of the observation of the corresponding outcomes that follow thoughts and feelings. It was only among the most sophisticated philosophers that I found anyone who understood the deeper levels of cause and effect."

Though the evidence of Dumani's premise was very palpable, and there could be no doubt that what he proposed was right, my mind still reeled at the implication. "So how do I know what's really real, then?" I wondered aloud, not without some consternation.

"That's not even worth thinking about," Dumani waved my question away. "Remember what I told you? You will go crazy out here in the Meluti if you question what's real and what isn't. Everything is real and isn't at the same time. That's the best way to look at everything. You should only concern yourself with what is obvious. Never get ahead of the obvious. All you need to agree with so far is that when you change the definition, your perception of reality changes. Isn't that so?"

"It is," I nodded, relieved to be restored to a simple, singular focus.

"Yah," said Dumani casually, "that is why so much magic can happen in the Meluti, you see? People changing shape from one kind of animal to another kind. And not only people." He laughed heartily to himself. "Also some animals can change shape, too. And mythical creatures exist here, like Tokoloshes and other things, too." Dumani arched his eyebrows to let me know of his earnestness. "Sometimes the people you meet here are not living people. They can be the ghost of a deceased person. And demons from the spirit world, they are found in this place. But only here, everywhere else they are practically extinct."

"How come?" I asked in fascination.

"Because, when the white man came, he changed the definition," replied Dumani. "Very strong definitions the white man brought. Very absolute, very separate, very arrogant. Time and space and linear reality. Very strong identification with the senses. But, out here, the old definitions still live. The Lapedi of the Meluti have held on to their reality. Out here, there is no time and space – everything is one. Nothing is separate, concrete. No identification with the senses, more with the imagination. The definition underlying this world is magic."

A hippo brayed in the water behind me to reinforce the enchantment of the world around me. Ngomani stood a little way from us, swaying his whole body and trunk as if in time with some ecstatic music only perceptible to his other-worldly ears. The vegetation around us was shrouded by a halo of radiant energy. Dumani radiated the same aura. Everything seemed content to be captivated by the dreami-ness of the moment and not have to go past soaking up the pleasant warmth of the mid-morning sun.

"So the forest is safe," I laughed, happy to be awakened to such a profound understanding of the nature of reality. "The world is safe."

"Ha ha ha," Dumani chuckled, "no wonder the philoso-phers of antiquity used to say that the half-wise will be dashed against the rocks by reason of their own folly. How easy it is to be seduced by reason when you don't have the key to the whole truth."

I was amazed to hear Dumani repeating the Hermetic axiom I had quoted to Maxine only the day before. Part of me wanted to share my amazement with him, but I felt compelled to respond to his mocking tone first. "Hang on," I said indignantly, "I'm getting tired of you patronizing me, Dumani. You were the one who just convinced me that my reality is created by the definitions I assign to myself, others and the world. So it is logical that if I define the forest and the world as safe, I'll have an experience of life being safe. Isn't that so?"

"You think so, white man?" Dumani cut in. "You think that if you tell yourself the world is safe then the war in the Republic will just go away and the dangers of the Meluti will make a path for you like Moses and the Red Sea?"

"But you're the one..." I began.

"I'm the one, I'm the one," clucked Dumani. "Do you

want the key to sorcery or not?"

"Sorcery?" I gasped, feeling the negative association of the word slap me across the face.

"Yes, sorcery!" said Dumani emphatically. "Are you like all the other babies? Are you looking for the milk of a happy story you can tell yourself so you can pretend that you're in charge of your life? Or have you come here to eat meat with the warriors who make their destiny in the realm of gods and demons?"

I looked at Dumani in puzzlement, feeling as if he had just shaken me fully awake. "Then tell me," I said, "what's wrong with using a positive definition?"

"Let's sit down." Dumani waved his stick toward the shade of a Marula tree beside the banks of the hippo wallow. I sat down on an exposed root holding my rifle barrel-up between my legs. Dumani hitched up his sarong and squatted down beside me. He studied my face for a while as if judging how best to explain his understanding to me, and then, with a small grimace, he began: "There was a time when sages taught that everything in the universe is vibration – thoughts, feelings, colors, fire, water, earth, existence, non-existence, everything. The only difference between anything is the rate or speed at which it vibrates. Why are you smiling? Do you think this sounds silly?"

"Not at all," I said, "it fits in with what scientists say about matter being made up of waves of energy or rays. I'm actually smiling because someone once tried to tell me about vibration and I wasn't ready to hear it."

"Very foolish to dismiss the principle of vibration," Dumani shook his head disapprovingly. "It is what separates the half-wise from the wise."

"Please tell me about it, then," I urged him.

"The big insight is not that everything is vibration," he said. "The key to super-conscious mastery is the realization that everything is on the same vibration as its opposite. Love is on the same vibration as hatred, as are hot and cold, or rich and poor, or well and sick. It's like a thermometer; you don't have one thermometer to measure cold and another thermometer to measure hot; they're just at opposite ends of the spectrum of the same temperature gauge."

"So how does this apply to definition?" I wondered aloud.

"Aha," cried Dumani enthusiastically, "don't you see that when you feel scared in the forest, you can tell yourself, 'There's nothing to be scared of; I'm safe; the forest is safe,' but you're still on the same vibration as scared and unsafe? The subconscious part of you that creates your reality is not compelled by literal words; it's guided by what the underlying assumption is, what an action is designed to achieve. So when you're in a forest shivering with fear and you're telling yourself, 'I'm safe; the forest is safe,' your subconscious isn't assuming everything is okay; it's picking up on the fear you're trying to deny. It's going to assume the power is in the fear, and then what it sees has the power, it creates that thing as your reality."

"But hang on," I frowned, "before, when I saw you and Ngomani as dangerous or benign, my perception of you both changed accordingly and then even my experiences changed. Surely my definitions do change my perception and experience."

"Yes," said Dumani, "but you were just reacting to your assumptions as they came up, and I was the one guiding your assumptions. My point is this: yes, definition does create reality, and," Dumani paused to get my full attention, "you won't change an unwanted reality by consciously applying a definition that is merely the opposite of the one that created the reality you don't like. You see what I'm saying, Mr. Vale?"

"I think I do," I said thoughtfully. "What I'm hearing is that by trying to negate the effects of one definition by affirming its opposite, you're only reinforcing the original definition."

"Yah," Dumani smiled, nodding his head with satisfaction. "You give power to the definition you don't like. That's not to say, though, that you can't create a false perception that makes you feel better."

"What do you mean?" I said.

"Well, sometimes you can tell yourself, 'This forest is safe; I'm safe wherever I go in the Meluti,' and maybe you feel no danger and think of no danger. Sometimes you can create a perception of safety. But that is not a reality of safety. Perception isn't the same as actual reality. The reality is that there are many dangerous things out here: hungry predators on the land and in the water, hostile people who don't take prisoners, desperate initiates on the prowl for resources, sangomas trading in human body parts, spies from other villages and other worlds. It doesn't matter what you tell yourself, if you go down this path ignoring the dangers hiding behind the bushes, you will not go far before you become a victim of your presumptuous denial – to quote the philosophers."

I stared at Dumani with renewed astonishment. Listening to him speak, I got the impression of a persona whose wisdom spanned every age and culture since the beginning of time.

"Dumani," I sighed, "you're confusing the hell out of me. First I feel silly for worrying about the dangers of the forest; now I feel silly for not worrying about the dangers of the forest."

"Do not despair, my friend," he said, "you are so close to the answer. The truth is that the forest is full of danger. To deny so would be very foolish and not lead to a good outcome. But it is an illusion that you are powerless over the dangers of the forest. Your fear is telling you what you believe: that you don't have the inner resources to navigate your way through the perils of this forest or, indeed, this world. That's an unconscious definition or assumption, that you're unsafe, that you are separate from your viability."

"So how do I connect with those inner resources that create my viability," I leaned my forehead into the two fists wrapped around the barrel of my gun, "without reinforcing my fear?" I mumbled.

"Now you are on the money," Dumani clapped his hands in approval. "Now you're asking the right question."

"So what's the right answer?" I looked up at Dumani expectantly.

"The higher against the lower," Dumani declared triumphantly. "You use the higher vibration against the lower vibration. You see that? Like when you're struggling being poor, you don't just think to be rich; that is just on the same vibration. Instead you can think to follow your true calling or doing what you love or something like that. Maybe you heard the story about the Enema Tycoon? No? He's a famous man in this country – all the Africans know about him. In the beginning he was just a poor subsistence farmer living in the far south of the Republic. His allotment was in the middle of some hot springs where nothing could grow because of all the sulfur leaching into the soil. He was an ignorant man; he didn't know that no matter how hard he worked, he'd never raise a crop that his family could survive on. One day he took his last goat to the local sangoma and asked him to remove the curse he thought his enemies had put on him. The witch doctor was a very wise fellow. After he threw the bones, the sangoma asked the poor man if there was a duty he had neglected. The peasant was a hardworking man; he had to think for a very long time before he could come up with something. He finally remembered that he had been called to volunteer his services at the compound of the paramount chief, but he had been given a special dispensation by his local chief on account of his family's struggles. The sangoma told the man that unless he went and did his service for the paramount chief his fortunes would never change. Even though the poor farmer was afraid his family would starve without him, he reported for duty at the village of the paramount chief near the Capital. While he was there, the man learned that the fashion in those parts was for the men to give themselves enemas with the mineral waters from hot springs. When he was released from his spell of servitude, he came home and started making enema kits out of tin pots and surgical hose, just like the ones he'd seen in the Capital. Soon he became very rich starting an enema craze in his district – he even charged the men in that area to use the hot springs on his allotment.

"Funny story, no? But this is a good one, because the sangoma took the peasant's attention off of his struggle to survive. He focused the man on something higher than himself and his problems – in this case, the principle of service. And it's the same with everything. If you have a problem with drinking, you don't just think of stopping to drink; you must think of your health above drinking or not drinking. Overseas they have a very successful program called Alcoholics Anonymous – you heard about it? Yah, those people, they learn to put their faith in a power higher than themselves. You see what I mean?"

"I do," I said, "I've learned about structure in magic training before. I even taught it to others in a book I wrote called *The Magician's Way*, about the seven secrets of magic."

"Hauw, you know about the seven secrets of magic?" Dumani exclaimed, his surprise tinged with approval. "Then you know that the fifth secret is about how, in any dynamic, the underlying structure will always create an inevitable outcome, and that in terms of consciousness, the underlying structure is determined by motivation. Like I'm saying, if you're desperate to make some money because you're struggling financially, then the power is in the poverty."

"I've got it," I laughed, happy in the realization that I shared more with Dumani than I had appreciated. "But if the higher vibration over rich and poor is purpose, say, and health is higher than sober or not sober, what is the higher vibration or definition above safe and unsafe?"

"Still stuck on that one, eh?" Dumani chortled.

"It's what we were talking about," I said hastily.

"True," Dumani conceded, making a conscious effort to reassume a straight-faced demeanor, "and the answer to your question is innocence."

"Innocence?" I said, failing to make the connection.

"Yah," said Dumani, "very important, this one. The fundamental task of a real human is not to survive in the world but to navigate their way through life. We are all being guided along the path of our highest good. The one who is awake can hear that guidance and know what they need to know and do what they need to do. To follow this guidance is our bliss, and also the source of our inherent viability. But you can't know the truth – you can't see the path – when you're stuck in your perceptions.

"Playing around with definitions is like moving the deck chairs about on the *Titanic* to stop it from sinking. You have a perception you don't like, so you change the definition to create a perception you do like. Your projections might change, but you're still trapped in the duality of your egoic nature, responding and reacting to the assumptions in your unconscious. You're still not dealing with objective reality – the reality, or the truth, that is free of your projections. To do that, you have to step outside of duality, into innocence, which is a state of consciousness – or awareness, more precisely – that exists outside of definition.

"In-No-Sense," he spoke the three words very deliberately, "outside of thoughts and feelings."

A loud splashing noise erupted beside us. I jerked my head up in fright. It was Ngomani wading into the water. The hippos grunted like squeaky donkeys in protest. They submerged, leaving a trail of bubbles as they headed downstream, walking on the river floor. The young bull elephant stumbled out into the channel until he, too, sank completely beneath the surface, with only the tip of his trunk sticking out. He emerged on the far side, clumsily sloshing his way onto dry land.

"He's after the dates on the bank over there," said Dumani, watching Ngomani with the amused affection of a doting parent. Ngomani lumbered up to a tall palm tree laden with bunches of fist-sized red fruit at its crown. He leaned his shoulder into the slender trunk and shook the tree with all his might. The giant dates fell to the ground around him in a thunderous tattoo. After the elephant gave a few more token shakes to make sure the palm had nothing more to give, his trunk snuffed lazily around for the fruit on the ground before popping them into his mouth. He stood staring across the water at us, chewing as contentedly as a tame cow.

"So how do you step outside of thoughts and feelings?" I said, anxious to grasp the secret to mastering my reality.

"One moment," said Dumani. He stood up with the help of his fighting stick and lifted the front of his sarong. Without any self-consciousness, he pulled a brightly painted bush nut from the glans of his penis. His face took on a serene expression as he urinated straight out in front of where we were sitting. After shaking the last drops off his penis, he screwed the colorful nut back on and let his sarong fall to his knees again. He squatted straight back down with a satisfied groan. His eyes caught mine before I could look away.

To resolve my embarrassment, I asked, "What is that monkey nut for?"

"To stop us getting an erection when we're in public," he said casually.

"Does it work?"

"Sure," he grimaced, "it's too painful when you get swollen. The brainless one soon learns to behave himself when it's on." He smiled to himself at some private thought. "We can get you a junior size one to wear."

"Thanks, Dumani," I smiled back disingenuously, "I don't think I need one."

"What about when you're around Dr. Carlyle?" he smirked.

"We're not, um, together," I stammered. "Her fiancé just died."

"Be very careful with that one; the world is full of sirens sweetly singing," Dumani mused. "Remember what I said: We are all being guided. The one who is not awake to guidance can only live by trying to decide which move suits his circumstances." The sour look on his face indicated that he found this to be a very distasteful way of operating.

"You were going to tell me about innocence," I reminded Dumani, eager for him to move on from my own shortcomings. I shifted uncomfortably on the Marula root as he gazed at me steadily in the eyes. So blinded was I by my sensitivity to my lack of wisdom that I didn't even contemplate that he might be suggesting something about my current relationship to Maxine.

"You know what we teach the didakta boys?" he said finally. "Three things." He held up three fingers. "You can find these themes in all indigenous or traditional initiation in every age and culture throughout history. Number one: the being within; number two: the wound; number three: all things are conscious. This might not sound extraordinary to you – just some mysterious words; intriguing at most. But whoever knows what these themes are about and can unify them, they have uncovered the secret of how their being has been put together and how they can take control of their higher potential. So follow closely when I explain them.

"First, the being within: that means you are not just a carcass with some gray matter computing the most logical way to survive. There's a spirit inside, a pure creative spirit connected to everything through all time and space. This essence has a destiny, a purpose to fulfill, and many gifts and talents that support the expression of that nature. This is our greatness. The ability to own what we truly exist to serve, and the actualization of that, defines our personal sovereignty.

"Second, the wound. You are born into human form and, as pure creative spirit connected to everything through all time and space, you must create a concept of individual existence. To create this separate identity, you are wounded in relation to who you are. You end up believing you are the physical vehicle of your spirit, and the spirit itself becomes lost within.

"Third, all things are conscious. Everything is alive, even the rocks and water and the stars. We are all one in the sea of life, one in consciousness. Nothing ever dies; things only ever change. There's a root substance to everything, and at that substantial level there is no separation of time or space or knowledge. Everything is connected."

A big bull hippo announced its re-arrival in the pool beside us, and when Ngomani responded by giving another palm tree a shake, the hippo signaled the all-clear to the rest of its pod.

"But what do these themes have to do with definition and perception?" I shook my head in puzzlement.

"Everything," said Dumani. "When you are born into your human vehicle, you have no notion of individual identity. It's accepted scientifically, even, that a newborn baby does not differentiate itself from its mother or its environment. It still has to learn to shut off from everything else and experience itself as separate through time and space.

"The Mayans, those people who lived in the Americas when the Spanish came there, they used to have a proverb that said, 'The future of the world lies in the newborn child; the mother must hold the baby close so that it knows it belongs in the world and the father must take it to the highest hill so it can see how the world is.' We Lapedi say the same thing. We say that your mother teaches you that you have a heart and your father teaches you to bring your heart to the world. That is the job of mothers and fathers. You following me?"

I was actually at a loss as to what Dumani's current tangent had to do with the themes of perception and innocence, but I was beginning to trust that, given a little time, the seemingly random threads of his lectures inevitably pulled together to make sense. I nodded in the affirmative.

"This is very amazing stuff, this. You must listen carefully; otherwise, you won't understand the key. The lives of many depend on you understanding what I'm saying. The vehicle we enter is our ego. The body, the mind, the feelings – it's all the ego. The ego is our vehicle, but especially the vehicle of orientation. It wants to know, how do we operate here in this three-dimensional reality? It is dedicated to the assumption that there is some way it is here – a way that things are – and, thereby, some way we need to be here. Of course, this is the fundamental flaw in our unconscious logic, but very important for creating separation.

"So how does our ego learn how it is here and how to be here? Very clever, the ego, like a genius. It looks for validation of its pure creative nature from the mother and the father. So you remember what the Mayans said? When you are a baby, you look for nurturing from your mother. You want to know that you can love and be loved, that you have worth, that you belong. Then when you start to walk and run, you look to your father for acknowledgment. You want to know that he sees your spirit and approves of your actions to bring it into the world.

"So you want this validation very badly, but there is no such thing as pure parenting. Somehow, you are not going to be met according to who you know yourself to be and how you expect that love and validation to happen. Now somewhere deep inside, you feel hurt and you want to know what causes this pain. So you explain it to yourself. You make decisions. You create definition and meaning. 'My mother doesn't love me when I'm trouble for her – I'm unworthy; I mustn't trouble others' – something like that. Or maybe, 'My father doesn't take notice of me unless I am the best at what I do – I'm not good enough unless I beat everyone at whatever I do.'

"All the time the ego is making up rubbish, beliefs that are not true: 'I'm not safe,' 'I'm powerless,' 'I'm unworthy,' 'I'm not good enough,' 'I'm not perfect,' 'I don't belong,' 'I'm not capable,' and so on and so on. Things just happen and we think those things...we take it that it means something about us. To fix the pain we feel when we are babies, we make up things that end up making us suffer for the rest of our lives. But all the time the ego is very happy. We are crying, 'Weh, weh, weh,'" Dumani cracked up at his own theatrics, "but the ego is laughing, 'Ha ha ha, I'm so happy because now I know how it is and how I must be.' You see that?"

I shook my head in the negative.

"The ego wants to know how it is here on the planet, in the physical world," Dumani went on before I had time to frame a question. "From the pain of unmet validation it makes up beliefs about itself, others and the world. Those beliefs then give the ego orientation, an understanding of how it is and what life is about. You see, like the person with not belonging thinks, 'Oh, I don't belong so now I must use my energy to fit in; that is who I am and what my life is about.' Or the one who does not believe he is good enough, he thinks, 'I am not okay unless I achieve important things; that is who I am and what my life is about.'

"Like yourself, you experience the drama of your life as one who is looking to find the direction that will resolve his place in the world. The anguish of your confusion and doubt is very real to you. Little do you realize that you are playing a game your ego made up when you were only a baby. Your mother, she likes to have control, and when you were little you learned that her heart shut down when you were independent minded or willful in any way. Before you even could talk, you decided that it was best not to know anything for yourself. Even today your mother makes decisions for you that you cannot defy. You are waiting for the women to decide, even though you don't like what they decide."

"That's so true," I shook my head in amazement. "I've never seen that about myself, or my mother, but it's right. In my family, there is always a battle of wills about who knows best, and I just always found it painful to get caught up in the competition for being right."

"Exactly," Dumani nodded gently, "and with your father so busy, you know not to get in his way. Always he is the important one; like a lion, he is the protector; he must eat first, get all the attention. So you must stay out of the way. Even what your mother controls you about is to stay out of your father's way. So now you always go away. Wherever you are, you think, 'This is not the place for me.' So you never know, 'Who am I; who must I be?' But all the time, it's just a game: 'I mustn't know for myself; I mustn't be here. And if I'm lost enough and out of the way enough someone can love me, someone can help me and take care of me.' You see, it's the baby running the show. But not just you; everyone in the world." He spread his arms out in a fatalistic gesture. "Everyone is a baby until didakta."

"So didakta is not just a physical ordeal to toughen boys

into men?" I said.

"No," Dumani scoffed, "you can't call yourself a man until you have been through didakta, but not because you are big and strong now – because you have grown up inside, because the being within is back in business."

"So, the didakta boys, they all know their wounds?"

"Correct," said Dumani. "You see, the wound gives names to everything. It defines everything. All of your beliefs amount to definitions about yourself, others and the world, and that's how you create separation. The more you describe something, the more you isolate it from everything else. This is why mystics like William Blake have been so opposed to the science of Isaac Newton, because mechanistic science is always defining and dividing, defining and dividing, until everything is lying cut into pieces like a butchered animal. But we cannot be here if we are not creating this separation, what your psychologists call individuation.

"The ego is very clever. It creates separation by creating definition and it reinforces the definition by creating a reality that confirms the definition. Then it knows how it is here and how to be here. It's very happy. Only problem, you're separate from everything, living inside your own bubble not knowing what's really going on – just thinking and feeling like you do."

"The first secret of magic," I reflected, "your thoughts and feelings aren't real."

"That's the one," Dumani laughed. "You really did have some magic training before, isn't it?" He squinted at me, cocking his head to one side. "I did suspect so before now, because every time you do something you stop and think about what you want first. You are good like that."

My mentor's nod of approval was some consolation for my embarrassment at how little I knew about the deeper levels of the subject I had once presumed to teach.

"It doesn't help if you are half-wise," I mumbled, "if you don't know how to fully apply it."

"Cheer up!" Dumani exclaimed. "You are so close to

knowing the answer." He held his thumb and forefinger a fraction of an inch apart. "We are subject to our perceptions because all the time the ego wants to know how it is. You remember I told you that it's the vehicle of your orientation? 'How is it? How is it?' All the time it's asking that. But never asking actual reality, because actual reality can be different from its beliefs. Imagine if that happens – reality being different from the beliefs. Then there is no orientation, no consistent way that it is. So the ego shuns reality and looks instead to its pre-established definitions for the answer, and then projects that worldview onto reality. You see what I'm saying?

"So if perception is created by the ego needing to know how it is all the time, and checking in with what it believes to get the answer every time, then how can you stop being subject to your perception? How can you be free of ego-reality? That is the puzzle, isn't it?"

Dumani waited for the obvious to occur to me. "Well, it would involve not needing to know, wouldn't it?" I ventured. "If you didn't need to know how it is, you wouldn't reference your beliefs."

"Sure," said Dumani gleefully. "You've got it. Good chap. That is the answer – you don't need to know how it is."

"But how do you stop needing to know?" I looked at him baffled.

"This makes you crazy, eh?" Dumani smiled. "You, always believing you don't know, wanting to know how you can know, so you ask your beliefs and they tell you that you don't know. It makes your brain go, 'Eeeh, eeeh, eeeh!'" He cried out in a high-pitched voice, at the same time imitating someone having a fit. Then he straightened his face again and said, "You just stop knowing what you know. You let it go and don't need to know something else. Like when people meditate, they stop thinking. The thoughts are still coming and going, but the meditator doesn't jump into the thoughts like they are clothes; he just watches the thought go by like a stick in the river."

"You just stop knowing what you know?" I said dumbly. I was dejected by the impression that the key to the mastery

I so desperately yearned for was way beyond my cognitive reach.

"Hand me your gun," Dumani commanded. "Don't worry, I won't shoot you. I think if you experience the vibration of innocence then you can step into that vibration any time you like."

I looked around me. There was no sign of danger anywhere. Ngomani had disappeared into the forest on the other side of the channel. Only the violent rustle of palm fronds and thump of falling dates signaled his presence. A few disgruntled moans sounded from the water as some of the hippos jostled for position beside the big male. I let Dumani take my rifle.

"That's it," he said, laying the gun across his lap with the barrel pointing away from me. "Now lean against the tree trunk and close your eyes. That's it. Now breathe. There you go. You can relax. No need to worry about anything. Even if you can't stop worrying about your family and the dangers of the Meluti, no need to worry about what you can't stop worrying about. Let everything be.

"Now, just imagine that you're walking through a forest – any forest, maybe this one, maybe another one. But very important to use every sense. Imagine the smell, the feel of walking on the ground, the sounds, the sights, even the taste in your mouth. Just keep noticing what it's like to walk through a forest!"

Dumani fell silent. I became preoccupied with being able to only imagine myself in a pine forest and not among native African trees. Though I did my best to stay focused, I kept worrying that my mental distraction would detract from the process Dumani was guiding me through. After a few minutes he spoke again: "Imagine that you come across a path in the forest. Notice what it's like to follow the path through the forest. No need to worry about anything. Even if your mind is busy. No problem. Just think about what you see along the path, the noises and smells, how it feels to be in the forest.

"You walk and you walk, and after some time you reach

a fork in the path. So you must take the left fork. You go down the path to the left and you keep walking, keep imagining, keep noticing. What's it like walking down this new path to the left?

"Now the forest begins thinning. Less trees everywhere and some clearings starting to appear. In the clearing, some violet flowers are growing. As you walk, there are less and less trees, more and more violets – until there are no more trees – only violet flowers. You look around and you are in the middle of a sea of violet. No worries in your mind. You just keep walking through the field of violets.

"Some time passes. You walk this way, then that way. Nothing but violet color in every direction. Then on the horizon you see some kind of a place, like a building. You walk there. You see that it is a holy place, a temple. You keep walking through the violets till you reach this edifice.

"You come to the temple. You stand and you look. You know this place. You feel something in your heart like when you meet an old friend. But also a little fear, a reverence for a power greater than yourself. You walk up the stairs and you go through the entrance.

"Inside the temple, there is a crib. You walk up to the crib and look down. Inside the cot is lying a baby, a symbol of innocence. You look down at the baby and you look at its face and you learn everything there is to learn about innocence. You can feel it, what it's like to be in wonder, to apprehend everything in the world for the first time. You look at the child in innocence and you go back to being unaffected by experience, to being empty of preconceived definitions and meanings. You feel like that baby, still connected to everything. You feel the sacredness, the divinity, that is still strong in the little one's consciousness.

"Imagine you can step into the baby, become the child in innocence. Imagine knowing innocence by becoming it. You become the child in the crib. You lie there in awe, outside all thoughts and feelings. You see the colors of the world outside and visions of the creator inside. You hear the chimes above your crib and the music of the spheres echoing through the universe. You gaze on existence with the pleasure of one who belongs to it without question, without fear of separation.

"As you lie there, a child in innocence, the earth opens up beneath you and you start falling gently and safely through a purple void. You fall away from everything you know. The thoughts and feelings and beliefs and definitions you thought were you are left behind; you see them as stars in the sky up above you, remote and far away as you keep falling through a purple void.

"You've been falling through the purple void forever. Gently, happily falling. The stars above you have disappeared. Only purple. But now you are slowing down. You are drifting back to Earth. You are the creative child in innocence drifting back to Earth. Slowly, slowly, you land back in your body here on Earth. Back in your old body, but now with the consciousness of the child in innocence."

I opened my eyes and blinked. My first observation was that the scene before me was exactly the same as the one I had closed my eyes on. The fat, aubergine hippo heads still rested tranquilly in the dark-indigo water between me and the forest on the other side of the channel. Yet there was a new dimension to the world around me. I first noticed it in the hippos. I fancied they were looking at me with smiling eyes. Then it dawned on me that there was something friendly about my whole environment, as if I were somehow telepathically linked to it and could hear its expression of goodwill toward me. The palpable extrasensory connection with my surroundings made me gasp out loud.

"You okay?" Dumani asked in a mirthful tone.

"Sure," I said breathlessly, "it's like the whole world has come alive." Realizing that speaking moderated the intensity of the awe welling up in me, I continued to describe my experience to Dumani. "Everything is so alive, it's vibrating. No wonder the ancient philosophers said everything was vibration; they could see it."

"You speak truth, my friend," Dumani shook his head appreciatively.

"Wow, everything is so clear," I marveled. "Normally I just see a forest in front of me, not the trees. I see a general picture, not the individual elements that the picture is composed of. But now everything stands out, everything speaks to me." I fell silent again, hushed by the flood of beauty inundating my senses. It was the first time I had ever really appreciated the brilliance of the lime-colored bulrush stalks and the laughter in the sunlight glinting playfully on top of the moody, almost black water or noticed the symmetry created by the plant life around me.

"Yah," said Dumani, "usually when we say 'I see this' or 'I see that' we don't really see what's there, just the vague outline. This is because the rational mind catalogues things for convenience. At a glance we can tell what something is and whether its properties are good or bad for us. We don't have to spend a lot of time analyzing everything we come across. If we didn't catalogue information, we would be like a baboon you see in the bush picking up a rock, and then some snake hissing at him, and then the baboon fainting with fright, waking up, picking up the same stone, snake hissing at him, fainting, and carrying on like that for hours. Much better to remember that this rock has a snake under it.

"The only problem is that then you assume you know everything. You scan the environment and you don't appreciate it, don't really take it in, because you assume you have it all worked out. You walk past a snake, you jump away from it feeling bad feelings about it, seeing bad pictures in your mind, because you know from your catalogue that this is a bad thing. You don't stop and see the beautiful patterns on his body and think, 'This is one of God's fantastic creatures at home in his territory.'

"Or you walk past a flower. Even now you say to yourself, 'Yes, very nice flower, colorful and pretty; no harm to me.' But you don't see the flower. You think you did. You even say to your friend, 'Look at that pretty flower.' But your mind didn't take it in really; it just says, 'Yes, yes, pretty; we know pretty; we don't have to take it in.'"

Dumani's point was underscored by the world my

attention had been drawn into at my feet. A stubble of dry grass clung to the bleached earth by a tangle of wiry roots. Arranged casually around it, as if by the design of a practiced artist, lay a sprinkling of leaves at various stages of decay, from waxy orange ones with swollen blue veins to crumpled desiccated specimens with the dark vestiges of arteries standing out like ribs on a carcass. Completing the natural little montage was a placement of brittle, gray twigs with insipid green lichen growing on their joints. Traversing the miniature landscape was a team of black ants dragging a rust-colored bug with iridescent purple spots on its wings. As they focused on their task, others of their type raced in from all directions to fend off a patrol of larger, pale-brown ants evidently bent on hijacking their prize. At the same time as I was engrossed in the existential beauty and drama of this little world, I was conscious that under normal circumstances I would never have even been aware of its existence.

"In innocence, we suspend the cataloguing function of the rational mind," Dumani said after a pause. "Then we don't think we know everything. We are really present to whatever we're with. We take things in as if for the first time. We see the patterns of life, the connection between things, the way everything is in that moment. That is why Western people love to go travelling – so they can experience the awe of seeing things for the first time. But you don't have to go anywhere if your heart is open. In innocence, everything is new all the time. The wonder of life never ceases to amaze you."

For a moment I tried to think what else about my sensory awareness was different, other than my enhanced vision. Then it hit me. It was the noise! It was as if I had been wearing earplugs before and now they had been taken out. A symphony of sound crashed in delicious waves against my eardrums. I had not paid any attention before to a herd of zebras barking on the other side of the woods. Now their high-pitched whelping sounded a back beat to the vibrant hum of insects and cacophony of birdcalls. Over this constant rhythm, the forest reverberated with the squeals and grunts and growls of every kind of mammal adding their voice to the cheerful song of nature.

I didn't recall seeing so many birds before, either. I wondered whether they had always been there or whether the state of innocence had the power to magically flush them out. Kingfishers and Malachites swooped across the water, flashing every variation of brilliant blue. Bishop birds puffed out their scarlet chests as they sat atop brown-velvet bulrush heads. Lily-trotters stalked adroitly among pink and white lotus beds, their dark-green bodies glistening in the sunlight and their blood-red beaks pecking incessantly at invisible morsels on the lily leaves. I noticed two big hazel bulbs about a foot apart, floating between the lilies just out from where we were sitting. I looked in front of them and, sure enough, there was the tip of a crocodile snout.

"Do you see the crocodile down the bank here?" I said out of the corner of my mouth.

"Yes, big chap, maybe fifteen feet," Dumani replied casually. "More on the other side."

As soon as he said it, I made out several pairs of eyes sticking out of the water in among the lily pads near the far bank. I was marveling at how the water birds swam or waded by the crocodiles with impunity, when a spotted pattern moving among the reeds behind them caught my eye. The yellowy-orange hide disappeared behind a thicket. I kept my eye glued on the reeds for another glimpse of whatever it was. Finally a large feline head appeared at the water's edge. Though I could not see the rest of its body, I could sense that the cat was coiled and ready to pounce. I held my breath in anticipation, wondering what it was targeting, and at the same time concerned that it was dangerously close to becoming prey itself.

Suddenly the cat leaped high into the air with perfect anticipation. A gray heron rose straight into the spotted predator's outreached paws. One of the crocodiles dived for cover as the cat crashed into the water beside it, clutching its prey. In an instant, the cat bounded back onto dry land and disappeared into the bushes with the wader flapping uselessly in its jaws.

"Eh, eh, eh!" Dumani exclaimed. "You see that? Mpongisa – a serval cat. Two kills already today. First the eagle catched that monkey and now this kind of cheetah with a bird. You see how he nearly jumped on that crocodile? Very cheeky. But it's like the didakta boys, isn't it? If you want food, you must take it from the jaws of the crocodile – as a metaphor, I mean."

I looked at Dumani. His face, too, was a world of its own. There was no mistaking the years lined in his features, yet it was as if that face were a transparent mask behind which I could see the countenance of a young boy grinning at the world. Everything about him expressed itself in fascinating contradictions, even the way he alternated between pidgin and the Queen's English. I could not help but feel a deep affection for this remarkable individual who was, I fully appreciated, introducing me to the soul of the world.

"Wow," I shook my head in astonishment, "the world has come alive suddenly. Is it a coincidence, or is it because I'm in innocence now?"

"Ha ha ha," Dumani chuckled gleefully. "It's always like this. When you bring a person outside their egoic perception, they always say, 'Oh, the sun is so bright; was it behind a cloud before?' They pick some weed and they start crying, 'Oh, look at this beautiful flower; it looks like a purple vagina. How erotic.' They talk like this, as if the sun were not shining before and the weed were not beautiful before. No, no, no," he shook his head emphatically. "When the veils of perception fall away, then the world in all its glory is standing before you. Until then it appears to us as a pale, washed-out shadow of itself.

"Even the danger you look for, you don't really see it. In your mind, yes, but not out here. Like these crocodiles – we walked for a mile and you did not see one, but there are four or five in every pool the size of this one beside us. The camouflage works because the busy mind rashly associates the animal form with what it is blending in with. Your brain says, 'Yes, a leaf, a stick, the bush, no problem. Where's the monsters I'm looking for?' But when you see without comparing to the catalogue inside, then what is there stands out; you see it for what it is. You notice, 'Oh, this place is full of crocodiles; there's an animal in those reeds; look, the bush is full of birds.' Nothing is overlooked for convenience."

Dumani looked down and regarded the rifle in his lap quizzically, as though he had forgotten it was there. He gazed back at me with interest. "You look like those didakta boys yesterday, seeing white people for the first time," he smiled. "What are you learning, my friend?"

Normally I would have considered his question before answering, but now the answer was already there in my mind, as obvious as everything I could see and hear. "Well," I said, "what I'm learning is that what I think and feel is going on isn't going on. In fact, what I think and feel is going on is hiding what's really going on. There's another world beyond what I think and feel...the real world." I sat with what I had said for a while and then added, "Although, when I act on what I think and feel is going on, I create a reality that is self-fulfilling – I keep myself shut out of the real world."

"Uh-huh," Dumani nodded in his genial way, "that is right. So true, isn't it? But what about using this knowledge outside of time and space?"

"Time and space?" I frowned.

"Sure," said Dumani. "Now the things that are in your line of sight and hearing become apparent to you. But what about beyond what your senses can apprehend? Beyond what you can see and hear and touch and smell? How can you use innocence to know, to formulate, non-linear awareness?"

I was dumbfounded by the question. I couldn't, for the life of me, even find a starting point to contemplate his proposition. I shrugged my shoulders lamely.

"Like, for instance, over there," Dumani pointed across the river, "where Ngomani went in and the serval cat is hiding, what else is in the forest? What's there that is in your highest good to know?"

"But that's a psychic capacity you're talking about," I said, elated by where I assumed the lesson was headed, "or are you saying there are physical signs to be read?"

"No physical signs," he said. "I'm talking about stretching past what can be physically recognized, to know in the way you knew who took your fishing rods. You came out here looking for the secret to super-conscious awareness and you don't even know you're standing on the bridge."

"Innocence is the bridge?" I said uncertainly.

"Sure," Dumani sang out, "when you don't know, then you know. Now you look at those bushes and you think, 'I don't know anything about what I can't see or haven't seen before or someone else hasn't told me.' But what if you didn't know that you are separate, what would you know then?"

As enthralled as I was by my experience of being "In-No-Sense," as Dumani put it, and did not think that I could be any more elated than I already was, the suggestion that I was on the verge of attaining my quest to discover the secret to divine wisdom sent me into paroxysms of sheer delight.

"Shit, Dumani," I laughed gleefully, "I don't know, maybe nothing. Maybe my mind would just be blank."

"You want to give it a try?" said Dumani nonchalantly, pushing his glasses up to the bridge of his nose. "Just close your eyes again. That's it. Lean back and breathe."

I took a few deep breaths, relishing the pure oxygenated forest air I was drawing into my lungs. I noticed a slight flutter of trepidation at the thought that I might not succeed in bridging to my super-conscious faculties or, indeed, that they might not even exist. Maxine's admonishment that I could never hope to compare with Dumani's talent was still fresh in my mind. But this subtle misgiving was drowned out by a childlike curiosity and excitement.

"Yah, that's it, just breathe," said Dumani. "Don't worry about anything. How does this work? Will it work? You don't know anything. That's it. Now just imagine you look inside yourself and there you find that child in innocence you became in the temple. There he is living inside you. Now imagine you climb back inside your creative child – the one who knows nothing – and as the child, still knowing nothing, imagine you step into the forest there on the other side and stand there. Just be there with no capability to rationalize or compare or understand. So, then, what are you aware of, what is obvious to you then?"

Dumani had hardly finished talking before my eyes opened wide with fright.

"What is it?" said Dumani. "You must keep your eyes closed and stay there as the child in innocence."

"There's something scary in there," I shuddered. "Or it feels scary doing this. Maybe I have a subconscious block to connecting with my super-conscious."

"No," said Dumani contemptuously, "no such thing as blocks. It's just your rational mind coming in. You already got something about what's in there, but very quickly, before you can even count, your rational mind has compared it to an existing definition in your consciousness and created what you are experiencing now. Your ego has told you there is something dangerous in there, so you're scared to look.

"If you look in a dictionary, it will tell you that intuition is the first thing the mind apprehends, before rationalizing. Intuition, super-conscious awareness, call it what you like, is a statement of the obvious, like you see the world around you when you are in innocence. It's just what's there. To think that it's good or bad, or that it makes sense or doesn't make sense, that's added after seeing just what's there. That's rationalizing. What's just there, that's our highest truth." Dumani lifted his fighting stick to the heavens. "So you must go back there as the child and not know anything, not know whether what is there is good or bad or making sense or not making sense. Just see what is there."

I found my way into my inner child again and imaginatively stepped back into the forest. As I did my best to maintain the vision of myself standing in the jungle, a sense of foreboding came over me that I could not dismiss. In my imagination, I couldn't see anything; I was virtually blind. I could vaguely make out that Ngomani was standing over me trying to roll me over with his trunk. I could feel the earth along the entire length of my body. I was lying down and I couldn't move. I was paralyzed and…covered in fur.

"What is it?" Dumani prompted.

"I don't know," I said, "there's nothing there. I can't make sense of it."

"Nothing?" exclaimed Dumani incredulously. "No feeling, no sense, no picture, no sound or thought? Just nothing?"

"Well," I clarified, keeping my eyes closed, "I do get something, but it's very vague. It doesn't make sense. It doesn't tell me what's there – other than Ngomani, but I already knew that he's in there."

"Okay, listen to me," said Dumani urgently, "you remember when you spoke to the Tokoloshe, yes? You just make up a sound and then that sound becomes exactly what you wanted to say. Intuition is like that. Innocence takes you outside of what your preconceptions blind you from seeing. But that's just a starting place, and this starting place is often just some vague impression – maybe a vague sense of something or an image; sometimes a few words. Next step, you have to turn that impression into rational information. You have to interpret it, but same like you do when speaking with a Tokoloshe. You just make it up. Then you find it makes sense after. You can't know Tokoloshe before you speak it; you know it after you speak it. You know what I'm saying, white man? This is important. Now tell me what you see. What is obvious about it? Make it up!"

"Okay," I said hastily, responding to Dumani's sense of urgency, "I'm lying down in the forest. I'm covered in fur, but it's not mine. I'm not an animal. It's not even me. It's not me!" I opened my eyes, startled by the realization. I continued speaking as fast as I could: "It's not me. There's someone lying there in the forest paralyzed. Ngomani is trying to revive him or help him up. Something about the fur. He's trying to get the fur off of him. It's killing him. He's dying. Oh my god, Dumani," I cried out in horror, "someone is dying in the forest there. They need our help."

"Is he asking us for help?" said Dumani.

"No. What? Ngomani is calling us. It's a friend of Ngomani's." No sooner had I blurted out the words than I felt ridiculous for uttering them.

"Here's your gun," Dumani flung the rifle in my direction and jumped to his feet. I managed to catch the gun just before it smashed into my face. "It's Sibongila, the scout."

"How do you know?" I said as I got up.

"The question is," said Dumani, glancing up and down the channel impatiently, "how do we get to the other side?"

I looked across the water helplessly. The hippos lay in a cordon right up the waterway, and behind them I could see two sets of crocodile eyes close to the water-lily fringe. The big crocodile that had been nosing about below the bank on our side had disappeared, which was more of a worry than anything I could see on the surface.

"What's the way?" Dumani demanded fiercely.

"Jesus, Dumani," I hissed, "you're the one who's from around here. Why are you asking me?" I was afraid that the answer lay in my crossing the channel.

"You're the one connected to Ngomani and Sibongila," he said irritably. "Tune in again. Go back as the innocent child and ask them."

Possessing none of the serenity I assumed the process required, I imaginatively embodied my inner child again and stepped over into the forest. Silently I asked Ngomani and the prone figure how we could get across to them in a hurry. Immediately a picture formed in my mind of Dumani swimming across the river between two hippos. I tried to imagine myself in the picture but my imagination would not entertain the image. Finally, I opened my eyes and looked at the portly doctor of philosophy, reluctant to tell him what had occurred to me. His staring eyes insisted.

"I saw you swimming across the river," I muttered. "You swam right between two hippos." Meeting his staring eyes, I spoke up strongly, "It's crazy, I know. What do you expect; I'm just making it up."

Dumani's face broke into a relaxed smile. "Of course

you're making it up," he said, "that's the language of the soul. It is wise that you don't come with me. Insurance. If you see something coming for me you can shoot it." He untied his buckskin bejuga and unfurled his sarong and placed them in a pile on the ground. With a little hesitation he took off his spectacles and placed them carefully on top of the pile. He stood squinting across the water, wearing nothing but the brightly colored nut at the end of his penis.

"You're nuts, Dumani," I said, horrified at the thought of him going into the water.

"No pun intended, I'm sure," he said without humor. He peered at the water intently. "There are times when you can go in the water and nothing can happen. You see that serval cat before, how he nearly jumped on that crocodile? He's not stupid. He knew that today he can do that. He checked first. Now, your heart is saying I can make it."

"I don't want to be responsible for your death," I shook my head in dismay.

"Well, then, if a crocodile comes for me, make sure you shoot him and not me, okay?" His eyes studied the water carefully. "So, which hippo to swim past? Not the ones with calf, they're crazy. Not the bull, because the ones around him are jealous. Maybe these two cows away from the rest; they're not playing games. Yah, that's my line." Dumani pointed in the direction of the two crocodiles on the far side.

I instinctively pulled the bolt of my rifle back a little to check that there was a bullet in the firing chamber. I was sweating with dreaded anticipation, as if I were witnessing a horrible premonition play out. "Okay," I said without any conviction, "I've got you covered." I brought the rifle butt to my shoulder and aimed the barrel out at the water.

Dumani eased himself down the muddy bank. He did not look back to me for any reassurance. All the time his head was directed in the line he planned on swimming. He waded out into the water as stealthily as possible until the water was halfway up his thighs and then sank his whole body in without making so much as a ripple. Kicking like a frog and dog-paddling with his hands, he headed at a painfully slow speed toward the hippos.

As he approached the hippos, I breathed a sigh of relief that he had most probably passed the point at which the big crocodile from our side of the river was likely to make a move. I was just beginning to worry about what would happen in a few more strokes when he reached the two cows he had to swim between, when a huge crocodile surfaced between Dumani and the hippos. The tip of its tail nearly touched the closest hippo and its snout was just a few arm lengths away from Dumani. I knew it was attacking because the whole length of its body was exposed. I aimed at the crocodile but couldn't shoot. The top of Dumani's frizzy black head was in my sights. I screamed out, "Duck!" and began squeezing the trigger. If I had to wait for Dumani to respond and then aim and shoot, it would be too late.

As the gunshot exploded in my ear, the rifle butt kicked painfully into my collarbone. When I looked down the barrel of the rifle again, I couldn't see Dumani or any of the hippos, only the crocodile thrashing about furiously. The water around it was churning into a red froth.

"Dumani," I called out in panic. "Dumani, you okay?"

I held my breath until the crocodile's flailing subsided. Finally it rolled onto its back and lay lifelessly in the channel with an ever-expanding pool of blood forming around its head. Something broke the surface with a massive gasp between the dead crocodile and the far bank. My spirits soared to see Dumani frantically splashing his way to shore. I ejected the spent cartridge and loaded a fresh bullet into the firing chamber of the rifle and held it up again, ready for any further sign of trouble.

As soon as he could stand, Dumani began pushing his way through chest-deep water. My whole body tensed with squeamish apprehension as he reached the water lily pads. He was just starting to fight his way through the tangle of submerged lily stems when he collapsed with a frightening scream. He stood upright again, crying out in pain, and lunged toward the shore with an even greater desperation. He had not gone far before he went down again with another terrible cry.

"What is it, Dumani?" I yelled, aiming my rifle while knowing full well that it was a pointless gesture.

Dumani managed to push on in spite of the sustained underwater attack. He limped onto the far bank with blood running from his legs and hips.

"Eish! Eish!" he howled, stamping the earth in agony. A string of Lapedi expletives issued from his contorted mouth. I only caught "mother – devil – snake – potatoes." Once the pain of his injuries had settled down, he stood tall and waved over to me. He made an incongruous sight: a flabby black man covered in blood with a bright red bulb hanging off the end of his penis. "Eels," he called, "bloomin' things!"

He went back into the water up to his ankles and rinsed the blood off his body. After he had cleaned himself to his satisfaction, he contemplated the dead crocodile for a moment. "You see that," he shouted, pointing at the inert monster. "If we'd both tried to swim, he would have catched one of us. Then maybe the others come and get the other one who is still swimming. Ngomani and Sibongila gave us very wise guidance."

Dumani splashed his legs and hips a few more times and then walked cautiously toward the forest. He took a few steps and then peered in one direction intently, took a few more, and stopped again to listen to the jungle, not unlike a nervous bushbuck crossing open ground. Ngomani made a strained trumpeting noise. There was no sign of him other than some treetops quivering in the jungle canopy. Dumani must have taken the elephant's call as an all-clear signal because he immediately relaxed his posture and strode unstintingly into the bush.

For my part, I stood on my side of the river replaying Dumani's audacious crossing over and over again in my mind, shuddering at the thought of how I could have so easily shot Dumani instead of the crocodile, or what might have happened if it had attacked him underwater. I thought back to my magic training and how I had never seen a fiercer demonstration of someone believing in the infallibility of their natural ability. Our hearts, I reflected with dreadful awe, would never ask us to do something that we could not survive. The memory of riding my bicycle over a forty-foot cliff came back to me as if it were yesterday. I was clear, though, that compared with the chilling risk of swimming across a moat full of crocodiles and hippos, it was a lame feat by comparison. Talk about facing your dragons!

After what felt like an eternity, but was actually only about ten minutes, a path of swaying treetops moving in my direction indicated that Ngomani was marching back to the water. As I anticipated, Dumani came out of the jungle after the elephant. He was carrying a grotesque bundle on his shoulders. He dumped it unceremoniously at the water's edge.

"Yah, it's Sibongila," he puffed.

At first I thought it was a man's body with some kind of furry coat bundled over the head and shoulders. A second look revealed that it was in fact a creature with the lower half of a human being and the top half of a baboon. Though I gagged in revulsion at the sight of the creature, I was nevertheless gripped by a morbid fascination.

"I was too late to save him," said Dumani mournfully.

"What happened?" I said. "Why's he like that?"

"Snake bite."

"A snake bite?"

"A snake bite that is not from a snake," Dumani spoke with strong feeling. "That is what I tell you – there are spies everywhere. But this one, whoa, he is very bad, like an archenemy. He can come as any snake. You see, it's the middle of winter now, no snakes around – but this is the bite of a big cobra."

"Why is Sibongila half-half?" I said, hoping not to offend with my ghoulish curiosity.

"He was trying to turn back into a man so he can breathe better," said Dumani matter-of-factly. "If you can keep someone breathing with a cobra bite, then they have a chance. But he got stuck. When I reached him, he was finished."

"What will you do with him?"

"I'm going to ask Ngomani to carry us across the river. We must take him back to the village."

"Fantastic," I shouted across the water, "now Maxine won't be able to deny the magic I've been telling her about." I immediately felt guilty for my misplaced triumphalism.

"You mean Dr. Carlyle?" Dumani shouted back. "Oh, she will be very happy now that the Snake is here. This is certainly the trouble she has been waiting for."

"How did you know she's waiting for trouble?" I asked, at the same time intrigued and feeling abashed for being in collusion with Maxine.

"I don't know how," Dumani replied as he looked about distractedly. "When you live your life guided by intuition, you know what you need to know."

CHAPTER EIGHT

Visions of Truth

There is no experience so incredible that it can keep one uplifted forever. By the time we got back to Mlumu Village, the sublime wonder of my experience of innocence and the delirious amazement of encountering someone who could actually change between human and animal state – a real-life were-creature – were transmuted to hopelessness. Perhaps my energy levels had been depleted by the magic dust experience of the night before and the adrenalin my system had expended that morning. Whatever the underlying cause of my mood swing, to me it felt as if I were simply waking up from a trance and coming back to reality.

Sibongila's corpse kept falling off Ngomani's back and every time Dumani and I had to hoist the grotesque carcass over the dumb giant's neck, the more limp and pathetic it appeared to me. It was also an abject reminder that it wouldn't be long before my loved ones back at the Irrigation Scheme had the life snuffed out of them and were left to rot in dehumanized piles of flesh. More heartrending than that, even, was the thought that I very likely would suffer the same fate, and that my children would live on without their father to share their precious lives with them and be there to guide and protect them.

I would have abandoned my mission in the Meluti at the drop of a hat had it not meant plunging on through the jungle asylum on my own. My best hope, bleak as it was, was to play along with the unfolding drama I had gotten myself mixed up in. Though I might have been a tad more optimistic if we were up against natural forces. As it was, we were dealing with were-snakes and who knew what else. I was not happy.

On the way into the village, we found two didakta boys tied to a tree. They looked like mutilated waxwork dummies. The bamboo poles that they had been thrashed with lay in smashed-up pieces around them. The cream-colored ochre had been knocked off every inch of their bodies, which were covered in gruesome cuts and welts. Their heads lolled unconsciously to the side. My heart sank even further.

"So, they have already caught some weak ones," Dumani spat disparagingly. "These are the ones who don't trust their own instincts to survive, who think they must prey on the village like vultures."

I had nothing good to say about the Lapedi and their barbaric customs, or Dumani's complicity in them, so I kept quiet. My suppressed judgments quickly festered into a smoldering distaste of everything around me: Dumani, the Mlumu villagers, their witchcraft and especially the Meluti itself.

On the outskirts of the village we were met by an agitated welcoming committee consisting of Chollo, David and a handful of Lapedi warriors armed with submachine guns. "Hauw!" the leader of the deputation exclaimed. "Is that Sibongila?" He pointed his gun at Ngomani's back.

"It is Sibongila," Dumani replied gravely.

"Hah!" the group gasped as one.

Remembering his manners, the leader held his gun up to salute us. "We see you, Dumani. We see you, son of Vale."

"Aye," Dumani responded, "we see you Mumuletu; we see you, men."

"We heard a shot," said Mumuletu, looking at me suspiciously. "Was our brother hit?"

"No," said Dumani, "he was bitten by a snake that was no snake." He pushed the were-creature from Ngomani's back callously. The villagers crowded forward to inspect the crumpled body. Chollo and David stayed where they were.

Chollo stared stoically ahead without meeting my eyes. David looked beside himself with anguish. I had a chilling suspicion that their discomfort didn't have anything to do with Sibongila's demise.

Mumuletu straightened up. "We must go at once to Veeti's boma," he said. "The Portuguese Snake was here, too."

"Here?" Dumani exclaimed.

"Yes, in our village," said Mumuletu. He dropped his head and mumbled, "He took the lady doctor with him."

"What?" I cried, feeling my simmering displeasure turn to rage. "Chollo, David, how could you let Dr. Carlyle be taken? Why didn't you protect her?"

"Be quiet, Mr. Vale," said Dumani evenly in English, "this is no time to let our feelings get the better of us. This is a time for cool heads. You have no idea of the danger we are all in."

"Go to hell, Dumani," I said as scornfully as I could. "I'm responsible for Dr. Carlyle. I'm not going to let anything happen to her."

The villagers stared at me dispassionately. I immediately regretted my intemperate outburst. I became awkwardly self-conscious of my heightened breathing, flushed face and bulging eyes. I imagined how ridiculous my agitated demeanor must have appeared to the natives.

Dumani was unruffled by my outcry. He studied my face intently. "You think you're losing your love just when you found her again, isn't it?" he said. "She's all you've got in the world, that's how you feel?" I couldn't meet his eyes. I was dumbfounded that he could interpret my emotions before I could even work them out for myself.

"We must go to Veeti's," said Mumuletu forcefully. "The council is gathering there." He pointed to a pair of warriors. "You two, get some sugar cane sticks and entice the elephant back into the forest. Watch your backs." To another pair he said, "Give us your guns; you carry our brother. It will be better if we bring Sibongila to the council with us. His spirit might be able to give us guidance."

As our group hastened to Veeti's compound, David sidled up to me. "Excuse me, sir," he tugged on my shirt-sleeve timidly.

"What is it, David?" I snapped.

"Dr. Carlyle, she went with those people because they say they have a sick person with them – someone who is dying. She went to treat this person."

"Did they say where they were going?"

"No, sir."

I regarded him closely to see what I could read from his face. Whereas the last few times I had seen him I had perceived an ingratiating, if self-conscious, slyness in David's demeanor, now I saw only a guileless despair. It was plain to see that he was nothing other than a loyal servant gravely concerned for his mistress. My annoyance at Duma-ni intensified. I wondered what game he was playing by telling me that there was a traitor in my party.

Neither the scene nor the atmosphere in Veeti's compound conformed to my expectation of a tribal council meeting. There was no circle of sagacious elders gathered in earnest deliberation, only a motley crew of villagers spread out around the boma with no apparent reason for being there other than they happened to be in the neighborhood. Veeti and his wife sat on the edge of the raised pergola floor with their feet on the ground. They appeared as forlorn as ever. Sitting beside them were three children playing a game of slapping at each other's palms. They giggled quietly behind their hands and chided each other in hushed voices for not playing fair. From the headband of bandaging hold-ing a wad of gauze to the side of her head, I recognized the girl in the middle as Yapile, the daughter we had operated on the morning before. Other than a slightly listless demeanor, she seemed to be doing surprisingly well. A line of women of varying ages sat squashed together on the other side of the pergola with their backs to the headman and his wife. An old crone among them interrupted their heated gossiping to scold the girls for their impropriety. A couple of boys sat on their haunches listening to the idle talk of the men, who all stood on one leg, leaning against the walls of the closest huts. A bag of tobacco with a boxer's silhouette on it was passed among the warriors, who took pleasure in studiously rolling cigarettes in strips of brown paper. Taking in the disparate, ineffectual-looking collection of villagers, I was not inspired with any confidence that this was a gathering of the wisest minds to be counted on in formulating an action plan to deal with the latest turn of events.

The gathering was momentarily excited by my appearance, though their attention was quickly diverted. A collective gasp of astonishment rose in the air when Sibongila's body was carried in behind me and laid out on the dirt between Veeti and the men leaning against the huts. I expected everyone to rush in for a closer look but they all stayed right where they were, frozen in shock. Everyone seemed to be waiting for someone to make sense of the situation before they blinked again.

"Yes, people," Dumani stood beside the corpse, "as you can see, it is your brother, Sibongila. He was killed by a snake who is not a snake. This white man found him with his mind's eye." Another gasp of surprise issued from the small crowd. "This is how we found him. As you see, we were too late."

"It must be the same snake who was here," said Veeti, transfixed by the were-creature. "The doctor went with him, apparently to save someone's life. We know that the Portuguese Snake only takes lives, so something strange is going on. All these years he has not made any trouble for us. Now he comes here, kills our top scout and lures away someone under our protection by false pretenses."

"Veeti," I said, "I feel bad for the trouble my party and I have brought to your village. It is up to me to clean up this mess. Dr. Carlyle is my responsibility. She was under my protection. Wherever they have gone, Chollo and I can track them down. I will deal with this snake." I patted my rifle.

My proposal was met with murmurs of disapproval and, in some cases, outright derision. Dumani took a step away from me, as if to disown me. When someone spoke to me, it was a boy of around twelve years old wearing nothing but a rabbit-skin flap over his crotch and a rabbit-fur armband. "You cannot track the Snake," he said from where he squatted.

"Why not?" I snapped.

"Because he took your boat," the boy replied.

"What?" I stared murderously at Chollo and David. "Why did you let them take the boat?" David gulped nervously. Chollo stared sullenly ahead of himself.

"You should not question servants over their masters' decisions," the boy piped up.

"Who the hell is this kid?" I said to Dumani in English.

"A member of the council," Dumani replied.

"But he's only a boy," I said. "What does he know? What's he doing at council?"

Dumani took me by the elbow and turned me to face away from the gathering. Behind me I could hear an agitated buzz of conversation break out.

"Have you learned nothing today?" Dumani demanded in a hoarse whisper.

"What?" I said dumbly.

"After all I teach you this morning," the bespectacled philosopher hissed, "you start acting like this now. You must not let the swing of the pendulum affect you. This is not a good time to come back to your senses."

"The swing of the pendulum?" I frowned.

"The law of rhythm," said Dumani in an easier voice. "The swing of the pendulum to the right is equal to the swing of the pendulum to the left. So say the ancient masters of reality. Whatever vibration you are on, you will feel the pull of the opposite pole. When you experience enlightenment, you will sooner or later be overcome by darkness. When you have a run of good luck, it will inevitably be followed by a run of bad luck. It is how things go. And when you experience innocence, you will at some point be challenged by your perception. Like you now, you have an experience outside of all the separation you ever held on to. You become free from doubt and fear. You are with everything as one, and that oneness informs you beyond what you can usually know. You experience your super-conscious power. You laugh to yourself, 'This is really who I am – a god.' Meanwhile, your ego is not pleased. It is very concerned that you are going to lose your individual notion of existence. All the separation it spent your whole life constructing, it sees that falling apart. So it wants to remind you of who you are. Then your identity starts impressing on you through thoughts and feelings. You become sad because you believe you are separate from the one you think you love. Then you become angry because your sadness pushes up your belief that you are powerless to have all the things you wish for in your heart. Finally, you resent everything around you because the world doesn't conform to your expectations.

"It goes like that for you. The Snake has got your friend – your mission is failing – so you want to do something quickly to take away the pain of your old definition and meaning. You look at the people who are supposed to help you – some simple men and women wearing Java-print and skins, and some naked children – and you think, 'Where are the serious people, the qualified authorities?' You just compare to what you know from before, your old catalogue.

"Your ego likes to pull you down into the rhythm of the pendulum, and you like it, too. You might feel lost or frightened or angry or despairing, but this way everything has a name, you know how it is. But if you want to be a grown-up, an initiated adult, you must rise up and let the pendulum swing underneath you. Don't believe the reality of the lower plane. Use your will to go back to not having to know how it is. Stand in the vibration of innocence. See how things are in the objective world and choose your response from there."

Dumani looked over his shoulder at the chattering swamp dwellers and then back at me. "You see that old woman sitting there, nearly blind with the cataracts, with the beehive hair?" he said. "She can call lions. If she goes out into the jungle now and she starts singing, the lions will come to her. All the prides in the area, they will swim across the rivers and come to her!

"What about that man with the stump, with no arm? You know how he lost his arm? A black mamba bit him on the thumb when he was making a mokoro. He knew he had a couple of minutes before the poison travelled up to his heart and killed him, so he laid his arm over the log he was digging out and told his best friend to chop it off.

"I can tell you something about each person that will make your head spin in amazement. You think you know some people who are better than them? Some people with designer watches and good clothes and looking like lawyers who can talk in a serious voice?"

I could feel myself deflating like a badly punctured tire. As the hot air left me, I became acutely aware of my anxiety over Maxine's disappearance. I regretted letting my arrogance get the better of me. When I stole a glance back at the villagers, I saw no sign of the strengths Dumani eluded to, only a fatalistic bewilderment. They looked more like a bunch of refugees awaiting forced repatriation to some killing field.

A fresh anger began welling up in me. This time it was directed at Maxine for her blithe disregard for the wider consequences of her actions. Dragging me into this mess was one thing, I thought, but involving a whole village of innocent tribespeople was depraved. A voice in my head told me that I should not even be surprised if Maxine was by now romantically smitten by her treacherous abductor. My heart seethed with dark emotions.

"So how do you stay above the pendulum?" I said sullenly.

"You must not think you know," he said. "Your thoughts and feelings convince you that you know. You feel like if you ignore them, you will lose a good friend. It's hard to tear yourself away from them. But you must; your thoughts and feelings are only telling you what you assume has happened or is happening or is going to happen. They are not the voice of the one who knows. The one who knows is that child inside you – the child in innocence. When it's time to raise your vibration, you can find that child and become him again. That is the most powerful vibration you can be on. It is the one that is above the pendulum. All the others are inside the rhythm of the pendulum."

I was distracted by a commotion outside Veeti's compound. Anguished wailing announced a procession of mourners heading our way. Shortly, a striking young woman wearing only a scarlet sarong tied around her waist and carrying a baby on her hip burst into the boma with an entourage of matrons in tow. Her hair was not short or platted in the normal tribal styles but sprouted out in a wild fuzz. Her eyes were as red and crazy as a tormented animal's.

"Where is my man?" she screamed. "Where is the father of this child?" She bounced the baby on her hip a couple of times absently.

Dumani pulled me out of the woman's way.

"Eish, there he is," she shrieked. "There is your father, little one. Are there no ancestors left in heaven? What cruelty have the gods visited on us today? Is this how I must tell him that there is another one in my belly?" She tilted her head back and let out a loud despairing moan. Out in the forest, some baboons began coughing in alarm. One of the matrons rushed up beside Sibongila's woman and pried the baby gently away from her. Two of the other matrons then took her by the arms and began pulling her toward her husband's corpse. She held back with the ferocity of a wild panther being goaded into a cage. Her head shook violently from side to side as she cried out, "Xa! Xa! Xa! – No! No! No!"

The female elders brought Sibongila's widow beside her dead husband and let go of her. She fell in a heap on top of his bloated body, pressing a long and loud fart out of the carcass. I couldn't bear to watch her sobbing uncontrollably into the were-creature's furry chest while its baboon head stared vacantly into space, its tongue lolling lifelessly from its mouth. I averted my eyes, sick with sorrow for the poor woman's loss. For her to lose her mate and be left a widow in this harsh environment was bad enough, I imagined, but who could fathom how terrible it was for her to see him in this disgusting and freakish form? But greater than my sympathy for the bereaved woman, even, was my guilt that Maxine's and my own selfish agendas were responsible for her pitiful fate and whatever other ills were about to befall Mlumu Village.

My eagerness to escape my own dreadful pain made me willing enough to follow Dumani's advice. I closed my eyes and took a few deep breaths, hoping to wipe my mental and emotional slate clean. Nothing happened other than my anguish closing in on me more than ever. I searched desperately for an image of the inner child I had imagined before on the banks of the hippo pool. A vague picture occurred to me. I did my best to imagine myself embodying that picture of innocence. As soon as I did, I felt a shift within me. My heavy emotions were still with me, but I immediately experienced them as separate from myself.

I opened my eyes, willing myself to see through the eyes of my child in innocence. The same sad scene played out before me. Sibongila's widow sobbed hysterically, her body convulsing in great spasms. All of the women came over to her and began rolling in the dirt beside her, wailing and moaning for all they were worth and hitting and kicking the dirt in petulant fits. The difference in me, though, was that I could tolerate this massive outpouring of grief without having to resolve it in any way. I could just be with it. From the perspective of my inner child, the whole scene, including my reactions to it, was a spectacular passion play that didn't need to be controlled by me.

As I watched the drama from my newfound detachment, a second layer of reality revealed itself to me. I saw that Sibongila's woman was not a wretched victim after all, but that by embracing her experience of loss so utterly and completely she was in fact transcending her circumstance. In that moment she was not cut off and lost. Instead, she was herself exposed to her own second layer of reality, in which she was with the spirit of her husband and all the ancestors who were welcoming him to eternity – and not just the spirit of her husband and ancestors, but all the spirits and devas of the animal and forest kingdoms. She was the opposite of alone; she was fully immersed in her inherent connection to everything through all time and space.

Sibongila's wife was in a full embrace with the Divine. The women rolling in the dirt beside her were not colluding in her misery; they were encouraging her ecstasy, partaking in it, even. And the onlookers were not standing by uncaringly, as I had originally assumed; they were standing by in silent tribute to the rite being performed before them, fully conscious of its significance and the energies at play. Never was there a man who had a finer, more fitting send-off than this.

With a smile in my heart, I leaned into Dumani and whispered in his ear, "This innocence business has got something going for it, Doctor."

Dumani's face remained deadpan. Only his eyes showed any cheer. "Like Jesus said, only as a child can you enter the kingdom of heaven." He spoke out of the corner of his mouth. "Very powerful principle, this one. Feels silly and childish, but more powerful than any other force man knows about."

The cathartic dirge rose to a crescendo. Someone began blowing on a tin whistle. Everyone in the crowd who wasn't writhing on the floor ululated and drummed their hands on whatever they could find to make the most noise on. The baboons in the forest joined in, barking so loudly that the atmosphere for miles around resonated with their fearsome calls. Finally, everyone, including the animals outside, ran out of steam. One by one the women began picking themselves off the ground until only the widow was left there, lying across her late husband like a limp rag. She did not resist when some of the villagers pulled her to her feet. When she was standing steadily again, she straightened her sarong and patted the dirt off of her body. Taking her baby back on her hip, she held her head high and with dry eyes spoke out in a strong voice: "My heart sings for my husband as his baboon spirit flies home to be with the ancestors. How fortunate we are that with his passing we could look into the Land of Dreams, where our souls are one with the Soul of the World."

Her words sent a shiver up my back, for they confirmed to me what I had sensed was the villagers' collective experience. A glow of sheer delight lit up inside me to feel my own heart connected to the mystical world she spoke of. The tribespeople came forward in single file to offer the woman their condolences and congratulate her on her splendid performance. She stood up proudly, to receive everyone's respects as a queen receiving tributes.

The last native to pay his respects was Dumani. As he walked up to her, he pulled the red feather from his head and, standing before her, placed it affectionately in her baby's hair. The gesture pleased the villagers greatly. A chorus of laughter and applause broke out around the compound. I couldn't hear what Dumani said; whatever it was, it left a beatific glow on the woman's face.

After Dumani backed away from her, there was an uncomfortable silence. I realized all eyes were on me. Sibongila's widow, whose name I had not caught, commanded me with her expectant stare to come forward. I shuffled forward self-consciously, scrambling to think of something fitting to say. The elation I had been feeling was swamped by the same sense of not belonging I had suffered the night before in the presence of the leopard woman. I could feel myself shrink in the face of the woman's majestic presence.

When I tried to say something, no words came out. I tried to swallow but my mouth was dry. The anticipation of the crowd did nothing to relax me. All I could think to do was to retreat into my inner child. Immediately I was with the words I wanted to say, and though I felt foolish for saying them, I spoke them anyway.

"My heart is heavy for your loss, lady," I lifted my head to look her in the eye. "I did not know your man, but I do know he was a true human being. I am thankful to him because I feel he died serving not just his village but me, too. Also, I am indebted to you because before today I have never looked into the Land of Dreams. Being with your suffering helped me see."

"Oh, oh, oh." The woman brought her free hand to her heart. Her face was composed in an expression of bliss; her parted lips quivered with feeling. "You honor us, white man. Yesterday you came here to pass by our world; now today you are a part of our world. We see you, sir. You are one of us. As for my pain, it is not suffering. Pain is what holds us in the world of waking. Suffering is what happens when we do not understand the purpose of our pain. My man, who is now late, he is the one to me who taught that all things are one; everything lives in here." She beat her chest. "Because of him, I have wings – I can fly."

"Aye, *impela*!" the crowd chanted their approval. "Aye, that's the truth!"

When he was certain the woman was complete, Veeti came forward sluggishly. "Thank you, sister," he said, "we must get on with the *indaba* now – the council. Will you stay?"

"Eh-heh," she nodded, "if someone can bring me a gourd of water. My crying has parched my throat."

Her attendants helped her to a seat on the pergola while one of the naked little girls ran to fetch some water from one of the huts.

"My people," the headman looked around the boma, nodding to each clique of villagers, "there are bad portents in the air. First, the sound of the thunder in yonder Lesoti ranges, more ferocious than we have ever heard. Then yesterday, the white couple came. It's true that I called them to save little Yapile's life, but they came for reasons of their own, and I doubt that it was for a social visit. Now Dominue, the mulatto from Portuguese Territory, arrives today and takes the female doctor. At the same time, Sibongila is attacked by a snake in the middle of winter."

Veeti held up his hands as a rumble of heated opinion swept the courtyard. I shifted on my feet uncomfortably as several of the villagers looked balefully in my direction. "Slow down, people," the headman urged, "this is not the way of the indaba. Bickering will not serve us in a matter as serious as this. We must look deeper than our own opinions and let the whole truth speak to us. Everyone will get a turn to speak and it is not our place to agree or disagree, only to listen. When everyone has spoken and the dust settles, the truth will be obvious; we do not have to trouble our minds or each other's. And don't forget to use the common Lapedi...for our visitor's sake."

Dumani leaned into me and whispered, "In the indaba, the skill of listening is not in trying to remember everything that is said and working out whether it makes sense to you or not. The skill is in just listening – and watching – and noticing what jumps out. Observe the obvious and, when it comes time to talk, state the obvious."

One of the men raised his hand. "Will you begin, Skonkwana?" said Veeti.

"Eh," the man volunteered. He rubbed his chin thoughtfully to give the impression of a considered contribution. "Veeti, you will recall that time when you decided against me in the matter of settling my daughter's dowry..."

Before the man said another word it was apparent that he was not addressing the indaba's agenda but airing a long-standing gripe. I had already lost patience with him. "What's this got to do with anything?" I hissed into Dumani's ear. "All he's doing is attacking Veeti about some ancient history. Why doesn't someone put him straight?"

"Just be patient," Dumani whispered back. "The magic of the indaba works because no one is controlling anyone else. This is what encourages the whole truth to surface from the deep. Veeti has set the intention of the indaba; now everyone must trust that the power will be in that intention, not in the egos sitting in the indaba."

"...and meanwhile those cattle were eaten by hyenas, anyway," the man called Skonkwana was saying. "Maybe they paid a sangoma to put a spell on you to make you not think clearly. Now things are not right in the village since then. Your judgment has been clouded. It is these people we must deal with."

Though I knew nothing about the village and its politics, the man's word rang hollow; it was obvious that he was taking a cheap shot at the headman. Nevertheless, when it was evident that Skonkwana was complete, the indaba responded with a vigorous, "Aye, impela – Aye, that's the truth!" Even Veeti acknowledged him graciously: "Thank you for your truth, venerable one."

The next person to speak their mind brought the conversation on track immediately. It was the man with one arm. "Dominue and this village have co-existed like a water python and a crocodile," he said. "Neither wants to upset the other when there is no value in a power struggle. Let's face it, the man's nefarious activities and his supernatural powers help deter outsiders from stepping foot in the Meluti. The question is, what makes it worthwhile for the Portuguese Snake to make a mortal enemy of Mlumu Village and the south side of the swamps?"

"Aye, impela!" the gathering responded.

"Your words are a thread of gold for our tapestry of wisdom, my brother," a high-pitched voice rang out. It was Veeti's wife. "The mulatto is one of the pieces of the puzzle my husband spoke of. The war between Chitswa and Lapedi is another piece, and the white couple, too. But one piece of the puzzle my husband did not mention is someone else who is not strictly to do with us. Sorry, Dumani, you too are another piece of the puzzle. Your presence here must be thrown in the pot with all other facts. For many years you have sheltered here from your brother's wrath. This will have something to do with you, I'm sure."

"Aye, impela!" went up the cry.

I followed the conversation just as Dumani had instructed me. I resisted protesting the bits I disagreed with or trying to make sense of what I could not follow; I didn't attempt to hold all of the information in my head and I continually let go of the conclusions I expected the indaba to reach. I focused only on what jumped out at me.

It was as Veeti's wife had put it. The indaba was weaving a tapestry of truth. Everything everyone said amplified what had been said before and brought to light the next thread of insight. I was amazed at the incredibly accurate information that was formulated in this way. Some of the information was common knowledge, like Dumani's fraught relationship with his brother, but much of it could not have been facts the villagers had prior knowledge of.

When the old lady with the cataracts got a chance to speak, she said, "The white people are not the cause of this trouble, but they have their beaks in the honey. Now the bees are angry. That female doctor, she is trouble. The ancestors tell me that she is looking for a man who will save her. She has been looking for this man for all of her life. But always she takes the man deeper and deeper into trouble to test if he is strong enough. Very dangerous, this woman. Her games are none of our business."

"Aye, that is the truth, mother," Sibongila's wife called out rapturously. "The white people are not the cause of this trouble. The spirit of my late husband shows me that they are lost – the doctor searching for an end to her pain and the man with her following her because he is lost. I see some children that he is looking for that he believes he will find when they find the man she is looking for."

In the ensuing silence a man coughed, indicating his intention to speak. It was Mumuletu. "Thank you for your truth, sister. I hear your words like an eagle's cry." He raised his automatic rifle in her direction. "We see clearly who everyone is, but no one has spoken what the trouble is about. Dumani is like a brother to us. For many years he has served Veeti as his wizard counselor. That is why it pains us to be forthright and say this trouble is about him. The foreign elements in the Meluti today are here because they want something from Dumani. There are forces at play here that are bigger than these white people and that Portuguese Snake. The outside world has brought its problems on our soil. I say that the problems must go back to where they came from!"

"Vela, vela, vela," cried Dumani as he spun around to acknowledge everyone in the boma. "True, true, true. Every word is true. With the great war between the Chitswa and Lapedi finally reaching its denouement, it is logical that those who threaten the surviving order will be eliminated. But it is not my brother who is after me. He was angry with me for making a fool of him, true, and it's also true that he had many years to kill me. He knows that I am not a threat to him. I have no interest in the material world he rules. No, something else is coming for me and it is not right that I involve you good people in my trouble. I will never leave the Meluti to hide abroad, as the white lady expects me to, so I must take my chance deeper in the swamps."

"No!" I shouted, immediately regretting my outburst. I could see the look of horror on everyone's faces. Their mouths were frozen wide with the unuttered "Aye, impela" stuck in their throats. I had just committed the greatest social faux pas in Lapedi custom – I had disagreed with someone in the indaba. There was a time, I'd heard, when that was a killing offense. I wasn't confident that the people of the Meluti had moved on from those times.

"No," I shouted quickly, "you must not leave the swamps to hide abroad."

A groan of relief went around the boma like a Mexican wave. "Aye, impela!" the belated chant went up.

"Will you speak, Vale?" Veeti arched his eyebrows at me lethargically.

"If you would like me to speak," I said. In truth, I was bursting to have my say. The indaba was like a well that filled up with every word that was spoken. It was as if that well were in me and, not only was it resonating with what everyone had said, it was charged with a multitude of insights that had occurred to me. Never in my life had I been so clear about what I had to say – or so sure of its veracity. I was wide eyed with exhilaration.

"You are right about everything," I began. "You are guided by your ancestors and the spirits of this place. They are right about Dr. Carlyle and myself. I agree that we are not your problem. The doctor is under my protection, and it is my responsibility alone to save her or not.

"There is more to this business, though. I come from outside the Meluti and I am guided by what I know of the world outside." Even as I spoke, new realizations dawned on me. I talked as fast as I could to keep up with my insights. "Firstly, let me tell you that this might be more your business than you realize. The Meluti will not be left alone forever. I have looked in wonder on the magnificence of many forests, seemingly vast and endless, only to see them ripped away so that there was only bare earth and some shredded roots sticking out of the ground. And each time I asked myself in despair, 'What happened to the soul of that mighty forest? Where has its power gone?'

"There are forces that can strip away your world in a heartbeat, if they decide. Yesterday I thought that the way I presumed the world was, was the only way it is. Out here in the Meluti I have learned that there are other ways. If you think that your world can only ever be the way it is now, you must think again. Like they did for me, things can change for you between one sunset and another.

"The world outside is like a cannibal feeding on itself. There is not much left to eat. There are resources here that the world is hungry for. Whoever wins this war will have nothing but massive debts. They will be under pressure to give permission to the ones they owe the money to, for them to dig up the earth and chop down the trees. Unless someone cares, the soul of this world will be hung out like drying meat."

I paused to take in the reaction of my audience, fearing they might not like what I had to say. To my surprise, they were following me with rapt attention. Many of them nodded their encouragement for me to go on.

"As someone who lives abroad," I continued, "the way I see it is that the Republic is just like a human being with a body and a mind, and the Meluti is the soul of this being. How can the soul say to its body, 'I will have nothing to do with you?' If the body becomes soulless, then where will the soul reside?

"Veeti, I see you, and I see that you are suffering a sadness of your own soul. You are weary of only keeping the world away and having nothing to give it. You may serve Mlumu well but you know Mlumu only serves itself." My words began to lose their resonance so I adjusted my tack. "What I mean is, yes, you guard these wetlands fiercely, but cutting them off from the world does not serve the world – or protect the wetlands either."

I turned to my bespectacled mentor. "Dumani, today you swam through crocodiles to save a friend. There is no one braver on the face of the earth than you. Yet for all of your courage and your wisdom and your power, you are afraid of one thing. You fear that the magic you love cannot stand up to the forces of ignorance. You feel that your traditional medicine was not enough, that you were sent away overseas to acquire a substitute.

"It was you to me who taught that everything must have balance. You and the Meluti can survive, but only as the balance to the body and mind of the Republic. You and your friends guard your ways so fiercely out here; maybe you should be as fierce in championing them in the rest of the country."

"Hauw, hauw, hauw," the blind lady cackled gleefully, "this white man is only white on the outside. He reminds me of his father's father. When that great hunter visited us he spoke like this, as if the spirits were talking through him. Praise the ancestors for bringing his grandson to us."

"You have spoken well, Lord Vale," said Veeti. When I glanced his way I did a double take. The gray pallor of his skin had transmuted to a vibrant blue-black. His eyes sparkled with passion. "Praise the magic of the indaba."

"Praise the indaba," the villagers echoed.

"How I thought the world was has been changed, too," Veeti spoke again. "Not over the course of yesterday and today like for Vale here, but now in this instant. The words of this indaba have woken me from a bad dream in which I was running from something I could never get away from.

"I see something now about this business that I did not

see before. It is a big distraction. When the hyenas want to take a buffalo calf, some of them make a big noise to one side of the herd. Then, when the adult buffalos rush to that side, the rest of the clan come in and catch the calf from behind. We are like those buffalo now, and the Portuguese Snake is like a hyena yapping on our flank."

He looked around the boma. When his eyes found the person he was looking for, he called out, as if to someone far away: "Jugolass, do you have your bones with you?"

"Eh," said the young boy in the rabbit-skin loincloth, "they are always with me."

Veeti either did not notice or chose to ignore the boy's surly tone. "Will you throw them for us so we might know what predator is hiding on our blind side?"

The boy picked up a skin pouch and moved to the center of the gathering. Squatting down on his haunches, he began sweeping the earthen floor in front of him with his hands.

"Who is this kid?" I murmured in Dumani's ear.

"He is the ndotsikatsi's apprentice," Dumani smiled triumphantly. "He has been working with her since he was four years old. Don't you see how he moves and behaves like a cat?"

The boy spilled the contents of his bag onto the clean earth. He methodically began scrutinizing and sorting a collection of bones and shells into two separate piles.

Dumani cupped his hand on one side of his mouth so that only I could hear what he said. "Very interesting this. Throwing the bones is the oldest form of divination known to man. 'Divination' – the very word derives from knowing what the gods want mortals to know. Before even when time just began, the Chinese people were looking at the cracks in bones to stimulate subconscious associations. Later they incorporated tortoise shells – to read their patterns. This evolved into the *I Ching*, the most complex divination system known to man. Even dice. You know dice? They originate from throwing the bones. Some shamans used to mark their bones on the sides with symbols and this evolved into the game of dice."

The apprentice sorcerer took his time replacing the one lot of bones and shells back in his bag. He examined each piece again to make sure it did not suit his current purposes. A few were returned to the surviving pile.

"What difference do the individual bones make?" I whispered.

Dumani put his hand to his mouth again. "Maybe nothing. Maybe by choosing the bones carefully he is defining these bones as the ones that will give him a good vision – he is priming his subconscious mind. But wait, there's more."

The boy put the remaining bones to one side with exaggerated reverence and very deliberately began tracing a perfect circle in front of him. When he had completed the circle, he stared into it for a while, then closed his eyes and began a quiet droning chant as he rocked back and forth on his haunches.

"This is what I mean," said Dumani. "You see how he draws a circle to throw the bones in? Circles have been associated with magic for a long, long time. This is because a circle is a blank space, and when you define that space as something, if you step into that space, even imaginatively, you will have an experience of that definition. You know why, yah? Because definition creates reality. So, say a sangoma wants to diagnose a patient's illness, he or she can define a circle as that illness and throw the bones in that circle. When she reads the bones in that circle, she is that illness – it speaks to her like that. Now the boy is preparing the circle to produce a vision concerning our intention. Even as everyone watches his ritual, they are also thinking about the answer to Veeti's question: what is the predator on our blind side?"

I tore my attention off the little witch doctor to watch his audience. They looked on in wide-eyed anticipation. Hand-rolled cigarettes died in their smokers' fingers, women clutched at their hearts and children reached out for an adult to hold on to.

"Can you use the circle without the bones?" I said.

"Sure," said Dumani, "circles are a very powerful medium. The bones prompt the subconscious even further, though.

Very powerful combination."

The boy picked up the bones and shook them in his hands. He looked casually around at his onlookers as he did so, and then threw the bones into the circle. He cocked his head to examine the lie of the bones. He pulled one of the bones out of the circle and cocked his head the other way to survey the circle without the bone he had removed. One by one he pulled each bone from the circle, always pondering the surviving arrangement intently. After considering the last remaining bone, he sighed and nodded his head with satisfaction, as if agreeing with something that had been said.

"What do the bones say to you, son?" a woman in Sibongila's wife's entourage called out impatiently.

The boy picked up the last bone in the circle and held it up to the crowd. "This one is the hyena on our blind side," he said bitterly. "This is the one who sent the Snake." He threw the bone contemptuously back in the circle.

"Well, then," cried someone else, "for heaven's sake, tell us who it is."

"I see a Black Eagle," spat the boy, "who visits his soldiers every night in their dreams. Every morning when the sun rises, the Eagle flies before his army. It is their sign of assured victory. When the soldiers from the other side see the Eagle, their hearts quake and they take off their footwear and run."

"But why does the Eagle send the Snake here to distract us?" Veeti entreated the boy.

"By sunset today his army will have all but won the war for the Republic," he answered the headman. "Tomorrow he will fly before his soldiers one more time and they will take their victory. The cleansing of the Lapedi people from the face of the earth will begin. The Black Eagle does not want to take chances, though. His spies tell him that there are ones come to enlist Dumani and the people of Mlumu to help defeat him with sorcery. Today he distracts us, but after tomorrow he will come to finish us."

A rumble of consternation rippled through the assembly. "What do you mean, people come to enlist Dumani?"

"Do you mean the white people?"

"Why does the Eagle want to come for us? We haven't given him trouble."

I looked at Dumani in panic. "What's he talking about? Black eagles?" The thought of ethnic retribution once again brought vividly to mind what would be in store for my own family when the Rebel army reached the Irrigation Scheme.

"My people," Veeti held up his hands, "we are still in indaba. Please, hold off thinking with your feelings for now."

"You see that? Only twelve years old and he can tell us all that from the bones." Dumani eyed the boy with affection as the little fellow studiously ignored the crowd by blowing dust from his divining bones before replacing them lovingly in their pouch. To the crowd, Dumani called out, "My friends, our astonishment makes us forget our manners. Is not the boy sorcerer's wisdom fantastic?"

"Impela," the crowd muttered absently.

"Aye, impela," said Dumani. "The white people's shaman, the one they call Jesu Christo, he said that only if you are a child can you be in heaven. He, too, knew about the being within. Not all white people are so ignorant about the Dream World." He paused theatrically. I sensed, as everyone else must have, that he was moving to reclaim his authority.

"My white friend here asks me who the Black Eagle is. His name is Colonel Commoro Graca, head of the Chitswa Freedom Fighters. Next to him Selele is an innocent rabbit, just a petty thief whose crimes are the product of dissolute greed; his ambition has led him to commit evil deeds. Graca is in another league altogether; his evil drives his ambition.

"When he was only a child he already grew up under the humiliation of colonial rule, seeing his people treated as a subspecies of humanity. Then the colonials washed their hands of the Republic and the Lapedi took over. Our police and soldiers cracked down on the Chitswa towns and villages, robbing Graca's people of their share of the national redistribution. His father was killed and his mother and sisters were used like whores before his own eyes.

"You can imagine the hatred planted in his mind. It's

true what the white people say, that power eats a man's soul, but not so much as does powerlessness. When people don't have any power, then they have to find it anywhere they can. Without the power even to throw a stone at his oppressors, he was attracted to the secret possibilities of the supernatural. He studied under the most formidable Chitswa sorcerers, who were willing to teach him their magic even though he had not been initiated and had learned nothing about himself yet. Now his wounded self is at the head of an army that exists for the sake of inflicting cruelty on a world that showed him no mercy. The Black Eagle's victory will be the beginning of a nightmare reign of terror for terror's sake."

Dumani's audience shook their heads lamentably at the grim picture his words evoked.

"That's the trouble with a society without didakta," an old crone croaked. "That is why we instill our codes of true humanness so fiercely and reject a world that has long since abandoned the old values."

"But what shall we do, Dumani?" a man said from where he leaned against the wall of a hut. "You are never one to tell us bad news without offering a contingency."

"I do not have the answer right now," Dumani said, "but in my heart I know that to involve the people of the Meluti – even if by trying to sidetrack us – has been the Black Eagle's undoing. If you study the history of evil men, as I have done, in their bid for absolute control they inevitably reach too far and in so doing they leave themselves exposed. Graca's magic might be more formidable than any other in the land, but we have something mightier on our side – our dedication to the highest good of all."

Veeti stood up on the raised pergola floor and looked around the boma. "My people," he spoke up, "it is vexing enough to think of dealing with the Portuguese Snake and his henchmen. But to think of whole legions of their type marauding through the Meluti is too awful to contemplate. If something can be done we must do it, and if anything can tell us what can be done, it is the boy sorcerer's circle. Let us all stand in the circle and see what it tells us."

"The circle knows," Dumani nodded.

The villagers shook their heads in silent agreement and closed their eyes. I wondered how everyone expected to fit in a circle with a diameter of only a couple of feet. When they remained where they were in shut-eyed meditation, I realized they must be mentally projecting themselves into the circle. I, too, closed my eyes and pictured myself stepping into the empty circle in front of the boy sorcerer.

At first it felt as though nothing was different in the circle, but as I continued to imagine standing in the space that had been defined as the source of the village's trouble, the atmosphere around me suddenly became very heavy. I was no longer experiencing a mild, sunny winter's day amid brightly colored rectangle motifs on mud walls set within a shiny green jungle. Instead, I was standing in a bleak waste-land resembling a de-bushed field. The earth was black and toxic; all of the nutrients had been leached out of it. Noxious vapors steamed from gaping holes in the ground. Nowhere in the bleak world that had opened up to me, from one distant horizon to the next, was there any sign of life other than the odd carrion bird combing the wastes for some organic morsel to pick at. A stale, inhospitable wind lifted my hair and parched the skin on my arms and face, warning me telepathically not to look any further in the direction from which it blew. Meanwhile, I could sense some unseen eye seeking me out in service to a dark, malignant force dedicated to extinguishing my existence. It was, I realized by the devastating mood of despair and emptiness accompanying the scenario, a vision of death.

As confronted as I was by the terrible image, I was equally enthralled by the realization that I was experiencing an actual vision of the kind I had only heard of characters in the Bible having. I willed myself further into the pitiless scenario, provoking the ill wind and the psychic eye to a more dreadful intensity. The crows and buzzards zoomed by me now at ferocious speeds, coming ever closer to being aware of my presence. The reality of the world I had stepped into was as compelling as, if not more than, the world I had just stepped out of. I tried to open my eyes, but they would not open. I was mesmerized by the overwhelming feeling of doom, like a rat hypnotized by a snake.

As I pressed on imaginatively into the dreadful landscape, the oppressive feelings suddenly lifted, as if I had made it beyond some protective shield of fear. Now the landscape was black and barren as ever, but without any accompanying emotional charge. I was standing in the objective world of a black-and-white movie without sound, informed only by the action playing out in front of me. What I saw amazed and uplifted me.

"So, my friends," I heard Dumani saying in a quiet, deferential tone, "are you complete with your visions."

If I was amazed at what I had seen in my vision, I was completely blown away by what the villagers testified to seeing in theirs. What was so uplifting was that we had all been left with a sense of hope, a feeling that something could be done to curb the Black Eagle's vengeful campaign, and, astonishingly, we had all seen exactly the same image.

"I came to a still place," said the first villager to share their vision, "and from that place I saw an egg hatch, and from that egg a Black Eagle flew off to lead his legions of zombies to war. I did not see the armies but I could sense their multitude and their might. Not even the impis of the Zulu king Chaka were so fearsome.

"With the Eagle gone, I looked inside the egg and saw a man lying there asleep. His heart was missing. I looked for it everywhere and I could not find it. At first I thought this man did not have a heart, then I realized that he had one but it was locked away somewhere safe, so that his heart would not stop him from using his magic for the purposes of his wounded nature. It was an ugly vision, worse than my memories of taking my grandfather to the leper colony in Portuguese Territory. Still, my heart is glad because I can see that if this man who leads the Fighters can have his heart back, then the Soul of the World might still be saved from his vindictive clutches."

Every man, woman and child who followed had seen

exactly the same thing and had been led to the same conclusion. As each villager shared his or her vision, the mood became more and more buoyant. Everyone could sense the power of their collective spirit rising to the occasion. Though I shared the glow of our psychic connection, I was the only one who seemed to remain grounded in the practical reality of the situation. Amazed as I was at the cohesive power of a group of people stepping into a commonly defined space, I was still mindful of the vast geographical distance and the regiments of hostile forces separating us from Colonel Commoro Graca. Even if something could somehow be done to restore the hateful warlord to his better nature, we had less than twenty-four hours to do it in. Without the motorboat, it would take us nearly that long to get as far as the Stanley Gorge. Though I was loath to shoot down their high hopes, I felt it was my duty to point out the facts to the villagers.

"I, too, saw the Black Eagle flying across the dawn sky to incite his brainwashed troops," I said when everyone turned to me expectantly, "and I, too, saw the man lying asleep with his heart hidden in a safe place. A voice inside of me also told me that if that heart could be put back in the man's body then his anger at the Soul of the World for his lot in life would be healed. It makes my heart glad to know such healing is possible even for the most injured among us. Yet my own heart sinks when I realize that we are too far from the Eagle to reach him in time. The boy sorcerer himself told us that by tonight it will be all but over, and at dawn tomorrow the Fighters will make their decisive move."

The villagers looked at me and then at each other with blank, uncomprehending faces. "What does he mean?" they muttered.

"What is he talking about?" Veeti turned to Dumani in puzzlement. "Does he know something we don't?"

"No, no, never mind," Dumani reassured the crowd, "he's confused. It is his first vision."

"You don't say?" several voices cried out while others clapped and laughed their appreciation.

"I forgot my first vision a long time ago," the crone with the cataracts mused wistfully. "It was before I lost my maidenhood, and I can't even remember that." The adults laughed uproariously while the children snickered behind their hands. "But this is a vision of great import. He should remember this one as long as he lives. It is no shame to be shocked by what we have witnessed. Not in all my years have I encountered a terror so twisted or determined."

Dumani entertained the crone's high-spirited observations with an indulgent smile. He acknowledged her by clapping his hands at head height. When he turned to me, though, his demeanor turned grave.

"You're still thinking in linear terms," he said to me in English. "This is not a mission that can be accomplished within the parameters of time and space." He turned to the boy sorcerer and spoke in Lapedi. "How can we get Graca's heart back in his body?"

The boy stood up. He regarded the crowd sullenly. While most people naturally tend toward helping others feel at ease, the boy seemed to enjoy creating dis-ease in those around him – not unlike his mentor, I thought. As the villagers began to fidget and avert their eyes uncomfortably, he stepped into the circle he had traced on the ground earlier. He stood trembling with his eyes closed and his arms outstretched. His face contorted as if being sucked back by the acceleration of take-off. Then his arms tipped back and forth as he glided over some imaginary terrain.

The villagers stared at him once more in wide-eyed suspense. In the jungle, a lion roared – the first one I had heard since arriving in the Meluti – but no one paid it any mind. Flies buzzed in and out of open mouths without their owners even noticing.

Eventually the boy's face relaxed and his arms fell to his sides. He opened his eyes and blinked, seemingly surprised to see the eager faces crowding around him. When he saw me, it was evident that he was having trouble reconciling my presence. The cultivated leer he usually wore had dissolved; his face was as soft and light as a cherub's.

"Someone will have to fly as an eagle to him," the boy sorcerer said, apparently enthralled by what he had to report. "When it is just before dawn and the Black Eagle leaves his nest, that is the time that his heart can be found and put back in its right place."

A cheer broke out in the crowd, the kind a company of soldiers might let off after their leader has given them a rousing pre-battle pep talk. The men folk clapped their fellows on the shoulder and bellowed battle cries in each other's faces. The women looked at each other in silent amazement or laughed happily at anything that was said within earshot of them. I was with the children in looking around trying to comprehend what all the excitement was about.

"You hear that?" Dumani touched me on the shoulder. His face was beaming. "The boy is talking about a soul retrieval ritual. If Graca's soul can be restored to him, he can wake up from his soulless sleepwalking. But we need an eagle who will give himself to fly through the Dreamtime to take back the Colonel his heart. Now we must fan out into the swamps to find a volunteer bird. Everyone is so excited because this particular ritual has not been performed in many years – maybe not in anyone here's lifetime."

"That's great," I said without conviction. While I had delighted in my intuitive connection to the villagers' visionary experiences, I could not comprehend their hocus-pocus plans to rehabilitate the psyche of a megalomaniac warlord. They had lost me – I simply could not relate.

"You don't sound happy," Dumani bumped me encouragingly with his shoulder. "This is good news, man."

"It would be good if they succeeded," I said, unwilling to concede any more optimism than that. Tears began welling up in my eyes. It was a cruel irony that the day I realized my quest for inner knowing was effectively the same day my world would end. If by now my family on the Irrigation Scheme had not already been slaughtered, by tomorrow they most certainly would be. It had already occurred to me that there was no escape from the Meluti, either. The frontier with Portuguese Territory was guarded by forces in cahoots with the Fighters. There was no chance I would see my children again. I would have to wait impotently with my Lapedi hosts for the Chitswa marauders to come and finish us.

"What you say, white man?" Dumani grabbed my arm to stop me from walking away from him. I could not meet his stern expression. "You want to run away now when the fighting starts? Don't you see? This is the apocalypse, my friend. This is the end. By tomorrow, all can be lost. That will be the end of this culture you have met here in the Meluti; that will be the end of you and me; the end of your family and the Irrigation Scheme; the end of the Lapedi people and the Republic. How will it be a good thing if any one of those things perish, let alone all of them?"

"I can't do anything about any of that," I cried. "What I can do is what I must do – find Dr. Carlyle." I could hear the desperation in my own voice. It appeared very real to me that Maxine was no longer an option in my life, but that she was all I had. I was aware that the villagers had stopped their own interactions to watch our exchange. I lowered my voice self-consciously. "Besides, wouldn't stopping Graca only enable Selele more than ever?"

"Come on," Dumani scoffed, "Selele's finished, anyway. He's irrelevant. So is Dr. Carlyle; she's an outside event."

"A what?" I scowled.

"An outside event," Dumani said. "Often, when someone goes for something of high value to their heart, there is a distraction to pull the person from their course. The distraction appears more urgent than the original goal. Commitment is the rudder that steers us in the direction of our highest good, but the ego hates change – it is dedicated to consistency – so it's always finding clever diversions. It takes a true human being to be able to stay on the right path, one who can see through themselves to the truth.

"Don't you remember why you are here?" Dumani challenged me.

"Exactly," I stammered, "to escort Dr. Carlyle through the Meluti, to get her and me out of here."

"You see," Dumani sneered, "right here, you have it." He waved his arm contemptuously. "You are living proof of what I'm talking about. Now I must remind you that you came here to find the last shaman, to take him out of here to preserve his spiritual lineage. You want to save the Republic and your family in the Irrigation Scheme. You want to be reunited with your loved ones abroad. Is going in search of Dr. Carlyle in the direction of this shaman you are looking for? Will it save the Republic? Will it save your family or reunite you with your children?"

Though the villagers could not understand what we were saying, I read their disapproval of me in their eyes. Chollo, as usual, was not looking at me but staring stoically at the boma wall. Only David sided with me, cheering me on with an enthusiastic nod of his head.

"But you told me there wasn't any last shaman," I said, pleased to think I had found a way out of Dumani's intellectual clutches.

"Not of the kind you were looking for," he said. "Not the one out there who can save you. But how do you know that *you* are not the one you are looking for? Above all, you came into the Meluti looking for wisdom. That is inside you. Now you are finding that. No use finding it and then not using it in service of the highest good."

"I can't just leave her in the swamps with that Portuguese Snake, or whatever you call him," I said stubbornly.

Dumani groaned contemptuously. "What, you think you can eat your cake and still have it after? When you go for the higher, you have to let the lower fall away. You can't create by magic if you make conditions about what to lose and not to lose.

"Don't worry," his tone took an encouraging tack, "if you go for the truth, things work out for all concerned. The gods pull everything together when you are connected. But when you try to fix things like your ego wants," he grimaced sadly, "when you chase outside events, then nothing works out for anybody. If you truly want to save Dr. Carlyle, forget about her and focus on your end result."

"But she's the reason I'm here," I said. "This is her mission."

"Yah," said Dumani, "she is the catalyst for the mission, but you have come to confuse her for the mission. As long as you do so, events will keep happening to you. Now's your chance to let go and let things begin to unfold."

I knew that I was standing on some kind of threshold and that if I used my will to follow Dumani across it, great freedom and power would arise for me. But the promise the idea of Maxine held out was familiar, and thereby far more compelling. I stood in mute paralysis.

Dumani's mood grew harsh again. "You know what?" He fixed me with a fearsome stare. His eyes burned like hot coals fanned by the wind. "Normally a teacher must let his student come to his own conclusions. He must teach him about himself and trust that the student will know the truth from there. Now there is no time for that. Do you remember that I told you there was a traitor in your midst? Well, it is her." He waited for me to register the full impact of his statement. "She is not here with you in the Meluti looking for what you are looking for; she is a ghost following you from another time and place. She is the one who does not belong with you."

"How do you know that?" I shook my head groggily, feeling as if it had taken a blow. I was faint with consternation.

"Never mind how, why, when," Dumani clucked. "Only thing is, is it true? That is all that matters to the initiated warrior. The battle he fights is in his heart – for the truth. How can one be guided down the right path if they do not value the truth above everything else? We can decide this business about Dr. Carlyle very quickly. Do you want to go for the truth?"

I nodded vaguely.

"Okay," Dumani cried. Turning to the boy sorcerer, he signaled for him to erase the circle he had just been standing in and draw a fresh one. "Makulu," he shouted, "make it a big one."

As the boy rubbed the old circle out with his feet and began carefully tracing his finger in the dust, Dumani drew the villagers around us with a flutter of his raised hands.

"The white man needs to know his truth," he told them. "Should he go into the swamps looking for his lady doctor or should he stay and help us find the eagle that will fly the soul retriever to heal Graca?" He pointed to the new circle. "This is the white man's heart."

The villagers pointed at the circle and chanted, "The white man's heart." They looked back to me expectantly.

"So please, step inside," Dumani ushered me toward the circle. I hesitated. I was feeling devastated enough; I was afraid that there might be worse to come. "Go on," Dumani urged me.

I took a deep breath, as if I were about to plunge into a pool of water. As I stepped into the pristine circle, I heard a few of the villagers mumble, "The white man's heart."

An ambience as powerful as I had experienced in the previous circle embraced me, though the atmosphere in this circle was as light and exalted as the other one had been dark and oppressive. To begin with, I experienced no association with anything or anyone. I simply felt a profound equanimity wash through me, a falling away of all strident emotional and mental activity, which I remembered happening to me in my magic training years before.

From the perspective I now enjoyed, there was nothing I could relate to with any negativity. There didn't seem to be a condition or circumstance that could preclude my viability. Loss, death, failure – they were all irrelevant concepts. The meaning implicit in all painful states of mind is the assumption that we can be separated from the source of our life and the things that make life worthwhile, but in my current state I felt connected to an endless supply of magnificent energy. The possibility that I could cease to exist or that I could be separated from what I cared about in life was inconceivable. A sense of unlimited possibility dawned on me, opening a floodgate of wonder.

There was no perception that I had brought into the

circle that I didn't see in a totally new light. When I reflected on my relationship with the residents of Mlumu Village, there was nothing personal in their attitude toward me, as I had previously perceived. True, they were indifferent toward me, but simply because they were unfamiliar with me, not because of some innate antipathy toward me or my kind. The potential for a cordial relationship with them was only as remote as my own willingness to reach out. I was warmed by an emergent certainty that we shared a common destiny.

As my attention shifted to the trouble in the Republic, the disturbing images of war that usually accompanied any thoughts in that direction were mercifully absent. There was no denial in my mind of the current hostilities or which side was prevailing, yet there was no inference that those affected, including my relatives, were powerless victims. Nor was there, for that matter, any sense that the outcome of the civil war was a foregone conclusion. The non-rational aspect of me the villagers had defined as my heart seemed to respect that whatever unfolded for anyone else was their destiny and, ultimately, none of my business. Whatever pain I experienced in relation to them was merely a reflection of my illusion of separation. Above all, though, my heart had zero inclination to dwell on anything that had not yet come to pass.

My fabulous state of equanimity and detachment did lead me to one concern. I was worried that my son and daughter and their mother wouldn't mean anything to me, that my emotional connection to them would be lost. This notion, however, was quickly dispelled. The mere thought of them brought a joyful smile to my face. All of my complex questions of whether we could be a family again and how that could happen were dissolved. Suddenly nothing existed in my consciousness except for their presence. I felt only love between us – a love that was as natural and inherent as breathing.

In turning my thoughts optimistically to Maxine, I fully expected to experience a similarly uncomplicated and uplifted connection to her, only more intense considering our long history and present association. But there was nothing! By which I mean nothing other than a vague image of her unaccompanied by any significant feeling one way or the other. Even though I tried, I could not evoke any tangible impression of her, whether as Maxine the dangerous woman, the heartbreaker, the long-lost love of my life or the heroic civil rights crusader.

From the sublime vantage point of my heart circle, I dispassionately observed my own distress at discovering how inconsequential Maxine was within the essential scope of my life. It was as though she truly was a mirage that had given me hope as long as I had the energy to hold her as real. Evidently my heart – the part of me that held what was truly relevant to me – didn't have any energy for her. Each time I brought her to the front of my mind, her image immediately slipped back into the dim recesses reserved for dreams we have woken up from.

Once I gave up on trying to manipulate her existence in the constellation of all of the things I had a natural affinity with, a pleasant stream of people, places and things flowed through my mind. Business ideas I had long let go of resurfaced as compelling possibilities; memories of moments spent with loved ones came back to me replete with nostalgic resonance; the exquisite aroma of French pancakes and cinnamon teased my olfactory nerves as if they were being cooked right beside me; the Spirit of Nature represented itself to me as a series of beautiful images imbued with a rapturous energy. Along with the many and varied associations I experienced, I saw the faces of those whom I appeared to have some current connection to. In no particular order I saw my mother and brothers, my children and estranged wife, David and Chollo, Dumani and Veeti, and to my great surprise, a man without a heart in his body and another dressed in presidential regalia.

The sudden appearance of Graca and Selele in my consciousness was not exactly a pleasant intrusion, yet their presence evoked a certain excitement, as if we all – I and everyone to whom I felt an immediate connection – were bonded in some profound adventure. A bleak expanse appeared in my mind's eye, featureless except for a vague path winding from the foreground to the horizon and a fish eagle perched in a dead tree at the start of the road. There was no dreadful sentiment accompanying the image, only a calm certainty that this was my path and that following it would take more than everything I had to give.

CHAPTER NINE

Shape-Shifting

"You know, I've been told by scholars from Latin-speaking countries that the root words of 'experience' combine to mean 'out of risk,' which tells me that our forebears saw life as a journey through danger. That is profound, isn't it? It tells us that what we hang on to from the past are the dangers we encountered and what we learned about avoiding them. When you're out here, it is easy to see how come we're fixated on survival." Dumani seemed totally relaxed, content to be poling a mokoro through the backwaters of Mlumu Island and prattling idly on about his favorite topic – human nature. To listen to him you would have thought that all of the troubles besieging us had been surmounted and everything was back to normal. Sitting in the front of the mokoro with my back to him, I could just imagine his eyes twinkling with appreciation at his own thoughts as he inhaled the lush riparian scenery.

He may as well have been reading my mind. Climbing into a mokoro was, for me, like stepping into another circle, this time defined as a death trap. The one Dumani and I had borrowed was a very crudely shaped dugout that wobbled frightfully at the slightest movement on my part. Its sides stood out of the water by only a matter of inches. The seat of my pants was wet from water we had taken on when we first climbed in. It would not have taken a hippo or crocodile any effort whatsoever to tip us over. Even an inadvertent bump against some underwater structure would have been enough to topple us into the primordial swamp.

David stood at the back of a second mokoro, poling it with remarkable dexterity. Even though Dumani had made it clear that David should stay behind us, his mokoro kept gliding up alongside us with alarming regularity. It might have been that Dumani's less-than-expert ability made it difficult for David to keep back, or perhaps he could feel his passenger's instinctive urge to take point. I guessed from the sour look on Chollo's face that he didn't like the idea of having to use the shotgun from behind us, if the need arose. For that matter, neither did I.

"Can I ask you something, Dumani?" I said, thinking back to the indaba an hour earlier.

"Sure," Dumani sang magnanimously. Still in English, he shouted at David, "Hey, you, next time you try to get in front, I'll feed you to the crocodiles. You think I can't hit you with this pole?"

"I can't balance if I go so slowly," David laughed good-naturedly.

"Well, why don't you look for your own channel?" Dumani clucked. "Go find your own eagle." Lowering his voice, he said, "These young men, they think they are better."

"Dumani," I persisted, "how come we don't know our truth normally? Why do we only realize it when we step outside our rational self-conscious awareness...into inno-cence or some higher definition?"

"Experience! This is just what I'm talking about," said Dumani as if admonishing me. "Experience – the journey through danger. Like I told you before, we have the wounds, the memory of danger. That is our own personal myth. What is a myth? Is it a legend, a story that is not true? No, it is a framework for understanding the meaning of our lives. Like here in the Meluti, the didakta is teaching the boys what life is about. Didakta is the societal myth that takes over from the personal myth. The personal myth is the danger we carry with us and the strategies we focus on to keep us safe from those dangers. Is the myth what is really happening and something we should spend our energy resolving? Definitely not, but we are fixated on it. We see everything in terms of our myth. We don't see what is actually happening, what our choices really are."

Dumani continued: "Did you ever study anything about alchemy? No? If you had, you would know about this. You see what they say, those old philosophers: you make the fixed volatile and the volatile fixed. What do they mean by make the fixed volatile? Because we start out in the darkness – what the alchemists call the negredo – where we are fixed in our ego's perception of reality. It's an illusion, fixed solid, crystallized.

"So, to master reality, we must break down the illusion, dissolve it. Putrefaction – decomposing, rotting – this is the alchemist's way." Dumani gave a disgusted snort. "Breaking down the absolute certainty of the rational mind, unchaining the spirit so it can rise up into the albedo, the light. It's an analogy for going into innocence. Now you see the light... your truth is revealed.

"But very important the next step," he continued. "You have gone from the fixed structures of ego into the volatile world of soul. What you find here is fickle, ungrounded – it tends to evaporate. Which means that now you must make the volatile fixed. If you don't fix the truth, crystallize it, it will dissolve again just like a dream. You see how real a dream is when you are sleeping? When you first wake up you think this dream was so amazing that you'll never forget it, but after you've had breakfast you can't even remember it. Because what doesn't fit in with the ego's serious business of survival gets left behind like an invalid who can't march with the army to the war. So when you see your truth in the albedo, you have to fix it with the rubedo – the alchemists' red tincture – your will. You have to mark the truth, acknowledge it, take it on with every atom of your being. You must consciously nurture it – stay focused on it until it is an indivisible part of your self-conscious reality.

"I read a book once by a famous author who won the Nobel Prize for Literature. In the book, the main character goes for a job and that one whose business it was asked him, 'What can you do?' The other one, he said, 'I can think, I can wait, I can fast.' You hear that?

"Out here in the Meluti, they say a warrior is someone who can wait. They don't run around taking orders from the ego; they are not reacting. But when the warrior knows his truth," Dumani whistled emphatically through his teeth, "then there is no more waiting around. You don't want to stand between a warrior and what he knows he must do."

What Dumani had said about making the fixed volatile and the volatile fixed resonated deeply with my current circumstance. I thought of Maxine and how fiercely my emotions insisted I should be doing something to track her down and save her from the mulatto smuggler the locals called the Portuguese Snake. It was as if every dilemma I faced were embodied in her image, and that everything would be resolved by her rescue. I had to force myself to imagine the road winding through the bleak landscape of my heart vision, with the fish eagle perched in a dead tree. For an illusion, Maxine appeared very tangible and appealing, while my supposed truth already struck me as extremely vague and improbable.

David and Chollo's mokoro came alongside us again. This time there was no testy banter between the polers. David nodded casually ahead of us. Chollo stared intently into the forest beyond where the channel bent out of sight.

"I've seen it," said Dumani in a low voice. He let David pole his mokoro ahead of us. He spoke to me out of the corner of his mouth, "Don't make any sudden moves. There's a welcome party up ahead."

There was no need for me to move; I was already as coiled for action as I could be. I didn't relish the thought of having to fire my rifle. The kickback from a single shot would have been enough to capsize our dugout.

"Why don't we just turn around?" I whispered, squeezing the rifle butt tightly into my shoulder.

"Because the eagle we want is this way," Dumani reverted to a conversational tone. "Anyway, it's just a group of initiates. They won't be in their full strength yet. Still, we must be fierce; there's nothing these boys would like to get their hands on more than some canoes and guns."

I wondered what Dumani meant by the didakta boys not being in their full power yet, though I was concentrating on the waterway ahead too intently to ask him. I was also intrigued at how all three of my companions had become aware of the imminent ambush when I still couldn't make out any sign of hidden danger, even though I had been alerted to it. There was no movement that I could detect, no alarm calls from any birds or monkeys, no unusual quiet or noise – everything was as it should have been. It occurred to me that the Africans must have been using their intuition, probably some technique similar to the one I had used to find Sibongila choking to death in the jungle. That was the big difference between them and me, of course – I was just learning about these super-conscious techniques, while they practiced them every moment of their lives.

The knowledge that my companions had supernatural powers at their disposal did nothing to raise my hopes of getting by the didakta boys safely. I did think of trying out my intuition to see if it would give us any advantage, but I figured that we already knew all we needed to know. I decided that if I was going to use anything I had learned before, it might as well be handing the situation over to my natural ability. Almost wetting myself with fear, I quit striving to anticipate my response to what was going to happen next and used my energy to imagine us continuing on safely with our mission unimpeded.

It was not easy to hold that positive vision. As we drew near the bend in the channel, all of my attention involuntarily went into scanning the thick jungle on either side of us. Though Dumani and David had slowed the mokoros down to drift at the same speed as the sluggish current, it still wasn't slow enough for my quailing heart. My arms turned to jelly. I was afraid that I wouldn't even have the strength to raise my gun when the time came to use it. Nor was there any doubt in my mind that it would come down to that. The certainty that an attack was imminent consumed my whole consciousness. Somehow, the fact that our assailants were hidden out of sight gave them enormous power. Floating along over open water in our precarious crafts, we were sitting ducks. I gave up all hope and surrendered to the prospect of being annihilated.

As our dugouts floated into the channel bend where we anticipated the didakta boys to be lying in wait for us, a blood-curdling scream rose out of the undergrowth on the bank to our right. "Hold your nerve," Dumani commanded me in a stern voice as more screams erupted from both banks. "Don't move yet. They're testing us."

A figure darted into a clearing on the left bank. I sat transfixed as the head of a lion appeared on its shoulders. The figure tottered about on its two legs as the lion's head thrashed from side to side, letting out a roar that sounded like it came from the bowels of hell. The figure tripped and fell. The lion's head vanished to reveal an ochre-covered body lying prostrate on the ground, apparently unconscious.

Dumani burst out laughing. David also laughed, though his was more a quiet chuckle. "You see that," Dumani cried mirthfully, "he's trying to shift into a lion to scare us." In Lapedi he called out: "Run away, boys, before I turn myself into a dragon and breathe fire over you."

I myself was far from amused. My sense that something bad was going to happen had intensified rather than diminished. I had the feeling that I was in a surreal dream, being attacked by would-be demons while my companions laughed at their efforts. It was especially weird that David was suddenly so at ease in the Meluti. Since when had he gone so native?

A missile flew in an arc out of the forest and splashed in the water beside the bow of our mokoro. It was a small arrow. Another one followed it, this time pegging into the lip of the hull inches away from my thigh. Soon it was hailing arrows.

"Mnyuno soga!" Dumani screamed. "Fornicating snakes! Poison arrows. Take cover."

I surprised myself with my own alacrity. Without even thinking, I rolled into the water, holding my gun in the air to keep it dry. As soon as the dugout began to stabilize, I let the rifle fall into the shallow hull. The iron tip of an arrow thudded into the wooden shell inches from my nose. I took as big a breath as I could draw and dived under the mokoro for cover.

Once underwater, I had a new fear to contend with. I opened my eyes, hoping that I wasn't going to see anything nasty. I was disconcerted by how good the visibility was. I didn't want to know what lethal creatures were lurking in my vicinity. An arrow streaked through the water beside me. I snatched it by the shaft in the vain hope that I could use it as a stabbing weapon if anything came at me.

Treading water under the mokoro, I frantically considered my position. I couldn't stay in the water for long without coming to the attention of amphibious predators, and while I remained underwater the didakta marauders could move in on me without my seeing them. I found it extremely disturbing that there was no sign of my three companions, either. With such good visibility, I should have been able to see them in the water.

Soon my lungs were bursting; I had to come up for air. I was terrified of getting hit by an arrow. The poison used by traditional hunters is so potent that a scratch from an arrowhead buried for hundreds of years can still kill you within hours. Heartened only by the fact that no arrows had fallen in my vicinity in the last fifteen seconds, I broke the surface of the water as surreptitiously as I could.

In my imagination I had expected many different scenarios confronting me above the surface, but there was no way I could have anticipated what I actually witnessed. An almighty din startled me into keeping my head up after I had taken a great gulp of air. To one side I heard the demonic howl of a colossal cat and from the other side the raucous hooting of a giant ape. Above these unearthly sounds came the terrified shrieks of humans fleeing through the jungle.

Looking across David and Chollo's empty canoe, I caught a glimpse of a massive black cat, at least three times the size of a regular panther, bounce off the trunk of a wild fig tree into the thick undergrowth. Swiveling my head in the direction of the other bank, I saw a massive Neanderthal-like creature with tufts of long wiry hair flowing behind it attacking the jungle with an uprooted tree in its hands. Peering desperately into my own mokoro for Dumani, I saw only my rifle and a large tortoise with its head buried in its shell. As I ducked underwater again to make sure nothing was stalking me, I wondered how in hell the tortoise had gotten in the dugout.

When I surfaced again, Dumani was standing in the back of the mokoro, pole in hand. "Hey, don't rock the boat," he scowled. "You want me to fall in?" Seeing my puzzlement, he said, "What you looking for?"

"There was a tortoise in here," I spluttered.

"You sure?" Dumani retorted.

The jungle had fallen silent again. I looked around for the big cat and the Neanderthal-like creature. There was no sign of them. Chollo was wading into the water on the side of the channel that I had seen the giant panther. Soon after, David emerged from the brush where moments before the Bigfoot, or whatever it was, had been running amok. He stumbled into the unconscious didakta boy who had tried to change shape into a lion.

"Shall I break this one's neck as a lesson to the others?" he called out to Dumani.

"No," Dumani called back, "we should not discourage them from being fierce. Besides, one who has the potential to shift into a lion will have great value to the village."

If I had been anywhere other than hanging off the side of a mokoro waiting for a crocodile to sink its jaws into me, I would have fainted in utter disbelief. It wasn't the supernatural phenomenon of shape-changing by itself that boggled my mind – after all, seeing the ndotsikatsi transforming herself from leopard back to human form and Sibongila trapped in a half human–half baboon condition had prepared me for the reality of were-persons – it was the scale of what I had just witnessed. Psychologically it was acceptable that a sorceress and a scout from the Meluti would have the special training and talent to turn themselves into animals – especially creatures that belonged in the real world. But in the same moment to see an uninitiated boy half succeeding in turning himself into a lion, and Dumani turning turtle, while Chollo and David shape-shifted into completely demonic entities, was too much. To witness servants from my own world, whom I related to as people of lesser capacities than myself, demonstrate such incredible powers was at once humbling and shocking.

"I wish Max and the people from the Irrigation Scheme could have seen this," I stammered through chattering teeth.

"Hey, don't try to climb in now," Dumani barked. "You'll tip us over. Wait till I push us to shallow water."

Chollo used a dead branch to snag his mokoro and drag it into the shallows. After climbing in, he poled it over to the far bank alongside Dumani's. Once we were all safely on board our respective dugouts, we proceeded once more with our journey downstream. My many disquieting thoughts were kept at bay by the discomfort of being so wet and cold. All three of my companions, I noticed ruefully, were dry as a bone.

Something in me snapped. I began laughing hysterically. The others muttered to each other in Lapedi, expressing their bewilderment at my behavior.

"What's so funny?" Dumani asked sharply.

It took me a while before I was composed enough to reply. "Just the thought of Chollo and David changing themselves into fearsome monsters," I sighed at the pain in my side, "and you changing into a tortoise."

"What's so funny about that?" Dumani growled. "It's very useful to be a tortoise when people are shooting you with poisoned arrows. I didn't have to jump in the water. Look at you, shivering and wet."

Something in the defensiveness of his comeback prompted me to ask, "Yes, but can you change into anything other than a tortoise?" I meant no disrespect, but the improbable image of a tortoise hiding in its shell in the empty mokoro sent me into another fit of laughter.

"We cannot choose our totem animals, the ones who guide us and lend us their shapes and powers when needed," said Dumani sternly. "They come to us during initiation. They are part of who we are. You can only ever become who you already are."

"I see," I said, regretting injuring my mentor's pride. Something else occurred to me instinctively. Before I asked the question, I feared I knew the answer. "So, who in Mlumu Village can become a fish eagle?"

"No one," Dumani's voice was grim. "We are the only party searching for an eagle."

I slumped under a heavy weight of dread. "Don't tell me," I groaned, "that it's up to me to wrangle the fish eagle."

"You saw it in your heart circle," Dumani countered.

"Yes," I said, "but I thought I was tied to the quest of the fish eagle by association – as moral support. I didn't think it *was* my quest."

"You need to pay closer attention to your visions," said Dumani. "You're the one who came here looking for the last shaman. This is your quest. You *are* the last shaman."

"What do you mean, I'm the last shaman?" I squealed in protest. "I'm not a shaman. I'm just a white guy trying to go back home. Everyone else around here can see things without using their eyes and turn themselves into other animals. If anything, I'm the last human being."

The weird feeling of being in a dream came over me again. I felt as if I were defending myself against absurd charges in a crazy court presided over by a mad judge.

"That is an interesting way of putting it," Dumani mused calmly. "You *are* the last human being among us. All of us out here have died to that illusion. Now we are the supporting players in your death. We are your initiators."

"But what about Chollo and David?" I said. "They're

from outside the Meluti."

"You think that engaging me in a rational argument will help you cling to sanity?" Dumani laughed dryly. "Things are not what they seem. Chollo and David are your sponsors, the guides who brought you here for didakta."

"What?" I gasped.

"Yah," said Dumani, "it is time to let go of everything. You are safe with us. Not even the didakta boys with poisoned arrows can get to you."

I decided that Dumani had to be messing with me. He was most probably just getting even with me for laughing at his totem animal. I sat up straight and reined in my scattered thoughts. "Sure, Dumani," I said, "whatever you say."

"Not what I say," he objected, "things are unfolding now, not happening. Yesterday you asked me if you could shape-shift and I told you that by today you would be doing it. So now it's today, and time for you to learn."

"Are you serious?" I said.

"No need to be intimidated," he said. "You don't have to straightaway change into another thing. Besides its literal application, shape-shifting is a psychic metaphor."

"A psychic metaphor?" I frowned, shrinking at the idea of my capability being so strenuously tested. I looked around for the other mokoro in the childish hope that David and Chollo's presence would help avert any unpleasantness. They were now drifting well behind us. It felt as if Dumani and I had detached from the rest of the world, the better to focus on the lesson at hand. I swallowed nervously.

"Sure," said Dumani expansively. "When we look at anything, we only ever consider it from the perspective of our identity. In other words, we see things as we believe them to be, not for what they are. Shape-shifting is a technique where you can know about something by becoming it, so you know it for what it is rather than what you perceive it to be."

What Dumani said didn't sound so frightening, though I wasn't sure that I understood him. "Are you saying that if I see a tree, maybe it's not a tree?"

"Eish, that water has frozen your brains," he tutted. "For example, imagine a stone. When you see a stone, you see it as an inanimate object – something solid, hard, lifeless, with no consciousness. But if you become it, you realize that it is largely immaterial and that it is alive and talking to everything else. It is still a stone, but its nature is different than you assumed.

"Or, if you see some beautiful girl, you can see her as a – what you call it? – a sex object. The mind likes to reduce everything down to a single dimension. But there are many dimensions to everything. If you shape-shift into that girl, then you can realize who she really is: her heart, what she likes, what she thinks."

"So how do you become something?" I said. "Or someone?"

"Very easy," said Dumani. "It's just embodying something, imagining becoming that thing, like when you stepped into the jungle on the other side of the water to find Sibongila. First, you go into innocence to neutralize your identity. Then you imagine stepping into whatever you want to know about. When you step into something in innocence, you become attuned to that thing's vibration. When you resonate with that vibration, you know the qualities of that vibration. So, really, the trick of shape-shifting is to imagine stepping into the vibration of the thing, not just the thing itself."

"It sounds too simple," I remarked.

"It is simple," said Dumani, "but not too simple. Something very powerful is happening, but in your imagination – behind what you can physically do or rationally contemplate. All you have to do is direct your imagination by choosing the vibration you want to be fixed on." He paused for a moment. "You ready to start?"

My impression was that I had already started. I might not have changed into anything else yet, but I felt very different. I had become unhinged from my usual sense of self. My everyday subjective perception had given way to an objective view of the world, as if everything I observed –

even myself – were from a transcendent perspective. I was high, except there was no accompanying euphoria or other ecstatic emotion. It occurred to me that I might still be in shock from the didakta boys' ambush.

"Just close your eyes and follow me," Dumani instructed me in a soothing voice. "Just notice how you are feeling: stiff, cramped, cold, lightheaded, maybe strange. That's just a starting point; nothing to do about it. Now imagine a low, slow vibration vibrating through your being. Imagine this vibration – red in color, slow and dull in speed, giving off a deep, low-pitched sound – vibrating through every cell, every fiber of your being, even the empty spaces between the particles. All of your thoughts and feelings, aches and pains, they are all coming into alignment with this ruby-red, slow, dull-sounding vibration. Imagine every bone and muscle and hair, even the etheric layers of your body, the energy meridians in your body, all aligned."

At first it was difficult to focus on Dumani's guided meditation. Its initial effect on me was extreme irritation. I became intensely aware of every itch and ache, how cold I was and the dull throb in my head. The hypnotic drone of his voice, however, eventually overcame my resistance. Inexorably, a bright red glow spread through my consciousness, infusing even my irritability and jumbled synapses with a solid, earthy pulse. A calm descended over me as the niggling aspects of me became inundated by the vibration Dumani coaxed in my imagination.

I was just getting comfortable with my whole consciousness suffused in a red glow when Dumani cranked the meditation up a notch. "Now, as your whole being comes into alignment with this vibration, imagine that it spontaneously intensifies. Imagine that it begins speeding up, and as it speeds up, it brightens. It turns bright orange. Also the sound it emits goes up an octave. It makes a higher-pitched noise."

As Dumani led me through each color of the rainbow, all the time encouraging me to imagine the colors more vividly and the speed and pitch of the vibration intensifying exponentially, I went from experiencing my thoughts and feelings and physical discomforts as distinct de-energized elements of myself to losing all awareness of them. By the time we got to indigo, every part of me had been absorbed by the highest aspect of my consciousness. The only thing my mind apprehended was a sea of indigo, vibrating at a speed so fast that it was almost imperceptible and emitting a pitch so high that it was inaudible to the human ear. Though I say I felt nothing, I did simultaneously experience an ineffable calmness – an exquisite confidence that I knew everything, even though in that moment I knew nothing at all. Dumani had once again transported me to a state of serene emptiness.

"Now, as your whole being comes into alignment with the indigo vibration, imagine it intensifying again. Turning violet now and vibrating so fast it seems like it's standing still. The pitch of the sound it throws off is so high it seems like it is silent. The violet becomes so bright it appears to be colorless. Really, the closest you can come to imagining the vibration now is trying to imagine pure emptiness."

I realized that I was so at one with everything that I had even anticipated Dumani's instructions. I sat quietly in the mokoro, relishing the bliss implicit in my highest vibration. "So, when you are ready, you can open your eyes and return to normal consciousness," Dumani finished solemnly.

I was reluctant to abandon the serenity I assumed was contained only within myself. When I finally deigned to open my eyes, I was greeted by a world even more exalted than my internal one. The cerulean sky was mirrored in the glassy stretch of water before us. On either side of us a wall of jungle cushioned the edge of the waterway. The emerald green of the foliage was so brilliant, it screamed. Everything my senses apprehended delighted me: the concentric ripples of a fish rise expanding placidly outward, the iridescent bodies of blue-and-orange dragonflies resting on the hull of the mokoro, the rich organic odor of damp vegetation and the fairy-like twittering of colonies of little birds harvesting lichen and aphids from overhanging branches – all existence was imbued with a beauty breathed into it by a divine breath. Like sublime notes in a stirring symphony, there was not a thing I noticed that was not of special significance or that did not have its special place in the scheme of things.

"Beautiful, isn't it?" Dumani said softly.

My serene state of mind made me appreciate how stressed out I usually was. It became starkly apparent to me just how guilty I had been feeling about abandoning Maxine to her fate with the Portuguese Snake, and how confused I was about my wife and kids, and how sick with worry I was for my family back at the Irrigation Scheme, and how self-conscious I was about my status among the Meluti natives, and how scared for my life I was. I could see how this sickening pressure I continually put on myself was designed to manipulate me into paying attention to – and behaving in favor of – my ego's agendas.

It was obvious, too, how these tensions blinded me to my most functional relationship with life – how blind I was to what really mattered to me in life, my true options. I understood there and then, in every particle of my being, that life wasn't a guided meditation – that tension was inherent to the human condition – but that great freedom and mastery would come to those who had the will to stop buying into their stress. The first secret of magic, after all, is that thoughts and feelings aren't real. How many times would I have to learn the lesson before I assimilated it? Not ever again, I assured myself.

"Now you see all the things in the world," Dumani spoke again, "unburdened by the names you have given them, free of your projections – but you still don't know them by virtue of having become them. You must try to become something: the pond or the sun or a fish – anything."

"What do I do?" I said languidly.

"First thing to do, choose something to become." Dumani chuckled at his own wit. "Then stay in innocence and imagine stepping into that thing. The important thing is that you remain standing in that thing. Don't be swayed by your experience not conforming to what you know from before – not being like your assumptions."

"You said before to stand in the vibration of the thing?" I checked.

"Exactly," he sang out, "you imagine standing in the vibration of the thing. You stay there in innocence, just noticing what it's like, what's there. Observe the obvious – do you remember that one?"

My survival instincts were not as deeply suspended as I had assumed. The first thing I chose to shape-shift into was the whole environment around us. I was intensely curious to know what was going on in our surroundings. I imagined a bird's-eye view of the swamps in our vicinity. Next, I pictured a heat wave as a representation of the swamp's vibration. Then I imagined myself stepping into and being consumed by that vibration. At first there was nothing other than a wave of white light strobing in my head. Undeterred, I kept imagining that I was standing in the vibration of the surrounding swamps. Eventually, the grating light faded to reveal a montage of wildlife scenes.

I could either picture or sense the position of crocodiles swimming away from us underwater or lying hidden in undergrowth tunnels on the banks.

"Lots of crocodiles," I whistled.

"Many crocodiles," Dumani chuckled. "Good you didn't see them with these eyes when you were hanging in the water before."

I refocused on being the vibration of our surroundings. I could see fish everywhere and especially had a keen certainty of where prize tiger fish or pike were lurking. Though I didn't visualize them, I could sense hippo in the vicinity. Acknowledging that I was starting to get into my head about why I could sense hippos and not picture them, I let the puzzle go. Right away, the vague sense explained itself. There was a lone male in the next pool.

Right at that moment, Dumani called out matter-of-factly to the other mokoro, "Have you picked up on the bull in the next stretch?"

"Yah, he's been in a fight last night," Chollo called back.

"When you get to his pond, you better take your mokoro through the reeds."

I indulged myself for a moment in being amazed at the effectiveness of my psychic faculties. No doubt the confirmation of its validity encouraged my creative spirit considerably. When I did go back to the vibration again, the inner vision of my surroundings was twice as vivid as before. I picked up on a massive python waking up prematurely from its hibernation. From a bough high in the canopy of the forest, it watched a hyena with two pups retreating stealthily from our approach. The hyena passed warily by a dying campfire. Inside a ring of stones, red-hot coals burned under white ashes. Whoever had made the fire was long gone. The forest was void of human energy.

Reassured that there was nothing malingering in our immediate vicinity with foul intentions toward us, I looked around for something more specific to shape-shift into. The first thing that jumped out was the gray inside wall of the mokoro. I visualized the dead wood's vibration and imagined myself stepping into it. I was astonished at how different the properties of the wood were compared to how I expected them to be. The mokoro had been shaped out of an ironwood trunk – it looked and felt as solid as stone. Yet its essence had a very aerated, hollow quality to it. The discrepancy between the apparent and the energetic nature of the wood threw me again. Without even realizing it, I was questioning how something so dense could be represented by such a light impression. As soon as I stopped resisting what I was getting, not only did the dry, spongy quality reassert itself, but I also knew with absolute certainty what it meant. Beneath its iron-hard veneer, the wood was rotting.

Next I choose a tall ebony tree muscling its way out of the jungle canopy to project myself into. Once again I was surprised at how different my perception of the object was from my intuitive insight. From the outside, the ebony's dominance appeared to derive from the power of its limbs – its ability, in other words, to shove its competition out of the way. But when I imagined becoming the tree, I realized that its power originated underground in its massive root system, which controlled an area ten times the size of its own canopy. While I had imagined its branches straining against the encroaching limbs of its virile neighbors, they were in fact very relaxed and stretching out luxuriously to savor the mild rays of winter sunlight. Equally surprising was the quality of profound happiness I felt, which I was sure belonged to the tree rather than being my own emotional response to connecting with the tree.

"You'll be running into that hippo soon," Chollo's caution echoed across the water.

I decided to see if I could use shape-shifting to check out what level of threat the bull represented. Once I had assumed the unseen hippo's vibration, my first impression was an odd sensation of buoyancy. As the hippo, my own mass was not evident to me. Staying with its vibration, I couldn't help feeling a flush of pity for the animal. I had picked up that its lower jaw was badly hurt. My impression was that it was in a very feeble condition, more than likely mortally wounded.

"Yah, here he is," Dumani whispered. I could not see past the wall of papyrus stalks we were gliding through. In Lapedi, he called out to the others, "He's had it. There'll be no more fighting for this one." Suddenly he cried out, "Hauw, hauw, hauw! Crocodiles everywhere. Jesu Christo, the flat dogs are coming from everywhere to finish him."

I heard David's laugh close behind us. No doubt for my benefit, he spoke in English. "Bush telegraph calling the scavengers to clean up."

We entered the hippo's pool hugging the bank on our right. He was lying half submerged close to the left bank. As we drifted by him, he was only ten yards from us. There were huge lacerations on his head and back. Any other hippo would have ducked under the water, either to hide or attack. This fellow didn't budge. He just lay there with the dazed fatalism wounded animals are so good at expressing. Arranged around him in a semicircle was a float of massive crocodiles. I estimated the smallest one I could see to be around thirteen or fourteen feet. Still more were streaming up to the scrum from every direction.

"When it's like this, you can go for a swim right here," said Dumani.

"Are you serious?" I gulped, watching a pair of crocodiles brazenly snaking their way past our mokoro.

"Yah, now they're not interested in anything except for that four tons of meat there."

The Africans joked with each other about the hippo's fate all the way down the next stretch of water. I was keen to take my mind off the wretched beast's fate.

"Dumani," I said over my shoulder.

"Yes, sir?"

"Can we shape-shift into people who are not in the same place as us?"

"Yah, of course. Every vibration exists in your consciousness. So even that one who is far away in time and space is still in you. You can shape-shift into anyone, but not only now, also at some time in their past...or their future. You can shape-shift into anything you want to know – how they think or feel, their beliefs, their health. Everything is vibration and every vibration exists in you."

I was thinking of Maxine. I recalled her sitting on the edge of the bathtub with her creamy breast almost falling out of her shirt. A flood of other memories concerning her came back to me. Some were of us playing innocently in childhood; another was the look on her face when Mother told her that she had to leave the Republic for good. There were many. I shivered at the feeling of her leaning passionately into me the night before we left for the Meluti, and I winced at the pitying look on her face as she told me, all those years ago, that we couldn't be together because she was going to South America with a boy from medical school. Now she was out there in the swamps in who knows what kind of trouble. But, if I felt sorry for anyone it was myself. Going by her form, she would be the one who survived and I would be the one who ended up in the ditch with flies buzzing around my eyes.

It was hard to form a clear picture of her because her

image kept changing according to which memory I associated with her. In the end, I gave up trying to hold a consistent vision of her. I just imagined a heat wave–like blur and defined it as her vibration. Her true face, I figured, would be revealed.

I spent a long time tuning in to Maxine. The first thing I got was that she was in no immediate danger. Yet there was still a dark cloud over her. The longer I remained in her vibration without judgment, the clearer it became what the cloud symbolized. Once I had gleaned enough about her current situation, I tested Dumani's theory and began tuning in to as many aspects of her as I could think of: her dreams, her past, her personality, her heart and more besides. Words cannot convey my astonishment at what I saw. As someone who had been closely associated with Maxine since early childhood, I had assumed that I knew her. I was astounded to discover that what I knew about her was merely the tip of the iceberg, and what's more, that she didn't know much more about herself than I did.

"Dr. Carlyle has not been harmed yet," I breathed a sigh of relief, preparing to report what I had discovered about Maxine's status to Dumani.

"There it is!" he yelled. He tried to stifle his enthusiasm but it still burst out of him as a half-muffled shout. "Will you look at that, men? The king of all fish eagles!"

"Eh! Eh! Eh!" an involuntary cry of astonishment rose from the other mokoro.

"This is him," Dumani hissed to me. "This is the one who can take the soul retriever."

"Which is me," I thought nervously. Up ahead of us on the left bank stood an enormous, dead tree. Its gray branches were so thick they could have been shaped into mokoros. Near the top of the dry branches, a giant bird was perched – so big I thought it was a vulture at first glance. A closer look confirmed that it was a fish eagle. Rather than the normal dark-chocolate-brown, this bird's body was pure black, which contrasted spectacularly with its snow-white chest and head. It sat with a regal aloofness, stabbing the waterway with a piercing eye.

"This is your chance," Dumani whispered urgently. "You must find out if he is the one."

"What must I do?" I hissed back at him.

"Just shift into his vibration. If he is the one, the rest will happen."

The swamps went silent. Time seemed to freeze in anticipation. Nothing moved except for the eagle's head. It craned its neck in our direction, calculating the significance of our presence. I closed my eyes and imagined a shimmering wave of energy rising from the core of the eagle's being. After taking a moment to release any doubts or exuberance, I stepped into the vibration as calmly as I could.

"Don't be the observer," Dumani's voice trailed off behind me. "Let go of yourself altogether. Fix yourself in the eagle's vibration."

As I let myself sink into the fish eagle's vibration, a frightening darkness swept through my consciousness. I was beginning to black out, but instead of pulling back, I willed myself to die to all sense of personal existence. At the point where the black veil covered my last fragment of self-consciousness, I came to in the consciousness of the eagle. If I had been the observer of the eagle's consciousness rather than wholly embodying it, I would have been taken aback at how unselfconscious the giant bird was. As the eagle, I had no awareness of my body, other than to see my down feathers ruffled by a slight breeze in the periphery of my vision; I had no aches or pains or issues whatsoever with my physicality. Nor did I have any thoughts of my viability: no memories of recent traumas bothered me; no concerns over the ever-present dangers of my environment occurred to me; I didn't feel hungry and I didn't have a care about where my next meal would come from. I wasn't preoccupied with the time of day and what contingencies I had to make for the following stages of day and night. I wasn't even thinking of companionship. The only thing I was conscious of was what I could see. None of my energy was being used for anything other than processing visual input.

Down on the water I could see the two mokoros drifting toward my perch. The creatures standing at the back of each log were clearly navigating the floating structures. Their companions perched at the front of each log were armed with some kind of killing sticks, though the same instinct that told me that also told me that the beings were not in an aggressive mood. Beneath the surface of the water, the pond I was looking down on teamed with big fish that had been chased downstream by all the crocodiles converging on the dying hippo. The approaching logs were bunching the fish up against the bank beneath me.

Among the shoals of fish, a group of five big specimens the shape and color of a full moon hung near the surface, looking out for which way they should dart. My eyes locked on the biggest one. The fins on its back almost broke the surface. It faced the approaching logs. My wings spread out involuntarily. Without even thinking about it, I launched myself off my perch and flapped my way effortlessly clear of the dead branches. Then I tucked my head in and turned into a steep dive. My wings were almost fully retracted. I used only the tips to steer me in the direction of the big fish. Within seconds I was on top of it. At the very last moment I pulled up and hit the water feetfirst, my claws sticking out like a pair of tridents. By the time the fish began to move, my talons were already locking into its flanks.

I spread my wings, expecting my momentum to lift me and my prey into the air. Instead I was wrenched back by the weight of the fish. The brute began to dive, pulling me down with it. I had to stretch my wings out across the water to stop from being dragged under. After several furious attempts to dive, the fish tried bolting along the surface. Although I couldn't stop the fish from running, my wings were freed to flap my body out of the water. As I kept my grip on my thrashing prey and beat my wings for all I was worth, I began drowning in the deafening calls of the creatures on the logs.

I came to in the mokoro to the excited cries of my guides. "Eh! Eh!" Dumani shouted like a little boy. "It's like a lion trying to pick up an elephant in his mouth."

"Hauw," David gasped, "this eagle is mad."

Even Chollo was moved enough to snort, "That fish weighs much more than the bird."

My eyes were drawn by a thrashing noise to my left. It was the eagle using its wings to swim its prey to shore. All the fight had gone out of the fish. It gave only a few token flaps of resistance. Once it could stand, the eagle sank its beak into the fish and backed itself to the edge of the water. I gasped at the size of the massive perch. It must have weighed over ten pounds. With the perch only half out of the water, the eagle held on to it with one giant claw and began tearing strips off the fish's body with its razor-sharp beak.

Dumani forced his attention away from the awesome spectacle. "What happened?"

"I was the bird," I panted, still feeling like it was me who had been fighting for my life in the water.

"You must get back," Dumani insisted. "You must fly him back to the village."

"But if I'm not me anymore, how can I direct him where I want to go?"

"You must not exist anymore, except for your will. You must carry your intention and fix it in the consciousness of the eagle."

The eagle eyed us suspiciously between voracious gulps of fish flesh. I was worried that it was going to take off at any moment. I hurriedly shut my eyes and did my best to visualize the eagle flying willingly to Mlumu Village to help me with my mission. Under the pressure of having to achieve such an improbable feat, I found it impossible to imagine the end result with any conviction. It was all I could do to acknowledge the limited scope of my imagination and affirm to myself the outcome I wanted.

When I shape-shifted into the eagle, I received a strong knowing of what it was like to be the bird and what was going through its mind, but it was still from an observer's perspective. Try as I might, I couldn't completely dispense with my own sense of self. To my dismay, the eagle took off. I heard its plaintiff cry high above us and opened my eyes to see it ponderously flapping its way in the opposite direction of Mlumu Village. Just as it was about to disappear over the treetops at the end of the furthest reach of water, I heard a voice inside my head say, "I will be there tonight when it is time." The words startled me, for they sounded more real than if a person standing beside me had spoken them.

"Oh, no, he's running away," David moaned.

"It's not the Master's fault," Chollo bristled. "He did his best."

"What happened?" said Dumani after waiting to be sure that the eagle wasn't circling back.

"Don't worry," I said, "he'll be there tonight."

"What do you mean?" said Dumani.

"The eagle knows what must be done," I said. "The volatile is fixed, not only in my mind but his, too."

A six-foot monitor lizard came snaking through the bulrushes. It snatched the half-eaten perch carcass and pulled it into the water.

"Hauw, look at that!" Dumani exclaimed happily. "Nobody wastes any time out here in the Meluti."

CHAPTER TEN

Taking Wing

Letter from Cynthia Vale to Sir Ken Franklin, OBE, August 1

My Dear Sir,

What a strange task it is to write to the living from what is practically the grave. If you receive this letter, then the worst has come to pass. In the event that I do not survive the coming days, I have entrusted my most loyal servant to forward my correspondence as soon as circumstances permit.

Do not be tormented by thoughts of my suffering at the hands of the Rebels. I carry my Beretta with me at all times and have no plans to be taken alive. We have billeted the children with expatriate families in the hope that the lives of landowners will be blood enough for Graca's vengeful hordes.

I am not only obliged to thank you for your kind message of condolence on my beloved Stan's passing, but I would like to express my everlasting gratitude for your years of support for the Irrigation Scheme, first as High Commissioner in the Republic and then in your various capacities at the Foreign Office. It is sad to reflect that in the end our unstinting mutual efforts to drag this part of the world from the dark ages has been no match for the savage heart of this continent and its people.

With so many communiqués to complete and so little time, I must leave you with my fondest wishes for yourself and

Lady Franklin.
  I remain yours truly,
  Cynthia Vale

***

The moon lounged high in the sky above Lake Stanley like a naked goddess. The enthusiastic jungle noises that had greeted the night had long since melted away. The only sounds overlaying the blanket of stillness were the muffled strains of talking drums wafting in from across the water and the occasional raised voice from the village behind me. I had not noticed them the night before, but tonight I could make out the faint flickers of firelight on the far shore.

There were no booms of thunder or flashes of lightning above the Lesoti plateau. Evidently the fighting in the Republic was all but over, awaiting only the coup de grâce to be delivered at dawn. The question of whether my family was still okay did occur to me, as did the thought of Maxine and the peril I knew she was headed into, but they were background concerns. My angst was reserved for my own plight. No one had told me what riding an eagle into the Dream World to fight Colonel Graca's demons actually involved. My imagination was free to run as wild as it liked – and it did!

"They told me I would find you down by the water." I heard Dumani's soft voice behind me.

I said nothing. I was loath to tear myself away from the enchantment of the moonlit night. The thought of having to separate myself from the serenity of that moment saddened me deeply.

"It is time," said Dumani. "Word is that the ndotsikatsi will be arriving soon to administer the rites."

I felt like an athlete about to enter an arena to play the game of my life, with the added pressure of not even knowing what the game was. I turned around. "Has anyone seen the eagle yet?" I figured that facing the ndotsikatsi would be less uncomfortable if I had proved myself by delivering the fish eagle.

"No eagle yet." Dumani didn't sound optimistic.

A pang of dejection flushed tears into my eyes. I had not realized how worked up about my mission I was – how much it meant to me.

"Look!" Dumani suddenly shouted, pointing over my shoulder.

I jerked my head around to see a close formation of three shooting stars streaking across the sky. Fantastically, they did not fall at an angle like regular shooting stars, but instead travelled horizontally above the mountain range. When they came in line with the point where the moon had risen, the little comet-like objects turned sharply and began flying toward us at an incredible speed. It felt as if they had locked on to Dumani and me personally.

My stomach hollowed as a dreadful realization overtook me. "Shit," I swore, "they're bloody cruise missiles."

"What you say?"

"Guided missiles." I stared at the oncoming balls of fire in disbelief.

Halfway across the lake the missiles broke formation and shot off in different directions. At first they appeared to be doing random acrobatics in the sky above the lake. It took me a while to realize that they were actually tracing letters and the outline of various symbols, though I couldn't keep up with their manic signals.

Dumani watched with his jaw hanging open. "Hauw," he giggled, "the gods are crazy."

Several times the orbs of light came together to dance above the shimmering water as a single entity before exploding in a shower of sparks back into their individual forms. Finally, they hung close together above the lake without moving and then, after a while, began drifting down like parachute flares. One by one they hit the water and went out.

"What the hell was that?" My feelings of sadness and dreaded anticipation had been supplanted by an exultant awe. I would have given away every outcome I ever hoped for to have just one person from my life outside of the Meluti witness what I had just seen.

Dumani chuckled with great delight. "Yew, yew, yew! You see that, eh, white boy? You can see lights, but never like that. When you see it like that, it's the gods telling you they love you, that they have some big job for you."

"What are you talking about?"

"When the natives see lights in the sky, they say that it is witches going about their monkey business. But in fact, this is a fantastic sign. Metaphysically speaking, these kinds of anomalous lights always precede otherworldly experiences. Before a fairy sighting, or a UFO sighting, or a crop circle discovery, or things like that, these lights come on. It's an omen that the foundations of self-conscious reality are shaking. A doorway is opening into the Land of Dreams."

Out over the lake, I detected a vague movement in the same direction that the three orbs had vanished. I thought I must have been seeing things. Then I saw it again. There was definitely something out there. Peering into the gloomy light of the moon, I made out the nebulous form of a bird winging its way over the water toward the village. As it came closer, I could see that it was a raptor of some kind. My heart skipped a beat. If it was my fish eagle, my supernatural power would be confirmed – but it also meant that I would be undertaking a mission upon which a lot more than my own pride would be riding.

The bird was flying at an unnaturally high speed, seemingly propelled by a force other than its own wings. When it was a hundred yards out, I could already distinguish its pale chest and head from its dark body. The moonlight glinted off its blue-black wings. My heart soared to see the giant fish eagle swooping in like a king riding to take his place at the head of an army.

When the eagle reached us, it suddenly dive-bombed Dumani and me as if we were a pair of pheasant chicks. We both covered our heads with our arms as we saw the eagle's claws reach out for us. There was a thunderous flapping of wings and a rush of wind as the bird braked above our heads. It flew in a tight circle around us a few times and then climbed ponderously back into the sky again. Once it was level with the tallest treetops, it stopped flapping and glided off in the direction of Veeti's boma.

Dumani straightened himself, though he kept his hands out in front of his face. "You see that?" he marveled. "The eagle coming to you and saying, 'Let's go.' Things are unfolding beautifully, my friend."

I straightened myself up, not sure whether I was more shocked by the eagle's feint or by the fact that it had actually arrived. The idea of me flying off on an eagle's wings to do battle with a warlord's demons was no longer a remote fantasy. It appeared to be really happening.

"This isn't a dream?" I shook my head incredulously. "I'm going to fly across the Land of Dreams to steal Graca's heart back, aren't I?"

"Sure," Dumani dropped his hands to his sides, "it looks like it – your first job as a shaman. Normally beginners practice by making some rain or breaking a romantic enchantment of a lovesick girl. But you are starting at the highest degree of difficulty. The future of the Republic and the Irrigation Scheme and the Meluti are in your hands."

"But how does it work? What do I do?"

"Come, let us go. We mustn't keep the eagle waiting. I'll explain while we walk."

As we started toward the nearest line of burning torches, I saw a figure rise off an overturned mokoro thirty or so yards to our right. There was no mistaking the outline of a pump-action shotgun swinging over the figure's shoulder.

"In strict anthropological terms," Dumani was saying, "this is a straightforward soul retrieval ritual. Indigenous cultures such as ours believe that all ailments and negative conditions are caused by a loss of soul. The shaman's job is to retrieve the soul. To do that, they need to fight the demons that stole the soul or caused it to fragment. You understand?

"Really, though, we know that there are no causes outside of ourselves. The demons are a metaphor for our own wounds. The soul is stolen or fragmented – by ourselves, way back in early childhood – long before it becomes apparent. When we are in the individuation phase of life, busy creating a concept of individual existence, we look for validation. Something happens; we have experiences that hurt us. Not necessarily because they are painful in themselves, but because they tell us that we are not valid. To resolve the emotional pain, we make up what that means – about us, about others, about the world. The definitions begin to replace who we truly are. You see?

"Now, with our new definition the pain is resolved, but there is a new tension. We now have beliefs that we must resolve. So we develop strategies to resolve our beliefs. As we get lost in resolving our beliefs, we become separate from who we really are and what we really came here to do. When this separation is extreme, it makes us sick – sick in nature, sick in body, sick in actions."

As we arrived at the torch-lit path leading into the heart of the village, two warriors armed with AK-47s acknowledged us with the cordial Lapedi greeting, "Yes, you who belong to us, we see you."

"Yes," I replied, "I see you, too." I continued the conversation with Dumani in English. "I see what you're saying. So how do you repair the damage? How do you restore the wholeness?"

"You ask good questions, and the answer is very important. The cure is to go back and witness the causal incident again without judgment. So the consciousness of the damaged person is clear that what happened did happen, but what they made up about it never was.

"When I was studying abroad, I discovered that there was a revival of soul retrieval in the modern world. Only, they call it regression work – taking the patient back in their memories to a time when something traumatic occurred. Maybe they have it worked out by now, but when I was there I saw that Westerners were only working with half the truth. It never occurred to them that the one witnessing the past event was the victim itself, the ego. No matter what the cathartic benefit is of reliving the painful memory, the ego still believes it means something. It can often be consoled by acceptance, gratitude or forgiveness – all very powerful principles. They help the patient move on, free up the unconscious preoccupation with the wound, which takes the power out of it – but only to some degree, not entirely. When we work at this lower level of consciousness, the poison is never entirely sucked out. The ultimate level of healing happens when the one witnessing the past does not take it personally. To heal properly, to wipe the slate clean in the consciousness, you have to witness from the point of view of the pure creative spirit, the one who knows that it means nothing. The witness, whether the healer or the patient, must stand in the wound in innocence."

Dumani stopped walking and grabbed me by the arm. I heard the footsteps following behind us stop. "Don't you know the Grail myth, that one about Parsifal and the Fisher King? The king was dying from an incurable wound and one day Parsifal gave him a cup of water to drink. Right away the king got better. He said to Parsifal, 'How did you know to give me water to drink from that cup? My brightest and bravest have been searching far and wide for the Holy Grail without success.' So Parsifal, whose name means 'innocent fool,' said to the king, 'I don't know. I saw you were thirsty so I gave you water to drink from the cup standing beside you.' What about that? Innocence! You see that? The king's physicians tried everything. No one could heal that king except the one who was in innocence."

Dumani now spoke even more earnestly. "When it is the vibration of the lower consciousness that is the witness, there may be some catharsis, even some kind of symptomatic relief. Structurally, though, nothing will change. The loss of soul will remain, the victimhood reinforced. Always the subconscious will find a way to reflect that powerlessness. But when the higher vibration of consciousness is the witness, that higher awareness permeates the lower vibrations, raises them up. Then true change is occurring. The wound is cleansed."

He paused dramatically. "You must stand in the torment of Graca's personal myth and reflect back to his whole self that it never was."

His words resonated with a sublime ring of truth. Following the acrobatic lights and the arrival of the fish eagle, they were even more exhilarating than his vibration-raising meditation. And yet a part of me was still exasperated that I didn't have a clue as to how to achieve the end result Dumani spoke of.

"But how do I do it?" I blurted out. "I'm here; Graca's somewhere in Portuguese Territory. What's the process? Are there words?"

"Don't panic," Dumani cut me off. "Do you think you won't find out when the time is right? The only thing you must do is resist the temptation to need to understand or to judge. Life is a journey fraught with horror and wonder. Your mission is no different. If you let go of the wonder, your mind will be led to horror."

Persuaded by Dumani's admonishment to have trust in whatever was unfolding for me, I gave up trying to fill in the missing pieces in my knowledge base. I was immediately flushed with a profound elation, apparently promoted by a connection I felt with the whole world as soon as I stopped trying to work it all out. Now my sense of awe and wonder was complete. I was no longer merely amazed or exhilarated – I was inspired.

It was in this exalted state that I arrived at Veeti's compound. Even as we approached the boma, I felt a fresh surge of anticipation as I listened to the excited buzz of the crowd gathered there. Arriving at the gates, I was taken aback by the scores of villagers packed into the modest enclosure. All eyes were on the fish eagle, which perched at the top of the leafless Marula tree overhanging the central hut of the compound.

Dumani pushed through the crowd ahead of me to the pergola. As we jostled our way into the center of the throng, I spotted several faces I knew from before: Mumuletu and the one-armed warrior, the old crone who supposedly could summon lions, the precocious sorcerer's apprentice – they were all there, along with several others. Veeti, his senior wife and their daughter, little Yapile, sat on the edge of the packed pergola. When they saw me, all three gave me the Lapedi salute. "Yebo, *Mlumzane*," Veeti's wife sang out. "Greetings, Lord." Something about her reverential tone suggested that she was proudly calling attention to her association with me.

Yapile gave me a fragile, heart-melting smile and quickly looked down. Veeti sprang energetically to his feet. "Mlumzane," he said, offering his hand.

"Hauw, Chief, quite a crowd you have gathered here," Dumani nodded his head approvingly. "It should be a worthy send-off."

Aside from several fires blazing in the compound, the boma was also lit by burning torches tied to the corner posts of the pergola and poles in the enclosure wall. My eyes were drawn to the eagle. It sat regally on its perch with its head fixed attentively to one side. I felt as if it were looking directly at me. In the no-man's land between firelight and moonlight, there was something spectral about the giant bird's appearance. I could almost see right through it.

I was not the only one to marvel at the thought of the fish eagle and me being coupled by destiny in such a phenomenal undertaking. "Can you believe that this magnificent beast has volunteered to carry the white man across the Land of Dreams?" I heard a villager ask in amazement.

"I've only heard stories about eagles flying people places," another was saying, "but why not, if we can get about as other creatures?"

"If you had known his grandfather, you wouldn't be surprised," Veeti's wife sniffed haughtily. "That old man – bless his memory – his totem was a fish eagle, too. The skies were safe in his day."

It was fantastic to reflect upon the suggestion that my grandfather had been a visitor to the Meluti and was initiated in the ways of the indigenous people. I might have been morbidly engrossed by the question of why his knowledge had not passed on to me, had I not been so thoroughly enjoying my sense of belonging among the people of Mlumu.

I could not help but compare my alienation of the night before to my current state of ease among the villagers. It was wonderful to be so openly accepted into their collective myth, and thereby their hearts.

Even so, I was aware of a persistent nagging within me that resisted losing myself totally to my joy. Perhaps it was my conditioned fear of going native, or maybe it was the investment I had in the world I had come from; whatever it was, something was still around to remind me that it was irrational nonsense to join an uneducated rabble of half-naked natives in making believe that an eagle was about to carry me off to change the course of a war by doing some kind of psychic surgery on the commander of the vanquishing army. I flinched at the thought of what my mother and brothers – or even Maxine, for that matter – would think if they knew what I was going along with right then.

Sibongila's widow was sitting on the edge of the pergola just a few places past Veeti's wife. When our eyes met, she said something in the Meluti dialect and juggled her breasts at me. With a salacious laugh she turned to share some joke with the villagers crammed behind her.

"She says she can now be the wife of the one who is called the Fish Eagle." It was David's voice. He was standing on the other side of the pergola, hand in hand with a nubile girl who looked up at him adoringly. I did a double take. It was astonishing to see Maxine's chauffeur standing there so proudly in a sarong and monkey-skin bejuga with guinea fowl feathers adorning his hair. The amber torchlight glowed incandescent on the rich brown skin stretched taught across his strapping chest and shoulders. I was amazed at the transformation he had undergone in the Meluti, from a fawning servant, servile and insecure, to a warrior capable of assuming demonic form. It impressed on me how pathetically we are reduced when we try to fit into something that we are not, and how great we are when we come back home to who we really are.

Staring at David and contemplating his greatness was a defining moment for me. I felt as if I were looking in a mirror. Not in terms of physical appearance or the qualities of his power. I could never be him. But in the sense of coming home, of being restored to my native nature, I could relate one hundred percent. I knew for sure that if I couldn't see the world through the eyes I had come to see it, and know what I knew via the awareness I had gained in the Meluti, then I would always be a pale shadow of myself.

"I see you, my brother," I called over to him, touching my left hand to my right elbow and my right hand to my temple. It was the first time I had ever used the salute with total sincerity.

In that same moment the soulfulness of the natives hit me. An animated energy, usually censored by my rational senses, oozed out of everything they possessed. The batik patterns on their Java-prints danced with life; the motifs on their bead skirts and chokers and the walls of their huts paid homage to the deeper design of the extraordinary world they belonged to; and the skins and feathers they wore exuded an added dimension of personality, extending the individual's identity to include a deep affinity with nature. There was something about seeing the tribe gathered in the enchanted bronze firelight, transfixed by the wraithlike eagle perched above them that evoked a force far greater, far deeper, and far more poignant than the intellectual arrogance that seeks to squash life by means of mechanical objectivity.

I heard Dumani say in my ear, "Just go with it."

I looked at him, puzzled. "Go with what?"

"With the wonder," he said. "Your culture is an elaborate system for denying what you feel and know right now. All your life it has guarded you against nature, especially your own nature – because it is wild and chaotic. Science and religion can seem different, but in their fundamentalist guises they are the same. Then they are just competing systems for ordering the universe.

"Culture is a beautiful thing when it refines our ability to express and experience soul. But when refinement becomes the end in itself, culture becomes the enemy of soul. It buys you with the promise that conforming to its objectives will give you fulfillment with safety. This is a very persuasive promise – and clever, too. Because, when you don't get what you thought you would, you think that there is something wrong with you, not the system. So, all the time you are running around working on fitting in with the system of your culture, and while you do that you are lost to your untamed nature.

"Like you, Vale, you worked so hard to be the model of what a man should be in your society. You wanted to be the one who could hold everything together, rise to the top and supply everyone else with the resources to help them in their upward mobility. And all the time you struggled to conform, believing that was where your safety lay, you never stopped to think that there might be something outside the system, outside the collective agreement of society. You never thought to let that struggle go and follow the calling of your wild self, nor did you ever consider that out of that adventure your life would flow and your true connections grow.

"Your culture made you a false promise. But now you feel your culture losing its grip on you. You feel yourself slipping into the water you thought you would drown in. Only, it's not death, it's life – real life. You know what I'm talking about?"

"I know exactly what you're talking about," I smiled at Dumani. "I feel it."

"That's why I say, let go."

"I'm letting go, don't worry. Since I stood in the circle of my heart, there is no other way for me except the way I am guided."

"That is good," Dumani said. "It is good to know that you have found what you were looking for."

"I found you." I tried to smile again, without success. I was acutely aware that the expression I was trying for did not match my true emotion. A feeling of deep grief began choking me in relation to Dumani. I looked at him in bewilderment. "Am I dying?"

"Yes," he said kindly, "you knew in your heart when you

set out for the Meluti that neither you nor Dr. Carlyle would survive."

"What now?" I thought sadly. Perhaps I actually spoke the words.

"Never mind, Vale," Dumani managed a sympathetic smile, "you are dying to this world, but you will wake up in another world. You must not think about what you will lose here. Think about how you can use what you learned from us to create what you love in the next life."

I realized that I was no longer standing up. I was lying down on the wooden slats of the pergola floor. Dumani was kneeling beside me. The light of the torch burning above us reflected like two flashing eyes in his glasses. Curious faces crowded in around us. I heard a weird chanting noise at my feet. The ndotsikatsi was standing over me with her eyes rolled back in her head, passionately conducting her symphony of incantations with a rain stick. The sound of showering water cascaded sensuously through my mind, accompanied by the backbeat of a djembe being tapped lightly somewhere in the crowd.

"I think I've jumped ahead in time." I looked at Dumani in alarm.

"Relax," he said soothingly, "it's the medicine. Put your head back and go with it."

I lay my head down on a rolled-up blanket and closed my eyes. All of a sudden, I was back in the crowd standing beside Dumani. The resumption of linear time was so abrupt, my head spun. I clasped a hand on his shoulder for support.

No sooner had my dizziness cleared than an enthusiastic murmur of recognition swept through the gathering. As if by magic, the crowd parted in an instant to form a spacious path from the boma entrance to the pergola. Down the path came an old woman wrapped in a blanket bearing the same patterns as were painted on the village huts. She wore a kindly smile on her face. Folded over her crossed arms were two leopard cubs. The murmur of recognition that greeted her became a rumble of astonishment.

"Hauw," Dumani cried with delight, "the ndotsikatsi has brought her children from her leopard wife to witness the occasion."

The ndotsikatsi was unrecognizable compared with her appearance the night before. Gone were the cat skins and demented demeanor, replaced by a charismatic serenity. While her face was shrunken and lined by old age, there was an exquisite beauty projected by the modesty with which she carried herself. When she stopped before me, my whole attention was drawn into the universe of mystical illumination swimming in her eyes.

She fixed me with a long stare before acknowledging her people in common Lapedi. "I see you all, my children. What a beautiful night for it, is it not?"

"Yebo, Ndotsikatsi," the crowd chorused like a classroom of children greeting a favorite teacher.

The ndotsikatsi looked up at the Marula tree. "And you, my brother, thank you for answering the call to carry this sorcerer on his journey. The fate of these sacred swamps fly on your wings tonight. We know your efforts will be worthy; we pray the ancestors sanction our course of action."

The eagle swiveled its head as she spoke. Then, as she concluded, it beat its wings and flew down to a lower branch. To the delight of the crowd, it cocked its head, as if to listen more closely.

"Eh, eh, eh," the villagers laughed, "look how the eagle understands the ndotsikatsi's words."

The sorceress turned to me with an indulgent smile. "So, the curse is already visited on you, son of Vale. Tonight you become a fish eagle."

"It is not a curse, Ndotsikatsi," I said. "I am honored that I can do something to protect the lives of those I care about." My words were not exactly sincere; they were more like those spoken by a subject in deference of their liege.

"Hah, then our four-eyed friend has not told you anything about what this journey involves. Dumani, you should instruct the boy while I make the preparations. Would you like to hold my babies, you two?"

I took one of the cubs from the ndotsikatsi. One moment the cat-sized cub was wriggling unwillingly in my arms, and the next I was sitting up in the Marula tree looking down at the boma in bewilderment. I could see the naked body of a man covered in white ochre lying prostrate on the pergola floor. An ancient woman whose breasts sagged to her navel stood writhing at his feet. She waved some kind of wand in her hand. All around the compound, and even spilling out into the laneways, a host of villagers swayed fluidly to the rhythm of an orchestra of drums. Their hypnotic chanting and clapping had a calming effect on me. After watching the spectacle for a while, it occurred to me what was happening. The fevered drumming and the dancing and clapping and singing were a send-off. The soul of the prostrate figure was being encouraged to take flight.

I remembered the sound of those drums coming from the natives' compound when I was a child. They used to carry on until two or three in the morning sometimes. When we'd ask a servant who had been playing the drums all night, they would straight out deny any knowledge. "No, no one play the drums last night." They would laugh as if we were crazy.

Now, finally, I had learned their secret. As we white folk lay tucked up in bed resting our bodies against the ardors of the physical world, the traditional inhabitants of the land were sending their souls out into the night on errands that we were incapable of understanding. I had a vision of drums playing all over the Meluti and beyond, while the soul of the people escaped from their bodies, rising up and coming together like a mist over the earth.

I noticed that blood was dripping onto the branch beneath me. I looked around to see where it was coming from, but there was no sign. Then I observed blood running from the nose of the ochre-covered body. Soon, everyone's noses started to bleed. The earth became a blood-soaked sponge.

"What's going on? Are you alright?" Dumani was peering at me with concern.

"I keep feeling like I'm going to black out." I shook my

head. The cub I was holding squirmed off its back and snuggled belly-down into my folded arms.

"It's the power of the medicine. Your body is reacting even before you take it."

"Medicine?"

"Yah, the medicine the ndotsikatsi is cooking up for you. You know where it comes from? South America. Yah, the Portuguese sailors brought it to Africa hundreds of years ago. Some kind of vine. The ndotsis, they tried to mix it with magic dust. When they did, they found out that this super medicine can help you unglue from the vibration you're stuck on. Once you take this medicine, you can travel to any vibration in your consciousness. It's like a super will."

"Why did she say it was a curse?"

"First of all, for you to become an eagle on your first attempt, you will need a dose so strong that there's a chance it will kill you. Second thing, because this medicine fixes you so strongly to whatever you think of, you experience everything in its extreme manifestation. There are things that will come at you as you fly through the Land of Dreams that will be monstrous. Though you only fly through the shadow of the Valley of Death, it will seem like the Valley of Death itself."

My mental state was so manic that the threat of dying did not deter me from going ahead with what I knew in my heart I had to do. The only thing troubling me was my fear of failure. "What if I don't make it, though?" I said, dismayed by the thought. "My family, Dr. Carlyle, the Lapedi people, the Meluti – everything will be lost. Aren't there people in the village – you or the ndotsikatsi – who are experienced in taking this...this medicine? If it is as strong as you say, and has the properties you say it has, how come anybody can't take it and become the fish eagle?"

"No." Dumani shook his head adamantly. "There are many who are experienced. This is the medicine that Veeti used to call you into his world to save his daughter's life. But the fish eagle is your totem – everyone who stood in the boy-sorcerer's circle today saw that. No one here would presume to change shape into your eagle. This is your mission."

"But what if I don't make it? They will all die!"

"That is right. But it is a risk we must take for the sake of something higher. You are the last shaman. If you do not make it, the Soul of the World will be lost forever. You can't leave it up to others. You must go. Your time has come."

In the next instant, I was back up in the Marula tree. This time the instantaneous relocation was not as jarring. My system was evidently getting used to jumping around in space and time. I looked on calmly as the drumming and dancing reached a fever pitch. Only the faintest outline of the ochre-smeared figure remained. Most of his substance had evaporated and hung above his body in an ethereal cloud.

"His nose is bleeding again," my brother Martin's voice floated through my mind.

"Can you fetch the doctor, please, Philemon," Mother called out from a long way off.

"The doctor has gone already, madam," an African voice called back from even further away.

"Typical," Mother huffed.

"Are you sure that it's necessary?" I snapped. I was back on the ground again, surrounded by women with dirty white clay in their hands. "It's bloody winter, Dumani."

"Sure you must," chuckled Dumani. "You must leave yourself behind, become a ghost. Don't worry, the medicine will warm you."

The natives around me looked on jovially, amused by my modesty. Little Yapile moved in beside me. She stared up at me admiringly. "I can take the baby." She put out her hands to take the leopard cub from me. I let her have it.

"Thank you," she smiled demurely.

I was touched by a wave of deep affection for the little girl whose life I had saved. I wished I had something to give her to let her know what a beautiful soul she was. An idea came to me. "David," I called out, "can you go to our hut and get me my phone, please? It's in my bag with my passport and things."

"Yes, sir," he said. "I will hurry."

I turned back to face the women standing by impatiently to smear my body with ochre. As it happened, I didn't have to wait for the ndotsikatsi's "medicine" to kill me I died right there and then as I stripped. Every article of clothing, starting with my fleecy jacket and boots, symbolized some layer of my external façade being peeled away. Until that moment, I had never been aware of how much power I had invested in my appearance. Not only could I imagine how ridiculous I appeared compared to the statuesque natives, I was also bereft of the very tokens signifying my elevated standing among them. I felt as small and vulnerable as an aborted fetus.

Mercifully the women didn't give me any time to dwell on my pitiful vulnerability. They attacked me with the zeal of children in a food fight. The shock of the freezing mud was mitigated only by the bruising ferocity with which they slapped it onto my body. Any entreaties to go gently only encouraged my assailants to attack with more vigor. As they smeared the ochre roughly across my body, grains of quartz cut into my flesh. It was all I could do to stop myself from howling in agony.

Sibongila's wife was the last of the women to plaster me. She waited for the others to back off before planting herself directly in front of me. A few snickers issued from the crowd as she weighed a big clump of clay in her hand and raised her eyebrows suggestively. I gulped. She took a step forward and smeared the muddy lump into my lower chest, just above my solar plexus. I gasped for air, my eyes wide with surprise. Her eyes did not leave mine. A smile played on her lips as she pulled her flat hand slowly down my stomach. The hand came to a stop just below my belly button. I was praying that it would not go any lower. But it did. In a quick motion, the young widow reached for the only part of my body unblemished by ochre. She made several thorough circular sweeps of my genitals and then danced back triumphantly into the crowd. The surrounding villagers laughed approvingly.

"Look, this white man has iron in his veins," Veeti's wife cackled. "Not even the most beautiful woman in the village arouses him."

David saved me from any further embarrassment by arriving with my mobile phone. Handling the device carefully with the tips of my fingers, I turned it on. The mood of those around me switched from hilarity to cautious curiosity. Once the phone was powered up, I quickly clicked on "Settings" and began playing the sci-fi ring tone. The natives' jaws fell open.

"Hauw, what is this witchcraft?" they muttered, trying to back away into the crowd. A few men stiffened, bringing their weapons to the ready.

I tapped the xylophone option. Now the Africans looked at each other in puzzlement. "Xixituba! How does it play?"

Next I played the honky-tonk tone. Everyone smiled in wonder. Some even laughed. "Eh, eh, what a clever musical instrument."

"It's just a small radio," a voice in the crowd disclaimed.

"It is a radio," I acknowledged, "but with this I can talk to people very far away. Even as far away as where the Queen of England lives."

"Is that so?" the disclaimer spoke again. "Why don't you speak to someone far away?"

"The speaking part doesn't work in the Meluti," I said, beginning to regret I had introduced the concept.

The villagers laughed with self-satisfied derision. "If we want to talk to someone far away, we just think about them and they hear us," another member of the crowd piped up.

"Like when Veeti summoned you," someone else said, "he didn't need an instrument to reach you."

"That is right," I nodded, "but can you catch another person's soul?"

"What?" a rumble of consternation rippled through the gathering.

"Yapile," I smiled at Veeti's daughter, "come stand here with the leopard baby in front of me."

Yapile came forward hesitantly. "It's okay," I reassured

her, "this will make you happy."

Still handling the phone gingerly with the tips of my fingers, I set it on camera mode. I pointed it at Yapile. As I moved the camera backward and forward to establish a decent composition, I could feel the villagers' leery anticipation so strongly it made the hairs on the back of my neck stand up.

"Hold the baby up higher," I said. "That's it. Smile." I clicked the shutter down.

I took three photos altogether. Reviewing them, I was pleased that the subdued lighting had worked in my favor. While the pictures resembled Yapile clearly enough, her image was diluted by a diffuse orange haze. They looked like close-ups of a startled apparition.

Selecting the best of the three shots, I showed it to Yapile. She gaped at her own image mutely. There was no way I could tell what her reaction was.

"Here, let me show the others." It was Dumani. He pried the phone away from me. "Look here, people. Look at this, will you?"

Yapile held the leopard cub tightly against her chest and stared vacantly ahead of her.

"What did you think of that?" I asked her. She nodded dumbly. "Did you like it?" She nodded dumbly again. I assumed she was in shock.

A mild commotion had broken out around us. Raised voices expressed either astonishment or disapproval – or both.

"What's he done?" Veeti's wife cried in panic. "He comes here and brings her back from the dead, and now he catches her soul. What have you done to my girl? What evil is this thing?" Her pitch became more and more hysterical.

"Whoa, everyone, whoa," I rushed to assure the assembled company. "I can take these likenesses out of the thing, if you like. But I'm going to give this magic instrument to Yapile. Then she can catch more likenesses, and play music, and one day, if she is outside in the Republic, she can use it to talk to people far away."

"Hah!" The villagers were dumbstruck by my incredible offer. To them, the phone resembled an artifact of the gods.

"Would you like the magic instrument, Yapile?" I laid my hand lightly on her shoulder.

"Eh," she said with what was no more than an extra-strong exhalation of her breath. She continued to stare mutely ahead of her.

"Oh, God of all other gods, this can only be His doing," her mother cried out again. "Well, girl, what do you say to the white lord before the gods take offense at your ingratitude?"

"A big thank you, Lord," said the little girl, her voice cracking with emotion. "I will be very grateful."

Women wiped tears from their cheeks while men straightened themselves and set their faces in stern expressions. "Dr. Carlyle's man will teach you how to work it," I said.

I knew the phone was no good to her in the Meluti, but I made a choice with more conviction than I had ever made a choice before that Yapile would one day get a chance to travel into the wider world and speak to people far away. The little girl's presence evoked within me a profound connection to an animating principle pervading all of existence. I was gripped by a deep love of everything encompassed by all of eternity and inspired to only ever act in favor of bringing into the world that which corresponded with the beauty of that feeling. It was in that moment that I understood why the villagers had such high hopes for Yapile – she was the personification of their collective soul seeking expression outside of the Meluti. But there was something else. The realization that I was looking into a mirror reflecting my own soul was so overpowering that I felt myself beginning to black out.

When I came to again, I was flying through the air at a phenomenal speed. The thrill of traversing the night sky at high velocity was so intense that I had forgotten myself altogether. From high above, the Meluti looked like a massive circular bed covered by a rumpled satin sheet. The dark, incandescent, indigo patches would be the forested islands, I figured, while the shimmering pools and streaks would be the lagoons and channels.

I had almost flown clear across the Swamps before I realized that I was headed in the wrong direction. Not even a fraction of a second elapsed between the time I remembered my true direction and my body reacting. With a twitch of my tail and wing-tip feathers, I was catapulted skyward by a thermal updraught. I rose up through layers of wind, each travelling in a different direction. When I reached an air current streaming south, I banked around and let myself be carried back in the direction of the Stanley Gorge.

"Now you can see why eagles have always been revered by humans since time began," I heard Dumani's cheerful voice in my mind. "They know all about the law of vibration. You don't see an eagle struggling to flap against the wind; they just rise up into the sky and fix themselves on a current going their way. The higher against the lower, he he he."

I tried lifting my head, but it was no use. I was lying on my back paralyzed. I could feel the cold, damp texture of vomit on my chin and upper chest. I grimaced at the astringent taste in my mouth while a nauseating sensation ran back and forth between my nose and throat. My body shivered in reaction to the internal assault of overbearing chemical forces.

In spite of my toxic condition, I felt great overall. I was experiencing everything – even my physical discomfort and rational alarm – from somewhere above my body. My mind kept on waking up to higher and higher levels of lucidity and expanded awareness. I became acutely aware of everything around me from an objective point of view, by which I mean I seemed to perceive things from the point of view of the things themselves. There was something incredibly liberating about beginning to exist beyond the confines of my physical boundaries. My whole consciousness was bathed in a wonderful sense of awe and serenity.

When I fully gave in to the sensation of becoming

unhinged from my egoic identity, I began to appreciate just how committed each and every one of the attending villagers was to my mission. I could sense their whole attention trained on the beat of the drums, which in turn resonated with and amplified the vibration of our collective intention. A profound empathy gripped me, instilling in me an unprecedented joy at being so at one with the heart of a human community.

Though they did not physically come forward, each individual's spirit visited my consciousness to bid me farewell. While some did offer words, it was more the sense that each person imparted to me a measure of their own greatness.

Chollo was the first to commune with me telepathically. In my soul's eye, I could see him standing at the gates of the boma with his back to the dancing. His grip on the pump-action shotgun was tighter than ever. Though outwardly his senses appeared to be straining for signs of danger, I could feel his heart swelling with pride. That pride was so palpable that he might as well have told me in Lapedi how overjoyed he was that I, his nominal superior of nearly forty years, was at last participating in his hidden way of life. It astonished me to realize that he had been waiting his whole life for this moment.

For my part, I now understood why Chollo had so steadfastly resisted anything to do with my culture, whether that be the language, the modern conveniences or the way of thinking. In understanding him so thoroughly, I also understood the ruthlessness of didakta. Even though I had begun to appreciate the ancient Lapedi initiation rite as a spiritual assimilation, I had still been interpreting it through my conditioned Western mind as some kind of toughening-up process. What Chollo helped me to comprehend was that didakta, more than anything, was a kind of entrainment. It was the tribe forcing the initiates out into the Land of Dreams, holding them out there beyond physical and psychological comfort until they had fully assimilated supernatural reality. The young men only came back when they had met their guides and totems and learned to rely on the integrity of their super-conscious abilities.

"You see me like a stone wall without expression," Chollo's spirit said to me, "but now you know that inside I am a lake full of happiness and laughter. I am laughing because I am always one with everything in the world, like you are now with me. I have no hesitation because nothing can happen that will ever separate me."

A weird sensation came over me as I experienced a disquieting loss of distinction between my African guardian and myself. My head spun at the strange insistence in my mind that Chollo was not in fact a separate individual from me, but the human embodiment of my own instinct. I would have blacked out again had the lion caller's essence not startled me back from the brink of unconsciousness. A picture of the old crone's feeble visage floated benignly into the recesses of my inner vision, only to be shattered by a thunderous roar permeating every shred of my infinite being. Nothing else existed in my consciousness save that ferocious sound and a quality accompanying it that projected fearlessly into the physical world. When the lion caller's energy retracted itself back into the collective spirit of the ritual congregation, I perceived that some of that unyielding quality remained with me, indelibly stamped into my psyche.

One by one, and sometimes two by two, the others came to me: the one-armed man, with his gift of courage; Mumuletu and Veeti, with their spirit of service and leadership; Dumani, with his keen intelligence and passion for the mystical aspects of life; the apprentice sorcerer, with his innocence; the ndotsikatsi, with her fusion to nature and familiarity with the Other World; and little Yapile, with her heart of gold. Still others came, evoking humor or compassion, rhythm, the feminine qualities of nurturing and creativity or the simple traits of honesty, loyalty, diligent labor and so on.

Whether it had something to do with my own inner resistance or whether it was her choice, Sibongila's widow was one of the last to appear to me. Her presence was mind-blowing. I was certain that I was in the company of a goddess. When I think back, I wonder if it was the glow of early pregnancy representing itself to my highly impressionable mind. She was like some luscious fruit that hung before me, commanding me to feast my mind on the sensuous vitality pulsing through her juicy, ripe, unblemished physique. I was in no doubt that all life sprang from her fertile being, that it was through this goddess that nothingness must pass before it could become something.

Lying there transfixed by the young widow's staggering beauty, I was aware that her appeal emanated from the sublime creative force I beheld in her. It explained to me her sexual confidence, which I had found so embarrassing. At the same time, I realized that what I had taken for lewd sexual advances was in fact just her way of proudly proclaiming her God-given nature. It underscored to me how opposite the natives were to my own culture in their open-minded relationship to sexuality. While the tribal people of the Meluti fully owned the fact of sex and their own sexuality, we civilized folk had an almost pornographic association with ours. We titillated ourselves with allusions to carnality while never fully admitting to the depth and passion of the primitive function within ourselves. If it weren't in fact true of Western society, it was true of me. Somewhere deep inside of me I was ashamed of my sexuality, and I knew that my shame buried something magnificent about me. There were many kinds of power that I had learned to hide to help others feel safe and comfortable.

Once I had received the gift of the widow's insight, her energy suddenly became indistinct from all of the other energies infusing my consciousness. David was the only person I knew among those present whose persona had not telepathically communed with me. I was in no way concerned that he had not done so, yet I did want to say goodbye to him. I searched for him in the crowd with my soul's eye and then shape-shifted into his essential form as I imagined it. It was like stepping into a void. His consciousness was completely blank. Not a single impression revealed itself. There was nothing disconcerting about the utter emptiness. On the contrary, there was an exquisite lightness and sense of pure possibility, as if I had stumbled upon the blank canvas of life upon which I could paint anything I wanted. A shiver ran through my body as it dawned on me that David was not a regular human being. The man whom I had judged to be the most insignificant and unassuming member of our party, and whom I had kept at bay with my suspicions and prejudices, was in truth a mystical familiar of what was highest in me.

At the precise moment of this realization, the steady hypnotic beat of the big bass drums gave way to a cacophony of cheers and shouts. I was looking down at the sweating mass of humanity beneath me as they saluted me with clenched fists and raised guns, and howled their approval of me. There was not even a trace of the ghostly being who had been lying on the pergola floor. I had become a fish eagle. I tilted my head back and let out a piercing whistle-like cry that sliced through the night.

CHAPTER ELEVEN

Soul Retrieval

There are many stories in our culture that tell of the horrors confronting humans who travel into the Other World. The protagonists of these tales invariably find themselves in strangely enchanted environments typically laid waste by malevolent forces inimical to human virtues. Typically, too, they are surrounded by weird creatures and distorted personalities representing the hero's fears and complexes. Overall, the experience is always unsettling, to say the least. But there weren't any stories that I could remember that told how weird it was for Other Worldly creatures to venture into our world. I was about to find out for myself.

I carved through the air at such a speed that the stars above me were blurry streaks in the sky. Far beneath me, Lake Stanley looked like a giant furnace discharging a silver-gold lava that flowed backward up the Muchocho, across the plains of the Republic and into a gleaming thread on the horizon. The delight of rediscovering my aerial nature, combined with the potency of the qualities the villagers had armed me with, infused me with a dashing optimism. I relished the challenge of soaring through the war-torn skies to do battle with the forces of death and destruction.

A rude shock awaited me at the end of the Swamps, though. My supernatural powers were not as invincible as I presumed. As I flew over the Stanley Gorge, my wings began to sag as if pressed down by giant weights. I had hit a wall of air as dense as water. There was no wind stream keeping me aloft any longer. I began losing altitude at an alarming rate. My wings instinctively tried flapping but they were too leaden to move. The stars now streaked away from me vertically as I plummeted to Earth.

There was no use struggling. The weight of the atmosphere was too heavy for me to contend with. I resigned myself to being dashed against the great slabs of rock on the western face of the Lesoti Mountains. I heard Dumani's voice echoing in my head. "There are things that will come at you as you fly through the Land of Dreams that will be monstrous."

With my head hanging upside-down, I looked out across the world that was racing up to meet me. I could make out a haze of dark clouds across the horizon, and through them, the dull red glow of a hellish inferno. Beyond the Irrigation Scheme, the whole of the Republic was burning. Now I knew what had hit me. It was the grief of a nation ripped apart by war: the heartache of mothers torn away from children, the suffering of those scorched and cut up in battle, and the shell-shock of the newly dead souls blasted out of their bodies. I had run into the vibration of that pain without realizing it and had unwittingly become fixed to it. Unless I shifted to a higher vibration, it was going to consume me.

My mind flashed through all of the qualities the villagers had bestowed on me, searching for one that could pull me up from my free-fall. It was impossible for me to focus under the pain of death. A pang of regret assailed me concerning my mission and how the good things that might have flowed from its success would never happen. For just a second I felt lighter – my fall slowed slightly. A little surge of optimism buoyed my heart, which made me feel even lighter. I almost came to a standstill.

When I began to think about what had happened to slow

my fall, I began plummeting again. I was only a couple hundred feet above the ground. But now I had an idea of what had held me aloft. With every ounce of will I could muster, I pushed aside the thought of crashing into the mountainside and planted myself wholeheartedly in the end result of my mission. If I were going to die, it was going to be with a vision of the green grass of renewal growing across the land, with the children of the Republic looking forward with fresh hope to a bright future.

As my vision took root in my mind, I collided into something and bounced skyward. I had hit a pocket of air only a tree-length above the ground. I spread my wings and swooped down alongside the cliffs of the mountainside, rejoicing at the sight of my shadow racing beside me. At the bottom of the mountain, I didn't rise high into the air again, but streaked across the plains low over the ground. Ahead of me I could see a thousand ghostly rainbows as the moonlight shone through the silken arcs of sprinklers irrigating a seemingly endless expanse of sugar cane.

My eagle breath was unperturbed, but inwardly I sighed with relief. I had just witnessed firsthand the nightmare confronting Other World entities that ended up in our world. Encountering all of the limited definitions that human beings subscribed to, all the wounds their past had inflicted on them, and the greed and jealousy and big ideas and arrogance and self-pity and all the other dumb, self-serving attitudes they used to compartmentalize themselves from their pain – it was like flying into a hailstorm of poisoned arrows, any one of which could cut and infect me with a reality that dragged me from my heavenly chariot into the mud of separation.

Before I knew it, I was circling around the old Vale homestead. No lights burned in any of the pavilions; all was dark. Only the moonlight glinted off the tin roofs and lay like silver frost on the lawns. I was overjoyed to discover that my family home was untouched by the fighting. Hoping for some sign of my family members, I flew lower for a closer look. All I could see was a pair of guards walking on the path between the main house and the guest bungalows where I had been sleeping only two nights before.

"I have a strange feeling that something is watching us," I heard one guard say to the other.

The other guard took his automatic rifle off his shoulder and held it in his hands. "I feel it, too. When you see lights in the air like we did before, you know that something big is up."

"This is not a war between human beings anymore. Gods and demons have taken sides."

"Don't let the white people hear you talk like that, though." The two men chuckled quietly.

Two porcupines rooting around in the vegetable garden looked up at the sky in alarm. They sniffed the air and turned to each other in puzzlement. Then, on some imperceptible signal, they bolted for the hole they had dug under the chicken-mesh fence surrounding the vegetable patch. The hunting dogs ran out into the garden and began yapping at the moon. Somewhere between the garden and the river a bushbuck barked a warning. I knew I should be moving on, but something held me back. I circled the homestead, trying to understand what I was waiting for.

A shadow fell over the rooftops, extinguishing the moon's reflection. I rolled my eyes skyward. There were no clouds. I looked back at the rooftops. It occurred to me that I could feel the shadow rather than see it. Nostalgic memories rose up at me in dark waves. Each wave radiated through me, warming me with some fond recollection of childhood. Memories of family togetherness and special occasions came back to me: birthday cakes baked by Grandma, Christmas presents being opened with wide-eyed delight, the salty smell of venison cooking over a campfire as my father regaled us with hunting stories, my mother arriving home with a carload of new clothes for her boys, shooting catapults that the gardeners had made for us using strips of rubber from old tractor tires. The more the combined sense of place and kinship and privilege and safety cheered me, the more of it I wanted. I circled lower and lower, expecting that the closer to the ground I got, the more potent and, thereby, more fulfilling the nostalgic vibrations would be. It wasn't long before I was feeling totally empty. I might as well have been caught in a net; I couldn't contemplate flying off without getting a boost of some fantastically happy, completely gratifying memory. My flight slowed down and grew more labored. I had to flap my wings to stay in the air.

Without being aware of it, I had fallen into my human habit of looking for energy from where I unconsciously assumed it originated. Next thing, I wasn't just feeling desperately empty, but a chilling presentiment of doom began to impress on me. Now the waves flowing through me no longer caressed me with fond associations. They were loaded with antagonistic messages. Sad memories began to crush my heart. I gasped for air as hurtful recollection after hurtful recollection assailed me: the times my father had abruptly dismissed me when I had reached out for inclusion, the times my mother's mood had hardened against me when I offered to help, the times I was made to feel silly when I expressed appreciation of anything native or compassion for the natives themselves, the times I was left alone because everyone else was too busy, the times I was laughed at because the ideas I expressed made no sense to the adults. All of these experiences, and many besides, combined to form a picture of a small boy – with startled eyes, his thumb in his mouth – standing outside the circle of important family players, looking in with no hope of ever belonging or contributing anything of value.

The pain of that invalidated sense of self was unbearable. As was the pain of the decision the boy made in response to it – that he had to run and hide as far away as he could from his family's heartbreaking rejection of his nature. The weight of that raw wound crushed down on me like a ton of lead. My will to stay aloft evaporated and I fell unceremoniously onto the lawn halfway between the big house and the bottom of the garden.

I lay on my sternum with my wings spread out in defeat. The hunting dogs came bounding across the lawn at me. As they bore down on me, I could see their teeth and eyes flashing gruesomely in the moonlight. My terror of being ripped apart was nothing compared to the depressing alienation pinning me to the ground. I bowed my head in resignation to my fate.

The dogs pulled up a wingspan short of me. They snarled menacingly, their hackles raised. One of them lunged at me and then pulled back with a whimper. The other dogs began whimpering, too. I stole a look at them. They were wagging their tails in excitement, not sure whether they should lick me or run away. The dogs seemed to recognize me.

A shot rang out from near the big house. The hot-pink streak of a tracer bullet carved the night in two.

"Demon, demon," a voice cried out in Lapedi. "The dogs have cornered a demon."

A short rattle of automatic-rifle fire sounded, followed by more phosphorous streaks. "Come on, you cursed hounds," a second voice commanded, "move out of the way so we can shoot."

"You better fly or they're going to fill you with lead," I heard someone say. This voice was in my mind, though. I intuitively knew that it belonged to the alpha male of the pack.

"I can't move," I thought.

"You must fly," one of the other dogs encouraged me. "Your heart is too good to die."

"Yes," another dog yelped, "we know a good heart when we feel it – you could be the next leader of the pack."

"The next leader of the pack," all the other dogs howled together.

When I looked up at the exuberant hounds, I wondered how I could have attributed the power of speech to them. They just shook their tails and whined affectionately. Yet the power of their love was palpable. The dumb look on their faces conveyed their deep, unconditional adoration of me. Their innocent joy at being reunited with me was infectious. The leaden weight of my defeatism began to lift as I took on the pack's enthusiasm.

"What's going on here?" Oliver's irascible voice cried out.

"It's the dogs, Lord Oliver. They have cornered a demon."

"Have you lost your mind, Pangees?"

The energy of the hunting dogs' unconditional love cleared my mind enough for me to refocus on my end result again. As I did so, a golden light burst through my whole consciousness.

"Look, it's starting to fly away," one of the guards yelled. A rifle shot exploded on the ground.

"Put your gun down, Chechwa," Oliver roared. "It was an eagle owl or something. Now you'll wake Madam Cynthia; we'll all be in trouble."

"No, Mlumzane, it was a fish eagle; they don't fly at night. It was a demon for sure."

"Mrs. Oliver was bloody right," my brother moaned. "We should be drug-testing all of you."

As I lofted up out of range of the trigger-happy guards, the crash course I was getting in operating in three-dimensional reality was fixed firmly at the forefront of my consciousness. I was quickly learning to be conscious of where my attention was going. Perhaps the most vital insight of all was that simply because I wasn't self-consciously aware of something, didn't mean that my attention wasn't on it. Just as my unconscious need for unmet childhood validation had unwittingly sucked me into my wound, I found that any painful thoughts and feelings would immediately begin getting heavier and start to drag me down as soon as I tried to deny them.

Flying over the war-ravaged Republic was like navigating through the flack of an anti-aircraft barrage. The terror and trauma of a million souls hit me in dark, unrelenting waves. And yet, though I could not ignore the collective horror assailing me, I found that I did have the ability to neutralize its negative effect on my psyche. By remaining unswervingly focused on my end result, I was entrained to my inherent connection to everything through all time and space. As the fear and grief and hopelessness wrought by the internecine hostilities flailed about in my nether consciousness, the main part of me sailed blithely above the effects of mortal victimhood. From my higher vantage point I could appreciate that nothing ever died, that everything only ever changed, and that the connection and possibilities inherent in our essential nature remained intact no matter what form we took.

The wonder of human truth and illusion struck me, buoying me to a transcendent state of mind. With every physical death, I could see the death of an illusion and a waking up to personal divinity. It was as if each so-called victim were a magical player being pulled out of an amazing game by their coach to look back with delight at a replay of a move they had just made. Human suffering, I could see, is only a product of the illusion of separation. Outside of that illusion there exists only a wonder for all existence and a passion to create the new – the next expression of divinity.

I was glad for the psychological preparation the long, harrowing flight afforded me. After following my instincts several hours southeast of the smoldering ruins of Manzimwe, I saw a sight sure to fill even the bravest heart with dread. Like a snake uncoiling itself, the silhouette of an eagle climbed the invisible staircase of a thermal current into the pre-dawn sky. It could only be Graca's totem heading out to incite his troops in their final day of retribution. There couldn't have been any natural thermals for the eagle to ride before the sun was out. Only enchanted creatures like myself could conjure them imaginatively. Even though the dark silhouette was miles away, I could feel the bitter hatred it carried on behalf of its human counterpart.

In the gloomy moments before sunrise's first blush, I floated down in the direction I had seen the black eagle fly from. As I descended, I was gripped by a sickening anxiety brought on by the prospect of coming face to face with the notorious commander-in-chief of Africa's most ruthless fighting force – not to mention the thought of everything riding on my mission. The only way I could move forward was by reminding myself that I was only playing a game of life and death, and that neither I nor anything else would actually be diminished if I lost – it wouldn't mean anything!

I allowed myself to be drawn by a magnetic force to an isolated encampment set up in the southern no-man's land between the Republic and Portuguese Territory. The sentries keeping watch on the perimeter of the bivouac didn't notice me landing on the huge radio antenna towering above the camp. Directly below me, by the light of a paraffin lamp, I could see a man sprawled out on a camp stretcher under an open-walled tent. A worn, gray blanket covered his body. An overturned jar lay on a small wooden table beside his head. Blood was running from his nose.

"So, this is Graca," I thought. "He doesn't look so dangerous lying there." It occurred to me that the bulk of his energy would be with his eagle self. He looked as frail as a man on his deathbed. His skin had no color. I sensed that he was suffering from a chronic case of the same illness I had originally perceived in Veeti. A knowing deep inside me spoke, using Dumani's voice. "Yah, you see, he drinks the South American medicine so he can perform his magic for his soldiers. He takes the medicine to have power, but after time the medicine has the power; the supernatural tricks have the power – not him. The false power has taken him very high to expose his weakness. Now he must crash to Earth. It is the way it goes when we give something outside of our heart the power."

Once I heard the word "heart" I suddenly understood what I found strange about Graca's presence. It was the absence of any sense that he had a heart. Though he evidently was breathing and had a pulse, my impression was of a human carcass void of any grace, animated only by a diabolical, single-minded programming. While I had become used to the vibrant passion of the Mlumu villagers, the energy of Graca's consciousness was flat and controlled. I shuddered to contemplate what suffering could have dehumanized someone to the point that not a scintilla of his essence dared to show itself.

Driven by an instinctive knowledge of what I had to do,

I imagined the vibration of Graca's empty heart cavity. No sooner had I willed myself to assume that dark vibration than it occurred to me that in Portuguese the word "graca" meant grace, and therefore, in his true nature, the Rebel leader would be the very opposite of his harsh, merciless persona. My first impression was not of some tyrannical beast, but of a sweet lamb-like nature full of trust and eagerness to engage the world. There was also an opposing tension accompanying that charismatic vulnerability, which told me that I had shape-shifted into the vibration of Graca's individuation phase – that time in his early life when he had begun to establish an individual sense of existence. While the innocent nature only wanted to move forward and spontaneously express itself, the conflicting force – like myself back at the homestead a few hours earlier – was waiting for something it perceived it lacked. I could feel the unrelenting longing to be held and adored and taken to the highest mountain and introduced to the world. The effusive spirit of the newly born Graca was not going to be applied to anything until that need for validation had been met.

The theme of feminine doting was strong in the infant Graca's psyche. I could hear his mother's contented laughter chiming in his ears as he sat happily in a blanket tied to her back, or when he suckled blithely on her bosom. There was also a flavor of many other females competing for his affection – aunties and sisters passing him among themselves, cradling him and bouncing him on their knees, all the while expressing their delight in him by singing Chitswa lullabies and nursery rhymes.

While there was some sense of the masculine, it was not strong. Apparently little Graca was yet to feel his father's influence. Nevertheless, he basked secure in the knowledge that when the time came to enter into the masculine's orbit, he would be in good hands. Clearly he perceived the energy of a capable man eager to fulfill his paternal role – meaning, a loving father who was there for him!

The atmosphere of family bliss did not last very long. I was only beginning to contemplate the blessing of such an ideal formative experience when a dark shadow fell over the sunny image I had started out in. The remote, protective masculine shield I had sensed was suddenly obliterated. Through the hole his father's absence left came a sinister force bent on eradicating the biological makeup of the baby boy and his kin. Scenes of doors being kicked open and the sound of gunfire drowning out terrified screams jarred my consciousness. The little lamb's world was instantaneously transformed into a nightmare as every fond and comforting association of his newly begun life was torn asunder.

Now it was dark and the infant sat all alone. Hungry, wet, cold, bewildered, he could still vaguely sense some of the human forms that had doted on him. The presence of many others he remembered had disappeared as dramatically and inexplicably as his father's. A forlorn pain in his heart told him that those who were still in his world were too far away to provide him with any comfort or sustenance. Their love had been transmuted to despair; they could not reach beyond their own suffering to care for him.

· The shadow did not lift; it only grew darker. Dressed in rags, the growing boy – now not much older than a toddler – scavenged in garbage piles to keep himself alive. Even though he saw his mother and other female members of his family occasionally, this contact gave him no joy. When they weren't being dragged off to service the needs of strange men, they were too full of sorrow and shame to be present with him.

While the grief of Graca's experience was almost too much for me to bear, I was at the same time gripped by a morbid fascination. To have the opportunity of witnessing a human being beginning to establish his psychological framework for life was in a way a privilege, an honor. I observed, spellbound, as the boy, seething with hatred and bitterness, began to make decisions about his experience – mainly that his kind were vermin, reviled and unwanted. That perception was compounded by the fact that his people had been powerless in the face of external violation. As a result, he had a vile contempt for himself and his own family.

Unsurprisingly, he formed the belief that in order for him to be viable in life – to get the love and the recognition he craved as much as the next child – he would have to be the one holding ultimate power. To be anything less than the predominant controlling force in his universe meant that he was nothing more than a stray dog.

I knew intuitively that I should linger with those strong feelings of shame and anger so that I could reflect Graca's own beliefs back to his consciousness. Somehow, it seemed important that his ego's version of history was fully acknowledged. I noticed that the longer I observed his harrowing perceptions, the more removed I became from them. As I became less identified with Graca's subjective perspective, so too did the nausea I was feeling begin to ease. I found myself gasping for air, as if my head had been kept underwater for a moment longer than I could hold my breath.

"Ha ha ha," I heard a familiar chuckle floating in the dim recesses of my awareness. "To be a shaman, to be a healer, it takes a deep appreciation of humanness. You have to empathize with the reality the sick one is drowned in – know the vibration they are trapped in. And remember, to heal properly, to wipe the slate clean in the consciousness, you have to witness from the point of view of the pure creative spirit, the one who knows that the wounded reality is an illusion. The witness, whether it is the healer or the patient, they must stand in the wound in innocence."

Dumani's voice sounded so real that I expected him to materialize beside me. I was disappointed when he didn't, having for a split second gotten my hopes up that he would take over the proceedings. I was forced to fall back on trusting that the force that had carried me there on an eagle's wings would guide me to the completion of my mission. Besides, Dumani had given me the clue I needed.

I imagined the vibration of Graca's pure creative spirit and projected myself into it. The beauty of his essential nature was sublime, representing itself visually as a cascade of red roses. Not only was my inner vision inundated with the sight of the flowers, I could smell their exquisite perfume, too. It was as if I had woken up in a Sufi poem in which the temporal mask of humanness had fallen away to reveal the true face of the Divine.

There was no need for me to try to figure out the meaning of my vision. The accompanying emotion spoke clearly of the magnetic appeal of the Rebel leader's true nature. Once I had assimilated that quality, my vision opened up to show me Graca as a man of great power. I saw him sitting in council, while others were persuaded to action by his benevolent guidance. In his greatness, the force of his benevolent wisdom inspired multitudes to come together in the cause of the collective good.

Immersed in the vibration of Graca's pure creative spirit, I turned my attention back to his individuation experience. If anything, I saw it in more graphic detail than his ego had allowed me to. The massacre of his village; his father being gunned down; his mother being raped; the multiple violations perpetrated against him as a child – I was not spared any of the grim incidents contributing to his wounding. Yet, from the perspective of someone connected to everything through all time and space, I failed to see those events in negative terms.

The first realization I was struck by was that for a soul as powerful as Graca's, only such a terrible wounding could ever set up an illusion strong enough to create his earthly vehicle of separation. And secondly, what was abundantly obvious to me was that what had happened to him was petty compared to his greatness. The truth was that his spirit was unblemished, undiminished, untouched. What had happened to the boy had happened...and it didn't mean a single thing about him – it was absolutely not a reflection of who he was or what he could create.

Not only did the past not mean anything about Graca, it meant nothing about the other victims of the atrocities. I could see the love and the decency of his family – qualities to admire, not despise – and I could sense their undying affection for him reaching across the divide of apparent separation. They lived on in his heart – good people who had not let him down, but who had served him well in helping to define his destiny.

In this light, not even the perpetrators of the atrocities could be judged. There was nothing personal about the actions of the abusers. They were only perpetuating injuries that had been committed against them. If anything, Graca's spirit had intentionally landed him in those specific circumstances so that the might of his unlimited nature would be concentrated on bringing justice to the world. This was not an apology for the genocide perpetrated against his people but an enlightened, impersonal perspective from which the vengeful megalomaniac could move forward with grace and help end the cycle of abuse in a positive way.

As I reflected on Graca's enlightened relationship with the internecine war between Chitswa and Lapedi, his explosive rage and compulsion to crush his enemy evaporated. From this perspective, there was no enemy. I had a vision of him taking his place graciously at a newly formed inter-tribal council, where he spoke with a calm and firm authority. His intention was projected by his voice alone, and I saw that his humility carried more weight than all of his fighters put together. Graca now trusted that for the highest good of all to prevail, he needed only make a stand for it in his heart.

There was something incredibly energizing about this higher perspective. The bonds constricting Graca's soul had been undone and all of his latent potential was assembling to begin the task he had been born to undertake. The feeling was as intense as being inside a nuclear reactor. Unbridled passion surged through Graca's entire consciousness as his long-forgotten dream came back to life. I could sense a magnificent joy well up in the emotional core of his being as some recognition took hold that it was possible for him to return to the human fold from which he had cast himself out. That warm sentiment expanded as the realization unfolded to include that he could make his true contribution to society and that, in turn, he could be sustained by the society he served. He did have the power.

The intensity of emotion I picked up on grew so strong

that I began to feel giddy. "Ha ha ha," Dumani cackled in the background. "You see, the fixed was made volatile and now the volatile is being fixed. The illusion is dispelled and the truth resonates through the whole being. The lost soul is back home."

Dumani's voice was an expression of my own joy at witnessing the transformation in Graca's consciousness. Not only was it pleasing to know that I had facilitated that transformation, it was also thrilling to experience the undaunted nature and passion of pure creative spirit. I was awakened to my own immortal nature.

Before long, though, the experience became too much for me. The intensity of emotion became too strong, the white light too bright. It dawned on me that I was being pushed out of Graca's consciousness by his resurgent soul. I began to fret about what would become of me as the white light grew overwhelmingly brighter.

CHAPTER TWELVE

A Rude Awakening

A blinding light shined in my eyes. I was staggering around on the deck of a ship in a turbulent sea, desperately groping around for something to hold on to. From somewhere behind the light came a startled cry.

"Hauw, Lord Mark, he's alive!" A chair scraped against the floor. "Madam Cynthia," the familiar Lapedi voice yelled out, "Boss Mark is alive." A door opened and slammed shut. The voice grew more and more distant. "Boss Martin, Boss Oliver, come quick, it's Lord Mark, he opened his eyes. Madam Cynthia, Mr. Mark he is waking up."

The ship nosed down and then reared up into the full face of the bright light. I held both of my arms over my eyes. My legs buckled under me.

Heels clicked urgently along slate paving stones. "For goodness sakes, I'm here, Philemon," someone who sounded just like my mother snapped. "No need to wake the dead."

"Thank you, madam," the Lapedi voice rejoined.

The heels clacked up a set of concrete treads. A distant door opened. The heels came strutting in my direction. Another door, close behind the light, burst open.

"Mark, thank God, you're alive," Mother's voice came flying through the light toward me. "Philemon, quick, close the curtains. Can't you see the sunshine is hurting his eyes?"

I felt a cool hand on my forehead. "Just relax, darling. It's alright. You're back with us."

I heard the sound of brass rings scraping across curtain rods. The bright light faded. Peering into the gloom I could see that I was in a room very similar to the one I always slept in at the Vale homestead. My mother was standing over me, a nervous black face peeking over her shoulder. I still felt like the world was rising and falling. A bilious knot gagged deep in the back of my throat. I had to close my eyes.

"Quick, Philemon, run and get a bucket. I think he's going to be sick. Come on, don't just stand there."

Bare feet pattered across the floor away from us. They were met by boot-steps coming the other way.

"Is he awake?" I heard Martin say breathlessly.

"Aha! Good of the slacker to join us now that the trouble is all over," said another voice in a tone somewhere between facetious and resentful.

"Shush, Oliver," Mother tutted, "he's just coming around."

"Where am I?" The effort of speaking brought up a spurt of bile that I just managed to catch in my mouth. I forced the bitter fluid back down my gullet.

"It's okay, Mark, the war is over," Oliver laughed sarcastically. "You can come out of your shell now."

"Oliver!" Mother exclaimed. "Stop antagonizing him. He's been in a coma for four nights."

Excited whispers erupted from where the nearest door had been opening and closing. "Go on, kids," Mother sang out, "get out of here. Your uncle is still very sick."

"Is he going to live, Granny?"

"Yes, of course, Jessica. Now you run along, all of you."

"What do you mean, where are you?" said Martin, once the buzz of children's voices had faded. "You're at home. Isn't it obvious?"

"How did I get back from the Swamps?" Again, the effort

of speaking made me gag.

"I have the bucket, madam," the Lapedi voice was back.

"Here," Mother encouraged me, "use the bucket if you need to."

I propped myself up on one arm and leaned toward the tin pail. No sooner was my face over the bucket than a jet of liquid blew out of my mouth, hitting the bottom of the vessel and bouncing back into my face. The rocking sensation ceased immediately.

"Oh, Jesus, it's all over his face!" Oliver winced.

"Oh, shut up! You've skinned and gutted hundreds of buck, for heaven's sake," huffed Mother. "Philemon, we need some towels."

"Here, madam, I have the towels."

"Oh, good work." Mother began patting my face and hair with a towel.

"How did I get back from the Meluti?" I croaked.

There was a brief silence. Mother stopped cleaning my face. I opened my eyes. Everyone was looking at each other with puzzled expressions.

"Oh," Mother laughed reassuringly, "you didn't go into the Meluti, sweetheart. You've been in bed for four nights. You've been sick."

The world began to spin. "No, no," I insisted, pressing my hands into the bed to stabilize myself. "No, I was in the Meluti. I lost Maxine. But I couldn't look for her. I had to find an eagle to take me to…"

My voice trailed off at the sight of the others staring at me as if I were mad. "I was in the Meluti," I shouted. "You saw us go down the river, Marty."

"Hey, take it easy, Mark," said Martin. "You must have been dreaming. You've been here all the time. So was Maxine until she heard that the fighting had stopped. She left to go back to Manzimwe Mission last night."

I looked carefully at each of my family members in turn. Their eyes were bulging and their faces were weirdly distorted, with red and gray smudges blurring their foreheads and cheeks. "Why are you messing with me?" I complained.

"Why are you saying that I was here all the time? I went into the Meluti. I learned how to become an eagle. I took Graca back his heart."

"What's this bullshit?" Oliver groaned. "Now he's got Meluti Madness...without even stepping foot in there."

"Listen to me, Mark," said Mother, "it's all okay. Everything is going to be okay. You never went anywhere. You went to bed the night before you were supposed to leave for the Swamps and you never woke up again till now. We've been worried sick about you. Maxine left you here for dead."

Listening to Mother's perplexing refutation was giving me a headache. I had to change the subject. "What happened with the war, then?"

"No one knows for sure," said Martin. "The Rebels practically overran the whole country. They were camped just up the road the night after you went into your coma. We were expecting the worst yesterday morning. But the final attack never came. The Fighters just suddenly started retreating... running for the hills. No one can explain it. Half their equipment is still on the side of the road."

"Actually, we do know," said Oliver, his tone crackling with levity. "The Africans reckon that the black eagle that leads the Fighters didn't show up at dawn. They thought it was a sign that Graca had lost his mojo. Maybe it was that eagle the guards were shooting at the other night. Maybe they hit it." Oliver chuckled at his own sarcasm.

I tried to accept that I had been dreaming. I conjured up my memories of being in the Meluti: going fishing with Dumani; bringing Sibongila's half human–half baboon body back; drilling into little Yapile's temple with a corkscrew; the ndotsikatsi transforming from a leopard into human form right before my eyes; gliding across the moon-kissed sugar cane fields adorned by gossamer rainbows. These scenes and many more came back to me more real than anything else I could remember – more real, in fact, than lying in bed sick surrounded by my mother and two brothers.

"No," I groaned, "you're not going to fool me. I was in

the Meluti. I was with Veeti. I saved his daughter's life. I found Dumani, the last shaman. He's Selele's brother, Cedric."

"Bloody hell," Martin muttered, "maybe he has got Meluti Madness."

"Call Uncle Jack," I said. "I saw people turning themselves into baboons and leopards. Uncle Jack, he'll tell you I was there."

"Come on, boys," Mother said. "We must leave him to rest. Philemon get him some…ah, you have some water. You watch him. Don't talk to him. He must sleep."

"Paper." I raised my hand to stop my relatives from leaving.

"What do you want paper for?" asked Mother warily. "You need some rest."

"I have to write down everything that happened in the Other World."

"What? No, darling, you must rest."

"Have to write. Have to write."

"I'll get him some paper, Mom," said Martin. "It might help him settle."

As the three figures filed toward the bedroom door, they appeared to me to be some ghoulish imposters departing a nightmare. I turned apprehensively to Philemon. Mercifully, he looked like a real human being.

***

The heels came clicking briskly down the pathway again. I lifted my head up. "It's the madam," Philemon said from his post across the room. "She's with some people."

"Tell them to go away, Philemon."

The house servant laughed nervously. "No, sir, I can't do that. But I think it's some other people, not Boss Martin or Oliver."

Muffled voices carried through the window. Mother's heels marched up to the bedroom door. "Knock, knock." My mother swept into the room. "Goodness me, Mark, are you still at it? You've been up all through the night. Look at these papers everywhere. Philemon, help me collect the paper."

"No," I yelled at her, "don't touch anything. They're in a special order."

"Fine," Mother sniffed, "suit yourself." She lowered her voice. "There are some Africans asking to see you."

A twinge of excitement gripped me. "Who?"

"The headman of Mlumu and some other man. I'm only letting them see you so they can talk some sense into you about the Meluti." Mother turned her head and called out something in Lapedi. I only comprehended the words "Veeti," "friend" and "in."

Veeti and Dumani entered the bedroom hesitantly, looking self-consciously from Mother to me. They both wore buckskin bejugas over scarlet sarongs. Each was attired in a gray pinstripe jacket with no shirt underneath and a pair of lace-up shoes with no socks. Completing their incongruous ensembles, their heads were adorned with a luxurious display of parrot feathers. Veeti's jacket fitted him almost perfectly, while Dumani's was too long at the sleeves and tight around the shoulders and waist. Both of them appeared more vital and robust, somehow, than I remembered them.

"Veeti! Dumani!" I cried. "I see you, my friends. How happy I am to see you. No one here believes that I was in the Meluti with you."

Veeti stared at me blankly. Dumani frowned and turned to Mother. "Can you leave us alone for a while, good lady?" he said in English.

"Well, I don't..." Mother was lost for words.

"I'll be okay, Mom," I assured her.

"Very well, but only a few minutes. He's been very ill. He needs to rest."

When he was sure that Mother was out of earshot, Dumani smiled and said, "How's the tooth?"

I had to think for a moment. "All settled down. Hasn't bothered me since the night before I left for the Meluti."

A pained look crossed Dumani's face. "It sounds as though you have taken our meeting in the Land of Dreams literally," he said.

"What do you mean, literally?" My head reeled in astonishment. "Did I not come to Mlumu Village with Dr. Carlyle
and save the life of Veeti's daughter? Did you not teach me
the way of higher wisdom – definition and meaning, innocence, observing the obvious, making it up, shape-shifting?
What about Ngomani and Sibongila? We found the scout
dead from snakebite. And the fish eagle? I took the South
American medicine and flew all through the night to bring
Colonel Graca his soul back."

"Wait, stop right there." Dumani raised his hand assert-
ively. "It sounds like a very lucid dream. I had one too, you
know, though not as elaborate as yours, I'm thinking. In my
dream I was exiled from the Republic. I was walking about
aimless and lost in the Meluti. Then I ran into you. It was
you to me who said that I was hiding and that it was time to
take my place at council again."

"So all of these things I mentioned, are you saying they
never happened?" I said, dumbfounded.

"No, my friend, I never said that. These things have all
happened, though not in this world. We came together in
the Land of Dreams to help each other with our respective
challenges. If we had not really been there, how would I
know that the council of national reconciliation had been
formed, or you know correctly that the scout Sibongila was
killed by a snake, or the headman know to bring his dying
daughter to you to save?"

Not all of what Dumani said sank in. "How did I go
there? To the Land of Dreams, I mean. It's not part of my
culture, or my beliefs, or experience."

"Dream incubation," Dumani said. "Never mind your
worldview, if the mind is prepared in the right way, anyone
can go there. A strong intention and concentration on a
particular matter, combined with a softening of the rational
faculties. Being rundown, traumatized – these conditions
help. Sickness will take the mind where minds don't like to
go." His words triggered a strange sense of déjà vu. "By the
bruises on your inner arm, I'd say you've been administered
big doses of painkillers intravenously. My guess is, multiple

overdoses of morphine tipped you over the edge."

"Morphine?" Sure enough, there were a couple of yellow-black patches around the crook of my right arm. When I fingered them lightly, they hurt. My head sank back heavily into my pillows. "I just imagined the whole thing," I groaned. "It was all just an illusion."

"What are you saying, white man?" Dumani barked. "Don't say things like that. The dreams we had, our meetings, they were real. Don't think that the Dreamtime is any less valid than waking time."

"But it's ridiculous. I imagined that I really became an eagle and flew across the night to take Graca back his soul. That's insane, isn't it?"

"When I was teaching you about higher wisdom in the Land of Dreams, I would have warned you about the dangers of taking things literally," Dumani's voice took on an "I told you so" tone. "If I teach anyone anything, that is the first thing they must know. You must just accept that in one world you became an eagle and flew across the night to take Graca back his soul, and in this world you have woken up with wisdom you never had before. All the abilities you speak of – innocence, interpreting subtle observations and energies, shape-shifting – these are concrete skills that empower you to stand in the circle of your highest truth. From there you can help yourself and others rise above circumstances – survival – conditioning – and see the higher aim in everything that you're faced with or undertake or aspire to. Is this not miraculous?"

It was obviously a rhetorical question because Dumani carried on without pausing for breath. "Many wonders come together in the Land of Dreams. I teach you lessons, you pass me information. You are not the only one who has dreamed of digging up Graca's buried heart for him. Many people have been working on him in the Land of Dreams – and on my brother, Selele, too. Now the civil war ends suddenly. Is this not an amazing synchronicity? Don't you see how we can move mountains, especially when we come together as spirit?"

The two men from the Meluti stared at me impassively. I stared back at them sulkily. After a while, Dumani spoke again. "I see you are crushed that this was not a literal, physical experience. You think that the phenomena you encountered have no value because everything happened in a dream. But you should not be identified with phenomena. That is childish – just another form of validation hunger.

"You did go to another world. Just not in this form." He waved his hand over my body. "You will find that everything that happened in the Land of Dreams is as real as day, but not real like we know it here. It just represents itself to you in a way that you can understand. Like the shamans of old, they went into the Other World and they experienced all the forces at play according to their worldview, in terms of totem animals and demons. You go there and encounter it according to your worldview. It's like the myth of alien visitation: they have been coming here all through the ages, but before modern flying machines, people saw their vehicles as sailing boats in the sky; now we see them as saucers or rocket-shaped objects.

"The phenomena are not relevant. It is the forces that came together that are relevant. You will find that everything that happened in the Land of Dreams is relevant to this world, and it is this world that you must put your energy into. Fixating on mystic hooey – the phenomena – that's just going to drain your energy, kill the dream. But if you direct the energy of the dream into the end results of this world, then you will create wonders, real magic.

"It is as the alchemists taught: when we rise into the heavens – what they called the albedo – we must use our will – the rubedo – to manifest that vision here on Earth. You should be grateful that you have experienced the exalted power of your imagination. This is the alchemists' secret fire they borrowed from the shamans. Don't put the fire out with thinking and trying to understand and comparing. Let it burn."

He stopped to say something to Veeti in Lapedi, which I did not understand. Turning back to me, he said, "The headman brought you a gift. Maybe this will help you appreciate the significance of what I say."

It was only then that I took any notice of the rolled-up piece of hide in Veeti's hands. He handed the parchment to Dumani, who signaled for Philemon to pass it onto me.

"What is it?" I said as I unfurled the tanned skin on the bedcovers in front of me. What I saw made me gasp in amazement. Etched in black vegetable dye were three portraits, one each of my son and daughter and estranged wife, Kirsten. To look at them closely, which I did over and over again, they were not fine works of art. Yet they bore a striking resemblance to their subjects. The physical characteristics and individual personalities had been captured so accurately that their life-size faces seemed completely animated. My senses were so fooled that the emotional effect on me was the same as if they had been with us in real life.

"Who painted these?" I asked in wonder.

"It was Veeti," Dumani replied.

"Veeti, these are very good," I said. "How did you manage to draw pictures of my wife and children? When did you see their likeness before?"

Veeti stared at me in puzzlement, and then looked to Dumani for help.

"He doesn't speak any English," Dumani said, using a tone that implied I should know better.

"That's why I addressed him in Lapedi," I replied sharply.

"No, it was English," Dumani insisted. "Try again."

As I self-consciously tried to repeat myself in Lapedi, only Veeti's name and the words for mother and children came to me. "But when I was in the Meluti, I was speaking fluent Lapedi," I frowned in dismay.

"Yah, you see," Dumani laughed, "in the Meluti, you would not have managed with the language. But in the Land of Dreams we can speak any language – Chinese, Arabic, anything."

After a brief discussion with Veeti, in which the headman made flamboyant use of his hands, Dumani spoke to me again. "He says that when you met him in the Land of

Dreams, you showed him those people's likeness on a little instrument that you said could talk to people far away."

"That's amazing," I said absently. I was electrified by the realization that I had indeed participated in a supernatural occurrence as profound as the one that had resulted in the *Mona Lisa of Africa*. Nothing could have better illustrated to me how the true wonder of the Other World was not merely the experience of that dimension, but what could be created on the earthly dimension using the power derived from that world. It was as if an undersized helmet had been pried off of my head, freeing me from a tyrannical concentration of existential angst. A tide of good humor flowed through me. Forgetting myself, I blithely attempted to engage Veeti in casual conversation, "When I was in the Land of Dreams, your daughter was asleep and could not wake up. I fixed her by making a small hole in her head. I trust the girl is well?"

The headman's face clouded with confusion.

"No, that's what I told you before," Dumani intervened. "He was guided to bring her to you. In the Land of Dreams, you told Veeti that one day she would become late and that you could bring her back to life."

It was my turn to be confused. "Where is the girl now?"

"At the gate," said Dumani.

"The homestead gate?"

"Yah, with security."

"And how is she?" I asked in alarm. "Is she late?"

"No. But she is in a coma."

"How long has she been unconscious?"

"Yesterday afternoon she started fainting. Then in the evening she passed out and hasn't come around since then."

"How did you bring her here?"

"From Mlumu Village, we rowed over to the Stanley Gorge all night. From the Gorge, the soldiers brought us here."

"Well, she needs to get to a hospital right away. She can be late at any moment now."

"No," Dumani shook his head adamantly, "we have already learned that the road to Manzimwe is closed.

Besides, Veeti will not entrust his daughter's life to anyone but you. It was not medical doctors who promised him in the Land of Dreams; it was you."

I looked at Veeti and Dumani's resolute faces. For a moment, I was speechless. "No," I suddenly cried, throwing the bedcovers off of me. "No, we have to get to a hospital. If the road to Manzimwe is closed, we'll take her to the Capital. I'll drive."

Philemon rushed to my side. "No, Master, you must lie down." As he struggled to push me back against the mattress, he began berating the two visitors in Lapedi. I hardly understood a word, other than a long string of expletives ending with "fornicating snakes."

"What do you say, you black mamba?" Dumani sputtered in English. "You are the one making things worse. Let him go." He shoved the house servant away from me.

"What in heaven's name is going on in here?" Mother's voice rose indignantly above the fracas. The Africans skipped away from the bed in fright. My mother stormed forward, followed by Martin, wearing a perplexed look on his face.

I sat up on the bed with my arms planted behind me. "It's Veeti's daughter," I said wearily. "They didn't tell you; she's at the gate in a coma. She needs immediate medical attention or she's going to die."

"What's wrong with her?" Mother brought her hand up to her heart in consternation.

"It sounds like she has an extradural hemorrhage."

"What's that?"

"I can't remember the medical terms, but basically a blood vessel has burst between her skull and her brain in the region of her temple. A blood clot is forming inside that space, creating pressure on her brain. If the pressure keeps building, she will die."

"Since when are you a doctor?" Martin exploded. "You haven't even seen her. You don't know anything."

"Actually, I have studied medicine for a while," said Dumani, turning on his plumiest accent. "Mr. Vale's diagnosis is quite plausible."

"I beg your pardon?" Martin frowned. By their expressions, I could see that both he and Mother were struggling to reconcile Dumani's half-savage appearance with his eloquence.

"Yes," Dumani nodded confidently, "the bruising on the temple, the dilated pupil, the paralyzed arm on the opposite side of her body, the lucid intervals culminating in a coma."

A sickening premonition occurred to me. "She hasn't got long. The pressure will soon be too great," I murmured.

"We'll take her with us," said Martin decisively. "We're leaving for Council now, anyway. We'll drop the girl off at the hospital in the Capital."

"She won't last that long," I shook my head. "If we don't do something right away, she'll have permanent brain damage, even if she lives."

"Do what?" Mother gasped.

"We have to drill a burr-hole through her skull to let out the blood," I said.

"And who's going to do that?" Martin made an incredulous face. "Our medical student friend here?"

"Oh, no, not me," Dumani put up his hands. "I think your brother is competent enough."

"With all due respect, he doesn't even know how to skin a buck without tearing holes in the hide," said Martin. "What makes you think he can safely drill into someone's head?"

Dumani looked my brother in the eye. "Veeti met young Vale in a dream. He brought his daughter all the way from Mlumu Village to be treated by the young lord. How is it that Mr. Vale knows exactly what ails the girl and what must be done, and you question his capacity to perform this life-saving procedure?"

"Now look here, my good man," interjected Mother, "this is serious business. If my son takes responsibility for the girl and she dies, whether at his hands or not, we could get in big trouble, you know? Not only do we have our relationship with our Meluti neighbors to consider, Mark could be charged with manslaughter – or worse."

Veeti followed the English conversation with a helpless expression. Though he didn't understand the words being spoken, it was obvious that he could tell my family wanted no direct part in saving his little girl – the light of his life and the hope of his village. I tried to imagine what it would be like to be in his place. Detaching from my family perspective opened my mind to an epiphany. My family could only ever see things in terms of their own experience, and their concern for me was always clouded by their own beliefs and self-interests. Trying to fit my truth into their perception could never work because my experiences and insights were unique to me. The mistake I had made my whole life was needing to reconcile my own knowing with what everyone else thought before I took action.

"It's okay, Mom," I said. "This is between Veeti and me. I understand all of your concerns, but if something isn't done right away the girl will die. If Veeti is prepared to risk my drilling into her head, I'm willing to give it a go."

Dumani muttered something to Veeti. The headman nodded with satisfaction. He looked visibly relieved. Mother opened and closed her mouth, but nothing came out. She was again lost for words. Excluding her authority in the matter had completely flummoxed her.

"Mark, are you sure?" was all the resistance Martin could muster.

"Yes, I'm sure," I said. "Marty, we'll need a power drill with the finest wood bit you can find. Philemon, can you take Veeti and Dumani to the gate and bring the girl to the games room? We'll do it on the billiard table. Mom, can you organize some sheets, towels, water and disinfectant?"

"Bandages?" Mother had snapped into pragmatic action mode. As the others made their way out the door, she shouted after them. "Oh, and Philemon, tell the guards on duty I want to see them at the end of their shift." To me she said, "Can you believe the stupid buggers not reporting a child in a coma? It just beggars belief."

I swiveled around to sit with my feet on the floor. "Can I ask you something, Mom?"

"What is it?"

"Can I ask you not to give the guards a hard time about the girl?"

"But, darling, they should be more responsible. I mean, to let someone practically leave a corpse with them and not have the initiative to do something about it."

"You're too hard on the staff, Mom."

"Whatever do you mean? If one doesn't keep discipline with these people, things fall apart. Just the other night the guards were shooting at demons on the lawn." Mother laughed to accentuate the ridiculousness of the incident.

"Haven't you ever been in a situation," I said, "where you're an outsider, where you have no power?"

"What do you mean?"

"These people have to adapt to your world, meet your expectations. It's a scary place, believe me. I admire their guts for turning up every day and subjecting themselves to our constant disapproval. Beating on them only makes them more stressed, and that makes them incompetent. They have no room to express their capability."

"I just get so sick of having to tell them how to do everything," Mother sighed with exasperation. "They never learn."

"Oh come off it," I couldn't stop myself from laughing at my mother's self-pitying tone. I thought of all the arguments against her assertion, like how ingenious the locals were at managing in the wilds without modern conveniences or how they managed to become doctors and lawyers and teachers in our Western system. Yet I had no energy to voice an argument that would only engage Mother's rational mind – in the reality that people create, they can always find evidence of what they believe. Instead, I found myself repeating my original point. "Mom, all I want you to think about is how it is for them. Imagine being a slave in an alien world."

"They're not slaves," Mother objected.

"No," I agreed. "I'm just alluding to the powerlessness of their position, their alienation. All I'm asking you for is to help the staff feel safer. You'll be amazed at the difference in their performance."

Mother pursed her lips and nodded thoughtfully. "Alright," she said at last, "I'll think about what you said."

"Thanks, Mom. There's just one other thing."

"What's that?"

"What's this about Council?"

"Oh, I don't suppose you know, do you? They're forming a council of national reconciliation. Selele's power base has been shattered, both locally and internationally. The only way he's going to stay in the picture, as far as everyone is concerned, is if he begins a genuinely inclusive political process. Hence all stakeholders have been invited to Council, even our friends from the Meluti. I gave them some of Dad's clothes to wear. I couldn't let them attend in just their skins."

"And is Martin going to represent the Irrigation Scheme?"

"Of course. He'll take Veeti and the other man with him."

"Don't send Martin, Mom."

"Why not? He's the eldest son. He's in charge of the estate now."

"I know." I stood up and walked gingerly over to the window. Two gardeners sat on their haunches under a flamboyant tree, snipping the lawn with shearing clippers. Brilliant blue glossy starlings and hornbills with yellow beaks the size and shape of scythes bounced around them. "But Oliver should be our representative at Council."

"What?" Mother was aghast. "I'm surprised you'd support Oliver, considering his antagonism toward you. Besides, he's very undiplomatic. He suffers the natives less than anyone. You know that."

"The past is over," I said, gazing out at the timeless world of the garden. "We all have to move on. Oliver is only the way he is because he's a frustrated orator. When he's the only white man surrounded by a hundred African elders he'll learn some respect, don't worry. For all of Martin's strengths, he's too stubborn to be a politician. Council is going to take up a lot of time. Martin belongs on the land."

"What's happened to you?" When I turned away from the garden, Mother was staring at me with a painful look on her face.

"What do you mean, Mom?" I said, automatically regretting whatever it was on my part that had hurt her.

"You're different."

"I'm sorry," I said, "I only wanted to tell you what I think. I'm not trying to bully you."

"No, no, it's not that." Tears glistened in her eyes. "You sound just like your father now. Ever since his death, I've been so afraid that I would be all alone in guiding the family through these horrific times."

I gave my mother a big hug, tears welling in my own eyes. "Everything is going to be okay, Mom," I sniffed. "There's a lot of wisdom in this family...and love."

When we disengaged from our embrace, Mother turned away from me so that I couldn't see her face. "Alright then," she said in a broken voice, "you wash up and get dressed. We must attend to this poor creature." From the door she called back to me, "Are you sure you know what you're doing?"

"I think so," I called back. The thought of attempting the critical procedure did cause me some trepidation, but it was not my only worry. A dark foreboding had begun to brew in my heart concerning the bad omen I had received about Maxine in the Land of Dreams. Though I had done my best to ignore any sentimental feelings toward her since my return from the Other World, I could no longer brush off a growing certainty that her habit of altruistic folly was about to prove fatal.

CHAPTER THIRTEEN

The Healing Assignment

Addendum to Mark Vale's Land of Dreams notes, August 4

It is not as if I feel like I am going mad, but rather, that my mind has been taken hostage by some very weird dimension of life. It is surreal, to say the least, to contemplate events that I have been a party to. If it were all just a figment of my imagination, that would be more reassuring than to think that I must now conduct myself according to an outrageously expanded set of assumptions about life. None of us realize how comforting the finiteness of our conditioned worldview is until it is wrenched away from us.

One of the aspects of my experience that exercises me more than anything is something I have no direct evidence of, though there are potential clues that, when combined with my innate knowing, seem to point to some startling conclusions. The question I ask myself is, why did Chollo and David both insist on camping out on the veranda of my bungalow the whole time I was in my coma, if not as a conscious choice to accompany me on my journey into the Other World? And did Dumani identify Maxine as a traitor – an imposter – because she was not, in fact, with us in spirit?

Predictably, Chollo steadfastly denies any knowledge of Other Worldly matters and maintains that he was only doing his duty to guard me while I was in such a vulnerable condition. David, who after serving Maxine loyally for three years, and who was prepared to follow her through the Meluti and beyond, chose not to accompany her back to the Mission Hospital. Instead, I'm told that just before I came out of my coma, he took off his European clothing and walked away into the bush wearing a sarong and bejuga, with nothing but an assegai and fighting stick in his hands.

Dumani warned me that it's best not to try to work everything out. Doing so only engages the rational mind, which in turn has to reference our belief system for answers, which of course removes us from objective reality. All paradoxes can be resolved if we but give our subconscious minds the room to put things together. And it's in those moments when I stop needing to understand everything that it comes to me, again and again, that it was David who was leading us in search of the last shaman. There is just one question that I would need to ask Maxine to find out whether my hypothesis is correct or not. If it is correct, it can only mean that we were unwittingly carrying a message from Selele to his brother, seeking the help of Dumani's supernatural allies in the fight against Graca.

So many realizations flow from this realization, and deeper questions, too. It brings to mind Dumani's obsession with spies. But if in physical, three-dimensional reality David was an agent of the Republic, what is he in the Other World? What is he to Maxine and me outside of time and space? Who is he really? It makes me shiver to think. And I know that if I don't think about him too much, if I don't rationalize him out of existence, he'll always be there to guide me as I travel through this phenomenal world he has brought me to.

From the diary of Jessica Vale, August 5

I can't believe how different things are around here since the fighting stopped. Maybe it's because everyone is so grateful to be alive. But things have changed a lot. Uncle Martin still likes to think he's the boss of everyone, but the hunting dogs don't think so – they follow Uncle Mark everywhere now.

The best thing is that Natanzi is coming to stay until school opens again – thanks to Uncle Mark. Dad is going to bring her from the Capital in the next couple of days when Council adjourns. We heard that Dad has impressed the indaba so much that there is talk of him being offered a senior position in the next government. Granma Cynthia says that Natanzi can help little Yapile settle in with us. I don't know how Uncle Mark persuaded Gran to take the headman's daughter in. Now she talks as if it were her idea. She says that Yapile has to stay with us so she can learn English; otherwise, she can't attend the Estate primary school.

The little girl is so sweet. It's fun showing her all of the technology things she's never seen before. I think the stimulation is helping her get better. It was really spooky when Uncle Mark showed her the phone he's going to give her and there were three photos of her already on it. Uncle Martin and my mom say that the photos are so fuzzy, they could be of anyone. Me and the other kids can see it's her, though. You can even see a bandage thing wrapped around her head.

***

It was the first time little Yapile had been in a motor vehicle in a conscious state. Whenever I stole a glance at her in the rearview mirror, she was staring at the moving scenery in open-mouthed astonishment. Just to see the vast expanse of savannah plains teeming with gnu and zebra would have been a marvel to someone who had known nothing other than the closed-in riparian forests around Mlumu Village. And to do so from the luxury of a vehicle moving twice the speed of the fastest animals she had ever encountered would have been even more incredible.

The little girl's greatest astonishment was reserved for other vehicles. Whenever we passed a car or a truck I'd hear an incredulous gasp from the backseat. "Hauw, another one!" It must have amazed her that just over the mountain range from where she lived there was an endless expanse of dry land where people commonly moved about in motorized transportation.

I wondered what she made of the occasional half-naked tribal folk waving cheerfully from their thatched huts. I was hoping that it gave her some sense of continuity to know that there were people outside of the Meluti who lived like she had. Though, I did sense that she wore the floral dress Mother had clothed her in with great pride. She even seemed to wear the excessive layers of bandaging around her head with an air of distinction. My feeling was that although she was still in a fragile condition, and not a little bewildered by the world she had woken up in, she was nevertheless very satisfied with her newfound circumstances.

Chollo sat beside me in the front passenger seat, as inscrutable as ever. He stared straight ahead, his face set like a grim, ebony mask. Every now and then he'd point into the bush without taking his eyes off the road and mumble something like, "Do you see that cheetah lying under that bush over there?" Mostly I couldn't make out what he was pointing out, no matter how hard I looked.

When it came time to turn off the main road that led to the Capital and begin driving toward the big mountain pass snaking precipitously up to Manzimwe, a swarm of butterflies started up in my stomach. Chollo sniffed heavily, as he always seemed to do when serious trouble loomed. He repeated his nervous habit of emptying the pump-action shotgun and reloading it. Most disconcerting of all, he once again saw fit to lay out a line of cartridges along the dashboard. "Vol-vol" he grunted, pointing at my hip to remind me of my own gun.

As we crested a steep hill, I could see a wall of smoke billowing up from the top of the mountain range to meet an oppressive cloudbank. Manzimwe was still burning. My heated conversation with Martin only hours before came back to me, and I wondered how wise I had been to defy his direct order not to return to the Mission Hospital.

"If the girl has to be checked out, take her to the Capital," he had said in answer to my reason for driving up. "It's too soon after the fighting. One of our scouts just came back from Manzimwe; they said it's a horror show."

"It's not only to get Yapile checked out," I leveled with him. "I've got a bad feeling about Max. Something bad is going to happen to her."

"Oh, and you know this how?"

"It's just a hunch."

"Oh, a hunch. Why didn't you say so?" his voice couldn't have sounded any more sarcastic. "Listen here, that woman is the biggest shit-stirrer this side of the equator. Of course something bad is going to happen to her. And she deserves it. She overdosed you with morphine and then ran away, left you for dead."

"You don't know the full story."

"I don't know? What do you know? You were lights-out the whole time she was with us. You know nothing. Just because you did a bit of bush surgery you think you're the main man now? Even if that jungle doctor was talking you through it?"

"She needs help."

"I'm telling you, you're not going anywhere. You've got to let her go. You've got bigger responsibilities than her."

I was dreading seeing the carnage that had been visited on Manzimwe by the Rebel invasion and subsequent retaking by the Republican army. Adding to my reluctance was my guilt at exposing a still-convalescing child to the dangers and unpleasantness inherent in venturing into a war zone. But ever since I had spoken with Dumani and seen Veeti's hide painting, the purpose born of my Other World journey had burned in my mind as fiercely as if it had been stamped in my consciousness with a branding iron. Deep inside I knew what Maxine meant to me, and I also knew that no matter what the danger, I had to do everything in my power to get through to her. And though I did not understand why, and would have preferred for it to be otherwise, the same knowing told me that it was crucial that Yapile come with me.

At the foot of the pass, we drove into an army roadblock. The scene was as berserk as a hornets' nest after being hit with a broomstick. Soldiers ran around in choreographed pandemonium, their eyes filled with exasperated rage as they screamed their heads off and waved guns at anyone who moved. Nothing at all seemed to be going how they wanted.

A military police sergeant in charge of directing traffic roared at me and gesticulated for me to drive closer, then stop, then move back, then forward. He was furious that I couldn't guess the exact invisible line he wanted me parked on. Losing all patience with me, he began striding toward me, aggressively waving a six-shooter and bellowing Lapedi obscenities. An infantry officer blocked the traffic controller and diverted his attention to a line of trucks trying to get rolling. The sergeant stormed off to do a deranged impression of a football referee breaking up an on-field fight.

The infantry officer marched up to my window. The look of disgust on his face told me that he could not believe the temerity of a white man showing up at his checkpoint in such hostile circumstances. In the Republic, they don't ask you for your papers like they do in the movies. They either like the look of you or they don't. If they don't, things go very badly.

Close by us was a pitiable case in point. A pair of soldiers used their rifle butts to keep a wounded civilian on his feet. He had been shot in the stomach. Some of his entrails spilled out of the front of his shredded shirt. His left cheek had been smashed in, leaving the eye on that side of his face hanging out of its socket.

I sat behind the wheel, every nerve in my body a live wire. My breathing was so shallow my head began to spin. It occurred to me that I could save myself and my companions a lot of grief by just telling the officer that we had taken a wrong turn, and reverse out of his nightmare jurisdiction. After all, bad as it was, the roadblock was merely the gateway to the grim gauntlet that lay ahead of us.

When I weighed the option of retreat against my original intention to go to the Mission Hospital, it was clear that it was just my fear doing my thinking for me. I put my attention back on my end result and let go of what it would take to get through.

"What's this?" the officer demanded.

It took me a moment to realize that he wasn't referring to anything in specific; he wanted an explanation for our presence. I swallowed nervously, knowing full well that our fate depended not only on my answer but also the conviction of its delivery. I took another moment to visualize myself getting safely through to the Manzimwe Mission Hospital. "Ah, good morning, Great Soldier," I said as boldly as I could. "We are heading to the hospital to get supplies for the soldiers guarding the Irrigation Scheme. And if we can help the army while we are here, we will."

"Hauw!" the officer exclaimed. "You speak Lapedi; you are one of us. I see you, sir." His eyes beamed with admiration and affection. He looked the inside of the vehicle over. "But we will have to give you real guns if you want to help us fight the Chitswa dogs," he chuckled affably in English. With a wave of his arm he dismissed me. "You may pass."

I was momentarily elated at the realization that, without even thinking, I had actually spoken fluently in the native tongue. My Lapedi had been miraculously restored to me at exactly the right moment. "You see," I turned to Chollo jovially, also speaking in English, "things are unfolding."

Any cheer I derived from escaping the potentially sticky situation was dashed by the sight of the wounded wretch beside our vehicle, sinking to his knees. Chollo stabbed his forefinger ahead as if to say, "Just shut up and drive." He needn't have urged me. I put my foot down hard on the accelerator and roared up the pass, wondering whether I should be grateful that virtually all of the traffic was heading out of town.

Had I known the scene of devastation that awaited us at the top of the escarpment, I might not have made such haste. The road was littered with the burned-out shells of cars and buses and armored vehicles. Nothing remained of the shanties and town buildings other than charred sticks and crumbling walls. Everywhere bedraggled natives huddled around smoky fires, doing their best to keep warm in the unseasonal drizzle. Two disheveled women stood in the middle of the road engaged in a tug of war over a dead dog, oblivious to the hooting traffic brushing past them. At frequent intervals we came across mean-faced militias standing guard over bloodied civilian prisoners kneeling in the dirt.

Right in the middle of where downtown used to be, I glanced in my rearview mirror to check Yapile's reaction, feeling terrible for exposing her to the harrowing scenes playing out around us. I assumed that her wide-eyed expression was a look of horror, but when I shape-shifted into her I was taken aback by her innocent perception of what she witnessed. To her it was not an appalling scene at all. Because her mind had nothing to compare it to, it was all just a fantastic blur of more people than she had ever imagined existed, all attired in an incredible variety of clothing and engaged in a diverse range of perplexing activities.

I was even surprised by my own reaction to the bleak scenario. There was no denying that I was sickened by what I saw. It chilled me to the marrow to realize just how ferocious the destructive urges in the human psyche were and how easily the fabric of a society could be shredded. Yet it was no longer a reality that I wanted to run away from, to avoid being caught up in. Somehow I felt like I belonged in this situation, that I was a part of its cause and equally a part of its solution. I knew that my painful emotions were a reflection of my humanness and I cherished them as such. But another part of me viewed the surrounding havoc through a different pair of eyes. And these eyes – the eyes of my pure creative spirit – did not see a tragedy before them. Instead, they saw a game well played, a beautiful human drama creating the fertile grounds for greatness to manifest and reshape the world in its own image. I could see that whenever any societal structure crumbles, it is not so much a loss as an opportunity to build a new structure founded on the values cherished by the human spirit. I could also see that my own spirit had planned for me to be sucked into this vortex of chaos, and a voice deep inside me told me that if I gave myself over to the chaos, surrendered to it absolutely, I would become an instrument of a divine resurgence, and through that, realize my own magnificent fulfillment.

***

The situation at the Manzimwe Mission Hospital was a lot calmer than I had anticipated. A couple of incinerated helicopter husks lay on the dusty field near the hospital's main entrance, and behind them stood rows of olive-green tents with red crosses stitched on their roofs. An orderly procession of people in white coats or camouflage uniforms made their way between the whitewashed hospital edifice and the tents. Other than a few pock marks in the walls and a blue plastic tarpaulin bandaging a section of roof, the main building appeared to have survived the fighting relatively unscathed. The same could not be said for the nearby church. There was nothing left of it other than a few A-shaped stumps where walls had once stood. An African priest in a black cassock led a small detail of women sifting through the rubble for intact bricks and any other recyclable materials.

A cordon of infantrymen around the hospital grounds explained the scarcity of civilians in the area. We were stopped by a line of soldiers with raised machine guns. Their officer came toward me with his pistol pointed at my head.

"What's your business here?" he shouted at me in English. "This is a hospital for army only."

I didn't blink. Looking him straight in the eye, I used the most indifferent tone I could muster. "I'm from the Irrigation Scheme. I have Selele's godchild in the back. She has to be treated for an extradural hemorrhage. She is very sick."

The officer aimed his gun at Chollo. "Is this white turd telling the truth?"

Chollo turned his head very slowly to face the officer. Even I shrank back at the sight of his savage countenance. "I don't understand the white man's language," he snarled, "but whatever he says, you would be wise to accept it as the truth."

The officer withered in the face of Chollo's ferocity. His

315

bottom jaw sagged along with his pistol. Chollo and I both continued to stare at him unflinchingly. "Okay," he said finally. He waved his men aside with his gun. "Let them through."

When we got out of the Land Rover, Chollo and I put on our Irrigation Scheme–issue fleeces and helped Yapile into the jersey we had brought along for her. "Come with us, Chollo," I said and led the way into the hospital, holding my pistol in my hand.

The entrance foyer was littered with wounded men lying on stretcher beds. A pair of startled soldiers standing beside a sliding reception window fumbled with their guns. "It's okay," I shouted, "we're just looking for a doctor. I need to see someone in charge."

The soldiers froze, their petrified eyes fixed on the shotgun Chollo had leveled on them. A nurse turned into the corridor on the other side of the foyer and began heading for the cavernous waiting room beyond. I ran toward the corridor shouting, "Sister! Sister!"

The woman turned around, a tray of assorted clinical supplies balancing in her hand. The front of her uniform was covered in dry blood.

"Have you seen Dr. Carlyle?" I shouted breathlessly.

"No," she shrugged indifferently. She eyed my gun with contempt.

"She's gone," a clerk poked her head out of the reception window. "She went to get her things."

The nurse in the corridor scowled at me before turning her back on me and walking away. She was evidently disappointed that I had found what I was looking for so easily.

My shoulders sagged. "Gone?" I cried. "Which way?"

"Maybe you can find her in her tent outside," said the clerk urgently.

I ran back to Yapile and took her hand. "Come, little girl," I said, "we must move."

Soldiers and orderlies jumped out of our way as we raced around to the tent village. A surge of anxiety told me I didn't have time to waste searching every tent. An orderly appeared from a nearby tent. "Excuse me," I called to him, "do you know where I can find Dr. Carlyle?" The man just shrugged.

Yapile squeezed my hand. I looked down into her big doe eyes, immediately regretting the stress I was putting on her enfeebled condition. "I know where the woman you are looking for is," she said softly.

"Of course you do," I said in English, "you're in innocence." The girl's face clouded in puzzlement. I switched to Lapedi. "Take me there. Quick, we must hurry."

Yapile began running down the first row of tents. When we reached the end of the row, Yapile turned and ran through another cluster of tents tucked in behind the hospital building.

"Wait," I pulled on her arm to stop her. "She's in these huts."

"Not anymore," she strained to keep going. "She's moving."

We ran around to the far side of the hospital. A jeep was starting up near the front of the building. A woman threw a duffle bag into the back of the open vehicle.

"Maxine!" I yelled. The woman apparently didn't hear me over the revving motor. She climbed into the front passenger seat with her back to us. She slammed her door shut.

"Maxine!" I called again. Before I even got her name out, an outdoor generator came to life beside me, drowning out my cry. The jeep began to roll forward. I tried to shake myself free of Yapile's hand so I could run after it. A gun blast exploded in my ear. Bits of debris blew off the jeep's right back tire and lower tailgate. The tire went flat and the vehicle listed to its side.

Out of the corner of my eye I could see a shotgun barrel poking over my left shoulder. I heard the clack-clack of the pump action, followed by another deafening blast. The left side of the jeep sagged to the same level as the right. The jeep stalled and rolled to a standstill.

Calming everyone down from that point took some doing. Within seconds both Maxine and her driver and my companions and I were surrounded by a swarm of highly agitated soldiers. Before we knew it, we were all up against a wall facing summary execution for carrying out an armed attack on a military facility.

As the soldiers argued among themselves whether it was necessary to shoot the females, Maxine's driver began cursing me in a thick Portuguese accent. He was a tall, lanky mulatto with a sallow complexion. His main concern in that moment was who would replace his busted tires. When I assured him that, assuming we survived our predicament, I could call on the Vale Estate to deliver him a spare pair of tires, he seemed placated. He stared patiently at the bickering soldiers.

The argument for executing the men and not the females hinged on the fact that Maxine's driver was wearing camouflage fatigues and Chollo and I were in Vale Estate security khaki and olives, while the woman and girl were in civilian clothing and therefore unlikely to be combatants. My defense was that if we had indeed intended to attack the hospital, it made no sense that we would start by shooting at each other. Unfortunately my logic didn't cut any mustard with the soldiers, who were bent on taking the trauma of the recent fighting out on the most convenient scapegoat at hand.

Our lives were only saved by the arrival of the commander we had encountered at the front of the hospital checkpoint. In his mind, Yapile's status had been elevated from Selele's goddaughter to daughter. That we were shooting at the lady doctor's transport to ensure she stayed to treat the girl suddenly made sense to everyone. The soldiers offered their profuse apologies, although they did admonish us for not explaining the situation properly in the first place.

Maxine was not as easily appeased as her driver or the soldiers. Under a leather bomber jacket, she was wearing the same shorts and T-shirt she'd had on the day she took me to see the *Mona Lisa of Africa,* but the fresh-faced exuberance was gone. The laugh lines around her eyes had turned to deeply etched crow's feet. Her "I'm so happy to see you" smile was in exile.

"Okay, so now I'm your prisoner. What do you want with me?" Maxine used a tone of voice so callous it made me flinch. She was slouched back in a folding chair in an attitude of defeated indifference. Her deflated demeanor made me think of all the times she had been imprisoned. I could see how this type of defense worked against interrogators. Her abject presence made me feel so empty that I had no appetite at all for engaging her.

I sat down on the stretcher beside her. Other than the one chair and the stretcher, the tent we had retired to for some privacy was completely bare. It had no ground sheet; the air smelled faintly of decomposing grass.

"Take it easy, Max," I said. "It wasn't my idea to blow your tires out. But to be honest, I am glad Chollo stopped you. I wanted to see you before you disappeared."

"But I was leaving on a medical emergency," Maxine spat. "Someone's life is in the balance." Her eyes fired up for a moment, and then went cold again.

"I don't think so," I shook my head.

"Excuse me?" Maxine came back angrily. She checked herself and changed to a tone of weary sarcasm. "Oh, I forgot, you know everything."

"I know enough," I said. "I know that you're acting like this because you're embarrassed."

"I'm embarrassed?" she arched an eyebrow condescendingly.

"Of course you are. You don't want to face me after overdosing me with morphine."

Maxine picked her head up and looked me evenly in the eyes. "I was giving you lifesaving medication. Anything I did was in response to your condition."

"I know you were saving my life, Max, but not from a tooth infection. You were putting me out of action so we didn't have to go into the Swamps."

"And I did this because...?"

"Because you love me, Max."

"There's nothing between us, Mark." A bemused expression crossed her face. "Is this what this is about?" she scoffed.

"Have you come to sweep me off my feet?"

"No, Max, that's not it. I have a family…a wife and kids. You and I aren't soul mates. But we do have a very special connection. You could say we're soul brother and sister. We were born to heal each other."

"Sounds like you're suffering from psychosis. I can give you something for that."

"I'm fine, Max. Since I woke up from my coma, I see everything very clearly. And I have you to thank for waking me up."

"Wasn't I the one who put you in the coma? The morphine overdoses, remember?"

I could see that I was not going to find a comfortable segue to what I had to tell Maxine. The time had come to jolt her out of her defensive cynicism. "I know why you kill men," I blurted, my voice breaking at the pain of what I had to say.

"What do you mean?" A shadow of anguish clouded her face.

"You know, Maxine. Or if you don't, you're the only person in the world who doesn't."

"What do you mean, I kill men? That's a terrible thing to say." Tears welled in her eyes. She tried in vain to blink them back. They began streaming down her cheeks. She folded her arms and clutched her triceps tightly.

"It started with your father…" I began.

"What? I killed my father?" Her face contorted in agony.

"No, no," I said quickly, "I'm just saying it started with your father. You think your father died in a hunting accident. That's what you've believed all of your life. But he didn't." Seeing the look of horror on Maxine's face, I had to use all of my will to go on. "Your father was killed by his lover."

"He had a lover? How do you know that?" Maxine's tone was mystified, not dismissive.

"It came to me when I was in my coma. I learned a lot of things. Your whole life flashed before me."

"But you were just dreaming. You would have been hallucinating."

"No, Max, not just dreaming. I wasn't hallucinating. I was in the Land of Dreams. You don't know it, but you helped me take a journey to the Other World."

"You? In the Other World? Like the *Mona Lisa of Africa*?"

"Like that, yes. Your lecture and the impression the *Mona Lisa* made on me must have prepared the ground in my consciousness. Combined with my longstanding yearning for wisdom and the intention we made to find the last shaman, the ingredients for a full-blown shamanic journey were all there. My fever and the drugs you gave me would have created the crack in my psyche for me to slip through."

"No, that's not possible." An intrigued smile played on Maxine's lips. Some of the pain had lifted from her countenance. "Is it?" She searched my face again, not disbelievingly.

"I'm telling you, Max, I was there as real as I am sitting here. I found out all sorts of things."

"Like what?"

"That I'm the last shaman. Well, that we all are. There are so many things I have to tell you. But now isn't the time. Right now, I'm here to return the favor you've done for me. You saved my life and I've come here to save yours."

"I don't know what you're talking about, Mark. Anyway, my life isn't important. There are bigger things in life than our own lives."

"No, Max, you're wrong. There is nothing more precious in the whole world than your life, and I won't stand to see you throw it away. Your father didn't die in a hunting accident. He had a lover. Apparently she wanted to end their affair, so she shot him and then claimed that she had killed him in self-defense – that he had attacked her, tried to force himself on her."

"This is what you learned in the Land of Dreams?" An edge of skepticism found its way back into her voice.

"Yes, and my mom confirmed the story for me, Max. I got it out of her. It's true, I'm sorry."

"Why are you sorry?" Maxine shook her head, no doubt trying to clear it of the overload of questions piling up in her mind.

"Because the adults at the time, including my mom and dad and your mother, they thought they were protecting you from the truth by telling you the hunting accident story. They didn't realize that they were aiding and abetting an unconscious pattern forming in your life. As a result of their denial, you couldn't resolve your pain around your father consciously, so you've been trying to resolve it unconsciously."

"What pattern?" Suddenly Maxine looked apprehensive, as if a door were being opened to a basement in which some ancient evil was trapped.

"To kill men." I paused. "To kill men by testing them beyond their limits so you can prove that they're never good enough."

I didn't say anything else. I waited for my words to sink in. Finally a look of comprehension dawned on Maxine's face. "Oh my god! I see it. I see it. Not just men. Is this why I'm always looking for a cause that is above the failings of mankind? Always being disappointed, and then pitting myself against greater and greater evils, forever trying to redeem myself and my father?"

"And just reinforcing that the masculine principle isn't worthy," I added. "Men, churches, governments, authority. But with men, it seems as if you were trying to initiate them, help them grow up, because your father wasn't grown up. Only, in the scope of your pattern – to fit in with your belief system – they had to die...like your father."

"So why didn't I want to let you go into the Swamps?" she said.

"Unconsciously, you didn't want us to go into the Meluti because you didn't want to sacrifice me in your dysfunctional quest. But there was also another reason. You didn't want your last illusion of the ideal masculine shattered. Deep down, you didn't believe that the last shaman would live up to your ideal. Even all of your theories about metaphysics – I think maybe you were afraid of putting them to the test. But the funny thing is, if we had actually gone, your ideals would have been born out – you would have found everything you were looking for."

Maxine shook her head from side to side in her hands. "You...you...must hate...me," she sobbed.

"No, Max, I love you very much. None of this was you. This wasn't your life. This all happened to you. The real you and your real life are standing by ready to unfold."

Maxine shook her head again and sniffed heavily. She looked up, mortified. Her face was blotched from crying. "I have to go," she whimpered.

"Go where?"

"Portuguese Territory. There's a man who needs my help."

"No way, Max!" I cried in dismay. "This is the pattern we're talking about. You're not going to treat someone; you're off to take up another cause." I jumped up and pointed out the tent door. "I know who that man is you were driving off with. His name is Dominue, isn't it? He's come here asking for your help. Colonel Graca, the leader of the Rebel army has had a heart attack, or something like that."

"Who told you all of this?" Maxine's face contorted again, this time in bafflement.

"I'm telling you, Max, I know things now, and I know that this is an outside event."

"What do you mean, outside event?"

"An outside event is when something happens that seems like you absolutely have to do something about it. Where, in fact, that assumption is an illusion – a trick of your perception steering you away from your true path. You know, like the sirens in Greek mythology who shipwrecked sailors with their seductive call."

Maxine nodded vaguely.

"You're not just planning on going to treat Graca, are you? You've fallen for the fantasy of going and ministering to the Chitswa refugees in Portuguese Territory – desperate people displaced from the Republic, harassed by the authorities over the border and preyed on by militia gangs. You couldn't have found a more abject cause!"

"Is that a bad thing? To help people like that?" Maxine spoke more out of genuine curiosity than resistance.

"No, it's not a bad thing, per se. It's just whether it's true for you. Is this the way to claim the value of your life's work? Everything you've worked for has come to fruition. Selele is finished as a dictator. Council is sitting now as we speak. Everyone in the Republic is represented: Lapedi, Chitswa, journalists, trade unions, tribal people, farmers, you name it. Traditional values and culture are coming back to guide and rebuild our nation. But there's a lot of work to be done, a lot of healing. From what I've witnessed on the drive up here, I can tell you that the input of the good people who willed this eventuality is more crucial than ever before. The question you have to ask yourself is this: is your energy better spent in the camps or on the big picture that will enable the people in the camps to come home?"

The way Maxine was staring at me made me stop. "You're different, Mark. What happened to you?"

"That's what my family wants to know," I laughed. "I told you, though. I was initiated in the Land of Dreams."

"Initiated? What happens when you're initiated?"

"You bring your creative spirit home – learn to live from the part of you that is connected to everything. You're aware of what you need to know, especially your path – and the illusion that blinds you from it."

Maxine arched her eyebrows. "I've never heard you talk about the Republic as *our* nation before. You were always on about how us Whities didn't belong here."

"Well, I don't feel that way anymore. I don't think I'll live here permanently again, but I'd like to bring people from overseas and take them into the Meluti. I have friends there who can teach them a lot."

"You have friends in the Meluti?"

"Sure, it's a long story. I'll tell you one day."

"And your family?"

"You mean Kirsten and the kids? That family? They're going to fly out here to be with me for a while as soon as the airport is open again."

"So, you've sorted things out with her, then?" I thought I detected a strain of regret in Maxine's voice.

"I wouldn't say that, but we spoke on the phone yesterday and it was just easy – a real joy, actually. There was a connection that was missing before. I suppose it was always there – I just hadn't claimed it, made the choice to receive it." I sat back down on the stretcher and took Maxine's hands in mine. Every bit of substance in my being deserted me in the face of the intimacy I was about to expose myself to. "The truth is, deep down, beyond my conscious awareness, the idea of you is what has been standing between me and a full commitment to Kirsten, my true soul mate."

I saw the alarm beginning to register in her eyes. "It's not your fault," I hurried to assure her. "Way back in my childhood pain, I identified you as the one thing that was sweet and noble, and decided that my association with you would be my shelter from the dark side of life. Ever since then, whenever I'm in pain, you're the option I rely on unconsciously to save me. And even though I'm conflicted about it, the sentimental memory of you always surfaces to haunt me. Then every time I begin collapsing into you, you have to push me away so that you don't hurt me.

"Now it's all over, thanks to your packing me off to the Other World, Max. You don't have to be my outside event anymore." I smiled weakly to acknowledge how unflattering my statement might have sounded. "You're the best friend I ever had, woman. No one has ever been there for me as unconditionally as you have. I wish I had known what you were worth all this time, instead of wasting my energy on romantic hang-ups."

Maxine brushed off my heart-spilling confession with a weak smile of her own. "Talking about romantic hang-ups," she sighed heavily, "what am I going to tell Dominue? How can I tell him I'm no longer going to honor my Hippocratic Oath?"

"Do you want to go with him?"

"Well, I did, but you've ruined all of that for me. I was excited about a fresh start in the refugee camps. Now I know that it wasn't based on genuine altruism. It was just me running away, chasing that ever elusive worthiness." She pulled her hands away from mine and rubbed her face. "I'm just so tired. I've been in surgery ever since I came back from the Irrigation Scheme."

"Why don't you come back to the farm with me and rest up until you're ready to decide your next steps?"

Maxine was quick to dismiss my suggestion. "No, I can't do that," she said. "You heard Cynthia. My privileges are all used up in the Republic."

"Nonsense," I said. "That was in the old Republic. Anyway, you know that she said all of that to manipulate you into babysitting me in the Meluti. I have no doubt you'll be the next Minister of Health."

Maxine kept her eyes on the ground and shook her head in the negative.

"Come on, Max," I cajoled her, "you don't have to be embarrassed about anything. It's only my family. The war helped us all realize what fools we've been, how wrong our priorities have been. You belong with us – the family of idiots."

A smile cracked on Maxine's face. I knew that I had won her over to my suggestion. After a little more coaxing, she let me help her to her feet. We left the tent with Maxine's arm around my shoulder for support and headed back to the jeep to retrieve her bag and let the tall mulatto know that she wouldn't be going back to Portuguese Territory with him.

When we reached the jeep, Dominue was nowhere in sight. Sitting in the driver's seat of his jeep was a man in an army uniform with the MP insignia on his helmet and armbands. He was diligently studying the matter he had just picked out of his nose with a fingernail evidently fashioned for that express purpose.

"I see you, Officer," I greeted him.

"You, too," he brought his hand up in a listless salute.

"Where is the mulatto?" I said.

The man sat up and straightened his helmet. "You know this man?" There was nothing apathetic in his manner any longer.

"Not personally," I said warily.

The military policeman lay back in his seat again. He

checked Maxine and me out as if deciding whether he could be bothered to talk to us or not. "They took him away. I'm waiting to drive the vehicle to headquarters after they fix the wheels."

"Who took him? Where? Why?"

"We got a tip that he was here. This man has been abducting foreign nationals under false pretenses and holding them for ransom. Not even a week ago, he shot an Englishman because the man refused to contact his family and employers for money. He is a snake, this one they call Dominue. They say that, before, he was a smuggler operating out of the Meluti Swamps. Only demons come and go from there." The MP appeared well pleased with himself for showing us our ignorance of worldly matters. My blood ran cold. I could only imagine what Maxine was feeling.

"You are well informed, Officer," I praised him. "But this man he shot, do you know if his name was Stratton?"

"Yah," he said, "Roger Stratton from that Human Rights League. I arrested him once. He was a good man."

I had to catch Maxine before she fell to the ground like a sack beside me. The MP gave a startled cry. "Hauw, what's the matter with the lady?"

***

The last order of business in Manzimwe was to escort Maxine to her late fiancé's grave in the small cemetery beside the decimated mission church. The clouds had sunk down to the ground and a fine mist shrouded our surroundings. A troop of baboons foraged through the unkempt graveyard. The female apes retreated with their young, leaving a rear guard of a dozen big males to slow our advance with a unified display of aggression. As we drew closer, they sauntered off, letting us know by their cool manner and ferocious barks that they were not intimidated by us.

Maxine found Roger's grave. It was marked by a cross of charred planks and his name spelled out with pebbles along the low six-foot-long mound of earth. I stood back a respectful distance, listening to the chatter of the women scavenging in the rubble of the nearby church ruins. I had expected a flood of tears from Maxine, but she stood staring at her lover's grave in stone-faced silence. The longer she stood there, the more I could sense her heart shutting down. A war was raging inside her, between her freshly liberated innocence and the battle-hardened enemy of life's injustices. I was at a loss as to what I should do to help her stay with the pain she was steeling herself against. One of the most important lessons I had learned in the Other World was that when we embrace our emotions, the definitions and meanings they convey dissolve, but when we seek to resolve them, we give the definitions and meanings life. The only thing I could do, I figured, to support her in holding out against her illusion was to stand in my own discomfort without reacting.

I was startled by the sound of someone treading across a bed of stones close behind me. I turned around to see who it was. It was Yapile, back from being checked out by Doctor Kanda, the hospital administrator. Her cumbersome bandages had been replaced with a simple piece of cotton gauze taped across her temple. She appeared so frail and gaunt that I was surprised she could stand, let alone walk. I turned to Maxine to let her know that I was going to take the little girl back to the car. Before I could say anything, a sweet melancholy singing started up beside me. Yapile had taken a step forward and now stood facing Maxine, singing out a Lapedi mourning song with the poise and passion of a seasoned opera singer. She seemed to grow in stature and vitality with every word that issued from her lips.

Behind us, Chollo held his shotgun over his shoulder and stared impassively into the misty foreground. Maxine did her best to remain unaffected by the little girl's heartfelt dirge. She smiled curtly at Yapile and looked back at the ground with her face set even harder.

Out of the mist, a chorus of voices began singing along with the girl. It was the women from the church; they swayed their way to the edge of the cemetery, followed by their priest, who added his baritone to create a rousing three-part harmony. The sound of their exalted voices resonated through every fiber of my being, releasing within me a torrent of emotion that drowned out all mental functioning. I was consumed by a crushing feeling of loss.

The steely look on Maxine's face melted into an expression of abject agony. Uncontrollable sobs began to convulse her body. With a heartrending cry she sank to her knees and then keeled over to lie weeping hysterically on the mound of earth covering her dead lover. The Africans launched into another song which, though I didn't understand the words, sounded like the perfect accompaniment to her catharsis. As I looked on in bittersweet sympathy, I imagined that I could see a lifetime of grief bleeding out of her. It was as if I could feel something dying. Yes, definitely – the death of a mendacious story that had kept Maxine separate from the beauty of her own heart. I hoped with all of my heart that, like Sibongila's widow in the Land of Dreams, in the depth of her passion she could see her soul at one with the Soul of the World.

Only when she was completely spent and lay like a limp rag did the singing cease. A woman who had disappeared halfway through the last song reappeared with a mug in her hands, which she gave to the priest. The priest picked his way through the small field of broken tombstones and rickety crosses, over to Maxine. He knelt down beside her and shook her gently by the shoulder. She looked up as if she had been woken from a deep sleep. The priest held out the mug of water to her. Maxine showed no inclination to accept his offer; she just stared at the cup, as if trying to make up her mind about something. Dumani's story about Parsifal and the Fisher King came back to me. A qualm of despair seized me as I realized that the war for her heart was not completely won.

The priest pushed the mug at her again, nodding his head in encouragement. She looked at him thoughtfully for a moment and then took the water from him. As she took her first sip, the women cheered. When I looked back at Yapile, she was clapping her hands in delight. Even Chollo had a grin on his face. The Africans could obviously sense that Maxine had made some kind of breakthrough, though I wondered whether they understood that, in accepting the drink from the priest, she had self-consciously used her will to let go of her wounded relationship with the masculine principle. When she had finished drinking, Maxine allowed the priest to help her to her feet and, with her hand leaning on his arm, lead her from the cemetery.

Once we were all aboard the Land Rover, I could sense everyone's buoyant mood. I could especially feel Yapile's excitement at heading back to her new life on the Vale Estate. Picking up on her eager anticipation made my own spirits soar.

"Well, here we are again," I said in English as I buckled my seat belt, "four of us heading down to the Irrigation Scheme. Except we've got Yapile with us instead of David. What happened to him, Max? Why didn't he come back to Manzimwe with you?"

"He said he wanted to go home to check on his family," Maxine's voice quavered. "I miss him a lot. He was so good to me. I used to call him my guardian angel."

My whole body shivered with goose bumps. "Who originally told you about the last shaman?" I leaned my head against the headrest, waiting to finish our discussion before turning the key in the ignition.

"Come to think of it, it was David who first started bringing us information about him." Maxine's reply sent a fresh wave of goose bumps crawling across my skin. "Why do you ask?"

I didn't see the point in overwhelming Maxine with my theory about David. All I said was: "I had a hunch it was him. He must have been an angel to give us such an incredible gift."

Maxine's cheerful laugh was music to my ears. "I hope I meet up with him again one day."

Chollo shifted in his seat irritably and cleared his throat meaningfully. He jacked his thumb backward to suggest I start reversing.

I turned the key and gave the motor some gas. As I

swung the vehicle onto the road to drive away from the hospital, I was hit by the full impact of what had unfolded for me since I first arrived there with a sore tooth. It also struck me that much of the gold I had gained was mirrored in my passengers: my inner being in the form of little Yapile, the un-gilded truth represented by Maxine, and my unfettered instinct to serve these highest aspects of myself as embodied by Chollo. I looked deliberately at the scout sitting in the seat beside me and smiled. "Well, old chap," I said in an exaggerated colonial accent, "it's good to have us all together at last. Now it's up to me to keep it that way."

It's unlikely that he understood a word of what I said. He stabbed his index finger at the road ahead. "Tuma, tuma!"

About the Author

William Whitecloud's connection to the magical nature of life can be traced back to his childhood in the small African country of Swaziland, where he was immersed in the super-natural worldview of the tribes people around him.

This association was reinforced when he immigrated to Australia in 1983 and began speculating on global financial money markets, using profoundly esoteric methods for predicting market movements. Over time William's attention shifted from observing phenomena at work outside of himself to finding ways he could practically apply magic to creating what truly mattered to him in his own life. This search brought him into contact with the alchemical principles of Hermetic Philosophy and the ideas of Robert Fritz, founder of Technologies For Creating.

Within months, he had begun to study and teach these superbly effective modalities for reconnecting with and manifesting what is truly important to the human spirit. William went on to found his own Natural Success modality, dedicated to empowering participants in discovering and living their authentic nature and purpose. Through his involvement in the program, he has worked with thousands of individuals, training and coaching them in bringing their dreams into reality. His ongoing search to discern the essence of what it takes people to connect with and live from their creative spirit forms the basis of his books, The Magician's Way and The Last Shaman.

William now lives in California where he devotes his time to coaching, writing, making films, enjoying his family, and letting life unfold by magic.

Other titles by William

THE MAGICIAN'S WAY

William Whitecloud's SECRETS OF NATURAL SUCCESS

Find out more about the author, his work, resources, and community at www.williamwhitecloud.com

Stay in touch with the Magic!

William Whitecloud sends out a regular newsletter to support you in living your super-consciously inspired life. For insightful articles, free support material, and news on his latest events and resources as they become available, SIGN UP NOW! **williamwhitecloud.com/signup**

Free Guided Meditation Downloads

Experience the sublime consciousness-raising techniques practiced in The *Last Shaman*, as guided by the author, William Whitecloud. For serenity, guidance, and higher awareness ACCEPT YOUR FREE GIFT!

williamwhitecloud.com/freegift

Take your own *Last Shaman* journey!

William Whitecloud will personally lead you on his African Soul Safari where you will visit the settings that inspired the book as you learn the wisdom and techniques conveyed through it. **www.africansoulsafari.com**

Connect with William Whitecloud here

www.instagram.com/williamwhitecloud/
www.twitter.com/willwhitecloud
www.facebook.com/williamwhitecloud